Robyn Annear lives in country Victoria with somebody else's husband. She is also the author of *Nothing But Gold, The Man Who Lost Himself, Fly a Rebel Flag* and *A City Lost and Found: Whelan the Wrecker's Melbourne*.

BEARBRASS

Imagining Early Melbourne

Robyn ANNEAR

First edition published in 1995 by Mandarin,
a part of Reed Books Australia

This edition published by Black Inc.,
an imprint of Schwartz Publishing Pty Ltd
37–39 Langridge Street
Collingwood VIC 3066, Australia
email: enquiries@blackincbooks.com
http://www.blackincbooks.com

The National Library of Australia Cataloguing-in-Publication entry:
   Annear, Robyn.
   Bearbrass : imagining early Melbourne / Robyn Annear.

   2nd Edition.
   9781863956550 (paperback)
   9781922231574 (ebook)

   Melbourne (Vic.)--History--1834-1851.
   Melbourne (Vic.)--Social life and customs--1834-1851.

   994.5102

Cover design: Peter Long
Text design: Anna Warren, Warren Ventures

For David and Rosie, my undoings

TABLE OF CONTENTS

PREFACE TO THE NEW EDITION

More Melburnians are aware of Bearbrass today than in 1995. There's a Bear Brass restaurant on Southbank, you can take a tour of Bearbrass, '*What was Melbourne's original name?*' is a standard poser with quizmasters, and ABC local radio's morning presenter sometimes gives his station call-sign as '774 Bearbrass'. But Bearbrass itself is neither harder nor easier to find than it was ten years ago. No matter how the city changes in shape, form and outlook, Bearbrass – dead-and-buried, trick-of-the-light Bearbrass – stays the same.

Not me, though: *Bearbrass* (the book) changed me. It awoke me, for one thing, to the value of an index. First time round, I opposed the inclusion of an index, determined that it wasn't to be *that* kind of book. Well, it turns out that it *is* that kind of book. As the passage of time distanced me from its contents, I came to share the readers' gripe. This new edition includes an index, as much for my sake as yours.

In the absence of footnotes, I've been called on sometimes to justify my 'facts'. How did I know (asked one reader) that Superintendent La Trobe swapped a flowered robe for 'something with epaulettes' on the morning of the Princes Bridge opening? I had no choice then but to own up to the time machine in my shed. Secrets – there's just no keeping them, is there?

ROBYN ANNEAR, 2005

INTRODUCTION

I n her history of the London suburb of Kentish Town, Gillian Tindall
wrote:

> ... just because you transfer the descendants of ploughmen to
> paved streets or turn villages into urban areas, you do not in
> fact alter human beings; they will still make their villages where
> they can.*

When I lived there, I made Melbourne my village. I'm not talking
about suburban Melbourne, where rusticity can be as close as the
corner shop: a few Scotch thistles, a galvanised iron fence and a flick-
ering Peter's ice cream cone can work magic on your sense of time and
place. I made my village of central Melbourne – and it's a village that
takes some finding. I think of it as Bearbrass.

Bearbrass was one of the names by which Melbourne was known
in its early days – apparently a mis-rendering of *Birrarung*, meaning
'river of mists' in the language of the Wurundjeri people. Other varia-
tions tried out by the settlers included Bareport, Bareheep, Barehurp,
and Bareberp. In my imagination, I've raised again the village (or 'the

---

*   Gillian Tindall, *The Fields Beneath: The history of one London village*, Paladin
      Books, London, 1980 (new ed. Weidenfeld & Nicholson, 2002)

Township', as it was called) that was early Melbourne, whose physical traces have been almost entirely displaced and pulverised by the out-gougings and up-thrustings of the Melbourne we see today.

Let me clarify what I mean by 'early Melbourne'. I'm talking of the period from the arrival of white settlers in 1835 until 1851 when the first gold rushes shook the town. Long before 1851, of course, Melbourne had grown well beyond a township, but its era of grandeur and Marvellousness was still far in the future: the Block was a quagmire and Collins Street had no Paris end. Early Melbourne was a *different* place – that's why I prefer to think of it as Bearbrass.

What fascinates me most is the shaping of the place, and its resistance to shaping. As soon as settlement commenced, the government, judiciary and men who called themselves masters did their best to make the place proper and meek and profitable. Their attempts and successes are well documented by historians, as are the men themselves. But the ground itself resisted – tree stumps held fast where thoroughfares were intended – and so, to a large extent, did common inhabitants of the town. This book is about the streetlife of Bearbrass – the people on the streets, the buildings on the streets, and those unyielding streets themselves.

I subtitled this book 'Imagining Early Melbourne' to make it clear that this is not a conventional history. I'm no historian; thoroughness and authority are not qualities I can lay claim to. This book about Bearbrass, the earliest Melbourne, is sometimes inaccurate, unfactual and fanciful – apocryphal, in fact. But *apocrypha* can also refer to something hidden, a secret, and I wanted to convey that element, too. Bearbrass is a hidden place; it relies for its existence on the imagination of the observer. It is my hope that readers of this book will carry their awareness of Bearbrass with them when they visit central Melbourne, and so rebuild the township. And just as I've overlaid Bearbrass with my impressions and experiences of the modern city, so readers will add their own snickleways, divergences and sacred sites – the wall that supported an ancient knee-trembler, the now-defunct cake shop that once sold the best Neenish tarts in town, the grate that ate your stiletto heel as you hurried to a big date ... and so on. Remember, *they will still make their villages where they can.*

This book is intended, most of all, as a counterbalance to modern Melbourne, as a way of saying: 'There *is* more to the place than car-parks, concrete and cafés.' And if I see just one person wearing an inexplicable smirk in Market Street or near Spencer Street station, I'll know this book has achieved its purpose – I'll know that they're imagining Bearbrass.

CHAPTER 1

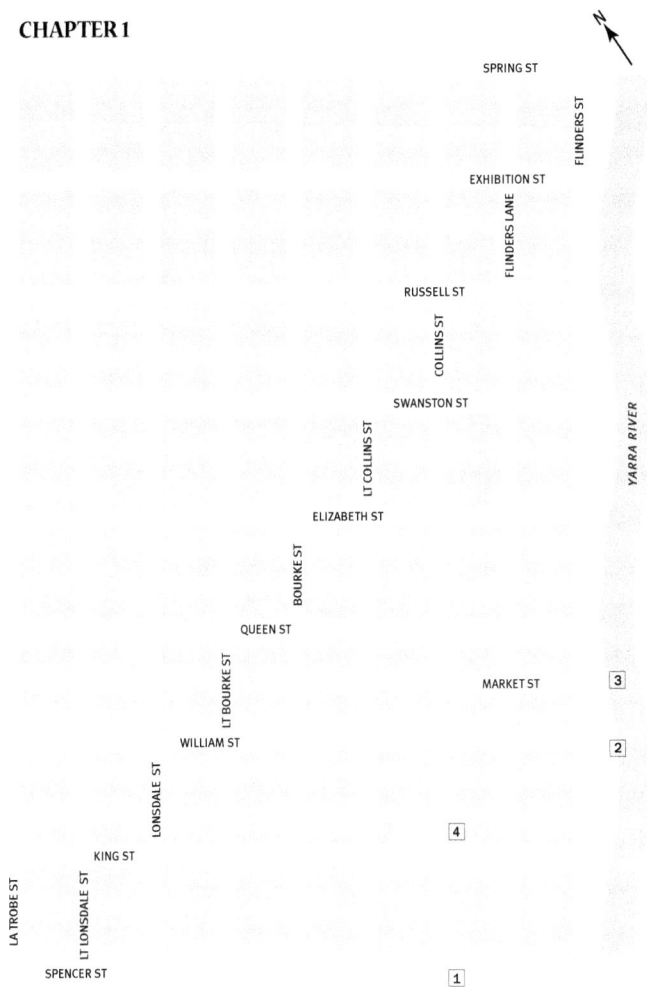

N

SPRING ST

FLINDERS ST

EXHIBITION ST

FLINDERS LANE

RUSSELL ST

COLLINS ST

SWANSTON ST

YARRA RIVER

LT COLLINS ST

ELIZABETH ST

BOURKE ST

QUEEN ST

LT BOURKE ST

MARKET ST

3

2

WILLIAM ST

LONSDALE ST

4

KING ST

LA TROBE ST

LT LONSDALE ST

SPENCER ST

1

1. *Batman's Hill*

2. *Mooring place of the* Enterprise, *August 1835*

3. *Yarra Falls*

4. *Site of* Enterprise *settlers' first huts*

CHAPTER 1

Founders and Shapers

Dreams of a noseless man

Transport yourself, in imagination or actuality, to Collins Street west of Spencer. Brave new city! Not till now – well, recently – did Melbourne's premier street break through the barrier of Spencer Street. Now its westward extension carries Collins Street over the railyards to Docklands, mimicking the long-lost Batman's Hill in the process.

Sit yourself in one of the tram shelters at the peak of the Collins Street hump. Eastward offers a new, elevated view of the city, while Docklands takes amazing shape to the west. Hunched atop a tall plinth, riverwards, a grey-white sculpted eagle – Bunjul, the ancestral creator spirit – watches over traffic on Wurundjeri Way. Trains grunting underfoot make your hollow hill shudder. Inbound or out-, they pass beneath the spectacularly seasick roof of the Southern Cross (née Spencer Street) railway station. With the new station unfinished at time of writing, it remains to be seen whether the traditional patrons – country train-travellers and chain-smokers in stretch denim – really will be displaced by well-heeled sophisticates, as the developers' concept drawings suggest.

This has long been a part of town that most people disregard, passing through in haste, if at all. The glamorisation of Docklands promises to change that, but I'm betting the seedy spirit of the station and its environs will prevail.

Up aloft on Batman's (reconstituted) Hill, though, it's not so hard to imagine a place that was – and might be – different. Well, good: that's why you're here.

∽

In January 1838, you'd be loafing against the trunk of a sheoak near the foot of Batman's Hill,* looking across to the government camp and with a fair view of the whole western end of the township. To your right swells Batman's Hill, a grassy flat spreads out to Burial Hill on your left-hand side, and a vast swamp (called the Lagoon or Batman's Swamp) stretches away behind you. The wood of the sheoaks that grace the summit and flanks of Batman's Hill is not much favoured by the settlers for fuel and building timber – a lucky thing for idlers like yourself. The trees' lush, rounded canopies cast welcome shade and their verdure relieves the otherwise uniform pale wheat-brown and dun of the settlement on a hot afternoon. Your drink would be a bottle of porter, the thermos being as yet undreamt of and a billy fire not worth the risk, what with that crusty wind from the north and nearly the whole town built of wood.

Batman's Hill (or hillock – only eighteen metres or so in height) peaks just south-west of the intersection of Spencer and Collins streets, whence it slopes down to meet the Yarra. On that southern side of the hill stands the home of John and Eliza Batman, their seven daughters and one Bearbrass-born son. You can't see it from here, but

---

* The Collins Street extension bridge, where you're sitting, rises to the north of the original hillock.

it's a substantial house, about the homeliest in the settlement, built of logs (of Van Diemen's Land timber, not the native sheoak) and mud, neatly white-washed with lime. The big sash-windows that face the river are hung with claret-coloured drapes, and a creeping rose vine twines about the front door. A sizeable orchard spreads out from the township side of the house.

Just as you're thinking of moving off to Jemmy Connell's for another of those black bottles and some shade within walls, the sound of metal wheels, accompanied not by horses' hooves but by human grunts and footfalls, alerts you to the approach of John Batman himself, from the direction of his orchard. Four Aboriginal servants, pushing and pulling, easing and trundling, bear Batman over the uneven ground in a makeshift perambulator of woven bamboo on an iron frame. This is not Batman's idea of travelling in style; syphilis has made an invalid of him. Constant pain in his feet and legs has made him dependent on this wickerwork Batmobile, and the bandage around his face (such a noble profile in his centenary portrait) hides the fact that his nose is decaying. The disease's recommended treatment is mercury, taken internally. It's one of those remedies that kills or cures, and Batman doesn't strike you as one of its success stories. His entourage is now making rough progress towards the hut of Captain George Smyth, opposite your 'window', where he'll join the captain in a slug or two of brandy, the usual speculation about land prices and horse flesh, and a few discreet hands of cards. Well, good luck to the poor noseless bugger.

∽

Batman died the following year, aged just thirty-nine. A parson named Dredge, recording the event in his journal, thundered to an imaginary congregation that 'his death from disease induced by loose and profligate habits ought to be regarded by the living as an admonitory instance of the truth of the sacred Scripture: *The wages of sin is death*.' But Batman continued to pay, posthumously.

Back in 1835, when he thought that he'd bought all the land here-abouts from the local Aborigines in exchange for a small consignment of geegaws, Batman had surveyed his new domain and declared: 'All I can see is my own, and all I can't see is my son's.' Well, as it turned out, to say that he must have had his eyes closed when he spoke would be an understatement. At that time, Batman had no son. When John junior was born at Bearbrass in 1836, it must have seemed like a blessing to Batman, who was already losing his nose and health. At least he now had an heir. But not for long. Young John was fishing at the Yarra falls one day, six years after his father's death, when he slipped into the river and drowned.

Even had both John Batmans lived to old age, Batman senior's *All I can see ...* pronouncement would not have been realised. The colonial government refused to recognise his 'purchase' from the Aborigines. Land at Bearbrass was sold piecemeal, with Batman just another bidder.

His family was left poorly-off after his death. His daughters were dispersed to the care of various protectors and guardians and within a couple of years his widow, Eliza, married her late husband's former overseer, William Willoughby. After the death of her son, Eliza left Willoughby and vanished from the town. In 1852, as 'Sarah Willoughby of somewhat abandoned character', the woman for whom Mt Eliza had been named was murdered in Geelong.

For a time, the Batmans' house on Batman's Hill was used as a government office. In the early 1840s it was suggested that the house should be preserved as a museum and library and the hill made the site for the botanic gardens. Neither suggestion was heeded. Not only was the Batmans' house not preserved, the hill itself was razed in 1863 to accommodate railway yards. Its earth and stones were carted off by horse and dray and dumped on the banks of the Yarra. So a walker along the river's northern side today can be said to tread the scattered peak of Batman's former hill.

Who *was* Melbourne's founder? Who cares?

John Batman is popularly regarded as Melbourne's founder, though his claim to that title was vigorously challenged by his rival, John Pascoe Fawkner. The two contestants are long since wormsmeat, but the squabbling and barracking goes on. Batman's cause had its heyday during the Melbourne centenary celebrations in 1935, when he was reinvented (or an earlier reinvention burnished) to suit the public tastes of that period: he was handsome, bold, decent – and tragic. You see, Batman did a clever thing: he died young. This practically assured him the status of tragic hero, from which the progression to glorious founder was a virtual formality. But let's give credit where it's due: Batman's elevation to founder was largely thanks to the unpopularity and relative longevity of his rival, Johnny Fawkner. If John Batman had never existed, Fawkner's detractors (and they were many) would have had to invent a John Batman; they couldn't bear to concede that the man who has been called 'the Derryn Hinch of his time'* could be the founder of their fine city. Batman was (mainly by dint of his being defunct) modest, agreeable, uninsistent; in short, a gentleman. Fawkner, on the other hand, was inescapable, vulgar, and managed to raise hackles by the mere act of drawing breath.†

But look – for the purposes of this book, the issue of *who-was-founder?* doesn't matter a toss. I don't really care whether Batman said, 'This will be the place for a village', or what he meant by it if he did (his map showed he had reserved Port Melbourne as the site for the township). Much is written about that elsewhere. This book is about Bearbrass – not about who found it or founded it, but about the place

---

* By former State Historian, Bernard Barrett.

† This is how R.A. Balbirnie described Fawkner (not by name, mind you) in a letter to the *Gazette* in 1839: 'His face was not one easily to be forgotten, it bore the stamp of disgusting sensuality – petty tyranny – brutish ignorance – and idiotic self-sufficiency branded on its every line. He was grossly vulgar in his speech, and wore upon his whole person the character of a doubly convicted scoundrel.'

and what was made of it. And the thing is, Fawkner was Bearbrass personified. The spirit of poor Batman is confined to his former hill; a bambooey creak and a whiff of gauze bandage, and he's gone. You'll find Fawkner everywhere.

Don't grimace: a somewhat conventional historical narrative

So far I've avoided launching into the conventional historical narrative, but I feel that, to introduce you properly to Fawkner and Bearbrass, some background is necessary. Now, don't grimace. Just think of it as a backdrop upon which to cast your Bearbrass shadow plays.

What is now the State of Victoria was, in 1835, the southernmost part of the colony of New South Wales, and was known as the Port Phillip District or Australia Felix. Tentative overland forays had been made to the district in search of pastoral land for the growing flocks of the colony's settled regions. Two attempts, both short-lived, had been made at establishing convict settlements on the south coast of Port Phillip. And the area around Port Fairy and Portland had begun to see some settlement by whalers and sealers working the waters of Bass Strait, and by the pastoral Henty family from Van Diemen's Land. But the colonial government had so far opposed settlement of the Port Phillip District because there was no official presence to orchestrate such development. Part of the Sydney government's concern was that unauthorised settlement would lead to clashes with local Aborigines.

John Batman was a sheep farmer of some influence in the north of Van Diemen's Land, near Launceston. He'd had his eye on Port Phillip pastures since the 1820s, but his overtures had so far met with government resistance. Eventually he formed the Port Phillip Association, a syndicate of fellow pastoralists and business types, and, in mid-1835, he sailed for Port Phillip with a contract to 'buy' nearly a quarter of a million hectares from the local Aborigines. In payment, he was to offer an assortment of blankets, knives, tomahawks, clothing, mirrors, scissors and flour – about £200 worth. He transacted his business with those whom he took to be the tribal leaders, the 'owners' of the land he wished to buy, and had the 'chiefs' sign the contract of sale. The purpose of this transaction was to show the Sydney government that his Association would deal fairly with the Aboriginal people of Port Phillip.

Batman left a party of men at Indented Head to protect his purchase, and sailed for Launceston. Upon arriving he made straight for his local watering-hole, the Cornwall Arms Hotel, and shouted the bar. At Batman's insistence ('and one for yourself') the publican, Johnny Fawkner, helped himself to a tot of cold tea and listened as Batman declared himself 'the greatest landowner in the world'. Within a month, Fawkner had himself got up a party of investors and plans for his own expedition to Port Phillip were well underway.

Fawkner was London-born but, as an eleven-year-old, had accompanied his convict father to Australia in 1803. This was Johnny Fawkner's first taste of a pioneering expedition, he and his family being among those sent to found a new convict settlement at Sorrento, at the entrance to Port Phillip Bay. A more exposed site would be hard to imagine and there was no fresh water in the area, so the experiment was soon abandoned. The Fawkners were removed to the brand-new settlement of Hobart Town where, after three years' labour, Fawkner senior was granted land for farming. Young Johnny worked for a time as a shepherd, then, at the age of twenty-two, took charge of the family's bakery in Hobart. Fawkner was, even then, quick to perceive and act on an injustice. With his earnings, he had a boat built so that his convict employees, whom he believed to be ill-used by officialdom, might escape by sea. Their attempt failed however and Fawkner's part in the plot earned him five hundred lashes and two years' hard labour at the miserable Coal River penal colony.

When he returned to Hobart in 1816, he carried on with his baker's shop but began also to sell liquor without a licence – the first manifestation of Fawkner's most striking hypocrisy: he spurned alcohol and despised drunkenness in others, yet he never flinched from selling the stuff. In 1819 he moved north to Launceston with his de facto wife, Eliza Cobb. Nineteen-year-old Eliza had been transported from England a year earlier for the crime of child-stealing. She was granted her certificate of freedom in 1825 and was later referred to as Fawkner's 'one-eyed, genteel wife' (they married in 1822). By 1828 Fawkner had built Launceston's first two-storey house, which he ran as the Cornwall Arms Hotel. He continued to make ructions with the authorities on behalf of those he considered oppressed, even establishing a newspaper to amplify his views. As a publican, he made the acquaintance of drinking men influential in that part of Van Diemen's Land, John Batman and his partners among them. Unusually for him, Fawkner would listen quietly as they expounded on their plans and aspirations for Port Phillip. They failed to see that (as a biographer has said of him) 'Johnny had to be first in everything.'*

Fawkner's schooner, *Enterprise*, carrying himself, his partners and their servants, left Launceston at the end of July 1835. The voyage had a stormy beginning and a combination of seasickness and a cash-flow crisis forced Fawkner to return to shore not far from Launceston, urging on his fellow expeditioners with the words: 'Go on lads and look for water.'

Not all of those on board the *Enterprise* were lads. Mary Gilbert, eighteen years old and four months pregnant, accompanied her husband James, Fawkner's blacksmith. Mary herself was employed as Fawkner's 'servant of all work'. She was the sole woman among the white settlers of Bearbrass for just over two weeks, but it can be imagined that the birth of her son, in December that year, was a lonely and frightening experience. Mary Gilbert rarely scores a mention as a Bearbrass pioneer, although a statue in the Fitzroy Gardens conservatory is dedicated to her. (On a recent visit I found her instead in the potting shed – a return to her earthy origins, perhaps.)

On 29 August 1835, the *Enterprise* moored on the north side of

---

* C.P. Billot (ed.), *Melbourne's Missing Chronicles*, Quartet Books, Melbourne, 1982, p. xii.

the Yarra basin, just below Queen's Bridge. The basin was formed by a rocky ledge across the river a little higher up, at the foot of Market Street. This ledge, known as the Falls, was called by the Aborigines *yarro yarro*; one of the earliest white arrivals took that to be the name of the river itself, and so it became the Yarro Yarro or Yarra Yarra River. Parts of the river were choked with snags and to reach the basin – the river's highest navigable point – the crew of the *Enterprise* had had to work against wind and current, warping the schooner upstream by pulling on ropes attached to trees on the bank. Overhanging trees lined the river banks, and branches and undergrowth had to be cut away to allow for the unloading of cargo and livestock – which included horses, pigs, dogs (less one killed on the voyage by 'Harry the Cook'), and a cat intended as 'companion and familiar' for Mary Gilbert.

Almost immediately after unloading, the *Enterprise* headed back to Launceston to collect Fawkner and further supplies. The expedition party remained at the Yarra basin to establish the settlement, building a few rough huts and a store in the vicinity of the present-day Rialto tower in Collins Street, ploughing land and sowing crops, and dividing up the river frontage between the six partners. Fawkner himself reached Bearbrass on 16 October; it is said that radishes were ready for the table by the time he arrived.

Not only radishes awaited Fawkner on his arrival at Bearbrass. A month earlier his party had been joined at the Yarra by a contingent belonging to Batman's Port Phillip Association. Fawkner's expedition party had been told that they were trespassing on the Association's land, but had thumbed their collective nose at the warning. (The government had not yet dismissed the Association's claim to the land.) The newcomers included Henry Batman (younger brother of John), his wife Catherine, and their four daughters who ranged in age from two months to eight years. Another in the group was William Buckley, the so-called 'Wild White Man', who had lived for more than thirty years with the Port Phillip Aborigines after escaping from the 1803 convict settlement at Sorrento, and had only recently been 'repatriated' by Batman's holding party at Indented Head. Buckley would be frequently called upon to act as intermediary between the settlers and Aborigines during the early days of Bearbrass.

Not two months old, the settlement already had the makings of a TV soap: too few women to go around, heated rivalries, assorted kids and animals, and a tall man with a mysterious past. Clearly, it would run for years.

Gristly soup

Antagonisms soon sprang up between Fawkner and his nearest neighbour, Henry Batman – in fact, between Fawkner and *everybody*. And Fawkner revelled in it. He loved being a pioneer. Having felt the sharp end of the law a couple of times in the past, he gloried in being on the spot as the rules were made at Bearbrass. He made a big noise, badgering and complaining and throwing his scrawny weight around. He was a terrier.

When the first representatives of the colonial government were installed at the settlement in 1836, they brought with them the acts and statutes of New South Wales. But remember that, until then, Bearbrass had been an outlaw settlement. Unlike Sydney and Hobart, with their origins as penal badlands, it had had no British Government whip-cracker at its helm. Bearbrass was instigated by small-town colonial businessmen for motives of profit and glory. The closest thing Bearbrass had to a leader was Johnny Fawkner – a cranky, self-promoting, teetotal grog-vender who had once bankrolled a convict breakout. Unlike those of the pastoral contingent, Fawkner was a townsman and he intended from the start to make a town, if not a city, of the place. He never saw Bearbrass as grazing land or a staging-point, a place just to make a few quid and then shoot through. He had big dreams – delusions, some might call them. Fawkner was ferociously loyal to the place from the first, fighting on its behalf against bureaucracy, outsiders, and all sorts of imaginary foes. Not for nothing did he call his newspaper the *Patriot* (though the fact that his initial, short-lived effort was called the *Advertiser* is also significant).

By the time the 'official presence' arrived on the scene, the force of Fawkner's influence had given a gristly, bothersome texture to the infant Bearbrass that the incoming laws and bureaucracy never quite managed to incorporate into their colonial soup. Bearbrass was as much shaped by Fawkner's energy and hypocrisy as by government surveyors and road gangs. Johnny Fawkner was what might these days be called, with parliamentary privilege and a fair degree of justification, a sanctimonious little prick. But he was the personification of Bearbrass.

CHAPTER 2

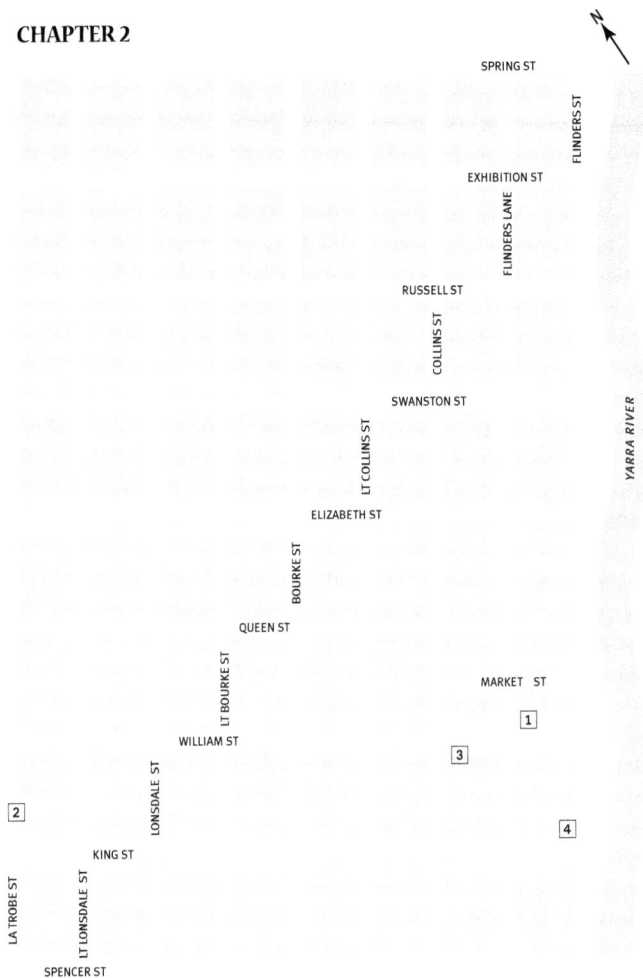

SPRING ST

FLINDERS ST

EXHIBITION ST

FLINDERS LANE

RUSSELL ST

COLLINS ST

SWANSTON ST

YARRA RIVER

LT COLLINS ST

ELIZABETH ST

BOURKE ST

QUEEN ST

LT BOURKE ST

MARKET ST

1

WILLIAM ST

3

LONSDALE ST

2

4

KING ST

LA TROBE ST

LT LONSDALE ST

SPENCER ST

1. Fawkner's first hotel, October 1835

2. Flagstaff Hill

3. Government survey paddock, site of first land auction, June 1837

4. Fawkner's £32 bargain – first allotment under the hammer

CHAPTER TWO

The Shaping of Bearbrass

The back bar at Johnny Fawkner's

Position yourself at the south-east corner of William Street and Flinders Lane today and the most striking feature is the squealing of the No. 55 tram as it negotiates the dog-leg. West of Market Street, Flinders Lane changes from a choked passage to a relatively airy two-way thoroughfare, brimful of multi-storey carparks. Sometimes it even sees sunlight. The tram hogs this first block of Flinders Lane's liberation to sneak its way between Market and William streets, en route to the zoo and beyond. Choose early afternoon for your visit to these parts and, if you can, make your way by the No. 55 – the city's most interesting tram route.

Turn back along Flinders Lane. Halfway to Market Street and down seventeen steps is the Tribute Garden, a courtyard scissored out between two buildings and leading down to the rear of the former Customs House, now the Immigration Museum. On stone tablets around the walls and lying flat under sheets of water are engraved thousands of names commemorating generations of immigrants to

Victoria. It's meant to be a restful contemplation space, and would be but for the roaring ventilators of the buildings on either side. Fetch yourself some sustenance from the café at the bottom of the courtyard, or bring your own in a bag. Then settle yourself on one of the rough-hewn timber seats – something like crouching koalas, only not as soft. For a flicker of time on a clear early afternoon, the sun triumphs over the thrust of the parking palace opposite, to cast some rays on this otherwise mildew-prone locale. Catch this moment if you can. Now, imagine a grassy slope leading down to the Yarra and a torrent of bombast cutting through your reverie …

∾

On this spot in the autumn of 1836, you'd be nursing a watery rum in the bar of Johnny Fawkner's public house. A chipped earthenware pudding bowl sits on the floor just inside the doorway, catching drips from the recent rain and tripping up customers. When you ducked in here at the height of the squall, Johnny enlisted your help in throwing a tarpaulin over the dining table in the front room, the leakiest spot in the house. The story goes that a grandly dressed roast swan took a posthumous dive off that table last Christmas Day, when an inpouring summer storm caught Johnny with knife poised to carve. After mopping up, the assembled company dined humbly instead on the first Bearbrass-grown potatoes. (There's a sack of these for sale in the bar – the sign affixed reads: *Pot 8 Os, 6d per lb.*)

The water in your rum owes nothing to the leaky roof and everything to Johnny Fawkner's parsimony. Four parts rum to one part water are what his housemaid, Mary Gilbert, reckons the contents of the serving barrel to be. And she should know: Johnny used occasionally to entrust her with the task of 'extending' the rum, until he caught her draining the one-fifth of rum into herself instead of the jug provided. Mary's in the bar now, mopping up rogue drips while her baby boy, trussed up in a blanket and sacking, snuffles on a bench in the corner. The poor mite is being kept from sleep by Johnny Fawkner in full voice.

Today's gripes are the usual ones: the Sydney Government and 'that villain' Henry Batman. Henry and Kate Batman are Johnny's nearest neighbours* and his principal antagonists (which is saying a good deal). Apparently Henry's dogs have been bothering the milch cows again and Kate abused Mary Gilbert and threatened to clout her with a ladle, and now the vilification is bubbling out of Johnny like sulphur gas from a hot spring. It's their drinking that outrages him the most. Of course, no one dares put the question, 'But Johnny, who sells them the rum?'; but a couple of customers splutter into their collars when he brands his enemy 'a specious hypocrite'. The Johnny Fawkner–Henry Batman saga is as good as a three-volume novel. True, sometimes it wears a bit thin, but in a town without a theatre Johnny Fawkner's rantings are as close as you'll get to public entertainment.

Fawkner built his house, which doubles as the settlement's only hotel, when he arrived in October last year. He would have liked to claim Batman's Hill for his residence, but John Batman was insistent that that land was his. Johnny backed off and instead selected a site overlooking the Yarra basin, where his inn would be certain to attract the notice of tired and thirsty arrivals by ship. The house is of Van Diemen's Land timber with a defective brick chimney built by Johnny and Jem Gilbert, Mary's husband. The rooms at the front of the house, facing the river, are reserved for 'respectable' visitors; the common run of customers is restricted to the dim, smoky bar at the back. (Most drinkers, however, bring their own flasks, jugs and tankards and take their liquor 'outdoors', beyond earshot of Johnny's haranguing.) Upstairs, an attic offers coffin-like sleeping accommodation where guests risk asphyxiation from smoke rising through gaps in the floorboards.

From Johnny Fawkner's attic window you can count most of the

---

* When the township's streets were marked out in 1837, Henry Batman found that he was living smack in the middle of the William Street roadway. How Johnny Fawkner must have crowed!

fifteen or so earthen huts and muddied tents that make up the settlement, all of them squatting amidst wind-whipped gums, tea-tree scrub, and long grass* flattened by rain. Smoke sputters from only a few chimneys. The scene explains why the bar downstairs has drawn more 'indoor' customers than usual. In spite of its disincentives, on a day such as this the back bar at Johnny Fawkner's is a refuge for settlers craving a little warmth and certainty.

What might Leonard Teale have made of the pre-Bearbrass landscape?

Like Johnny Fawkner, I'm a townie. I'd have been an exemplary colonist: off the ship and straight into the business of subduing and civilising the native landscape. Fawkner had tasted the rough life at Sorrento and Coal River; likewise, I've done time without blankets at Blanket Bay and tackled the wild scrub and leeches of Tasmania's west coast. And I'm not at ease with nature. In the thick of all that scenery and silence, I yearn for the clamour and mediocrity of town life. Ship me to unspoilt Bearbrass and, like Fawkner, I'd have had a decent house knocked together quick smart and set about making a town of the place.

Depictions of the place pre-settlement are somewhat lost on me. I've read descriptions of the site's natural features and seen sketches and paintings that show the landscape when it was still largely unaltered by the infant settlement, but somehow my imagination fails to catch. I see a place that was flat, hilly, grassy, swampy, treed, and sort of beige – a pleasantish but dullish rural scene. That's not to say there weren't moments when the moon was cocked just so and the wind leant on the reeds by the river till they moaned and a mopoke

---

* The grasslands of the central city ('green as a leek, and nearly breast high') were trampled and scythed and ploughed, and gradually receded as the settlement expanded. A visitor to the fledgling settlement as early as 1836 presumed that 'Bearbrass' had been derived from 'Bare-of-grass'. The topsoil, set loose from its webbing of grass and roots, took flight as dust in Bearbrass summers and made glorious mud in the winters.

sang out ... you know, the stuff of which Leonard Teale recitals were made. And to the Aboriginal inhabitants, the place certainly had value beyond beigeness and the odd bird call by moonlight. The site selected for the township was also the place most favoured by the Kulin people for inter-tribal gatherings. Bearbrass changed that, of course.

I guess my view of the pre-Bearbrass landscape is Eurocentric, imperialistic – all that. But when I scrape at the surface of a central city building site, it's not to find traces of the place's native grasses and seed pods; it's the fencepost and the firebrick and the paving stone I'm looking for. I'm interested in the shape that was *made* of Bearbrass.

The grid and Hoddle's cheroot

In 1850, an anonymous critic of the town's lay-out wrote that the surveyors' credo seemed to have been: 'The site must be made to suit the plan – not the plan to the site.' They went on:

We have planned our metropolis as we should plan a coal pit.
Pope's couplet, slightly modified, exactly describes Melbourne –

> *'Street answers street, each alley has its brother*
> *And half the city just reflects the other.'*

It's true: when you consider the irregularities of hills and contours and the curving shape of the river bank, the stern rectangular grid superimposed on the site does look a mite stiff. Perhaps it was a mistake. Maybe Robert Hoddle, the chief surveyor, sent the Governor a blank sheet of graph paper in error, using his innovative design (in which he had given the town the outline of a boxing kangaroo) to light a cheroot. More plausibly, he simply applied 'a plan in the Sydney office', the standard design for colonial townships. No space was allowed for a public square, considered a breeding-ground for 'the spirit of democracy'.

Martin Sullivan, an historian of early Port Phillip, has suggested that the township's lay-out was due, at least in part, to a determination by the authorities that the new settlement should not be user-friendly to the 'submerged classes' as Sydney had turned out to be. Sullivan writes:

> *the town planners had made it difficult for them to congregate in a labyrinth of narrow streets, lanes and alleys as everyone knew they did in Sydney. In Melbourne these men and women were visible; consequently they were less menacing, more controllable.* *

Like fish in a barrel. Whatever the process or motive, the result was a town laid out in ten-acre squares with streets ninety-nine feet (30 metres) wide. The angle at which the street grid was placed was roughly determined by the river, and the grid's western end butted up against Batman's Hill – these features set its two fixed boundaries.

Boundaries

A handful of natural landscape features had been given new names by the settlers and remained as points of reference in the developing town. These included Eastern Hill (originally 'a gum and wattle tree forest'), Batman's Hill ('clothed with she-oaks'), Flagstaff Hill, and of course the Yarra River. Early critics of the town's design argued that more should have been made of these features: that the town ought to have been shaped by them, rather than merely contained by them.

Flagstaff Hill formed the northern boundary of the original town survey, with Lonsdale Street the northernmost thoroughfare. The name originally given to the hill by the settlers was Burial Hill, as it was the site of their first cemetery. Six burials took place there before an official graveyard was established at the southern end of

---

* Martin Sullivan, *Men & Women of Port Phillip*, Hale & Iremonger, Sydney, 1985, p. 28.

the present Victoria Market site. Despite the sombre presence of six graves enclosed by a black-painted picket fence, the hill was a popular beauty spot and provided the best vantage point for sighting ships coming up the bay. It could well have been nicknamed Nob's Hill, as Lonsdale Street in that vicinity (between William and Spencer streets) became the town's earliest fashionable neighbourhood.

The same critic who likened the plan of the town to that of a coal pit, lamented that Flagstaff Hill had not been made the centrepiece of a town designed on classical, rather than purely functional lines.

The brow of the hill beyond the flag-staff, commanding a view of Hobson's Bay, the Melbourne Plains, and the distant mountains, would form an admirable site for a public promenade, which might hereafter be adorned with statues and vases, and formed into a terrace, with a steep escarpment towards the lagoon. Avenues of ilex and shrubberies of mimosa, etc., would render it a delightful retreat in the summer heats. From hence a road, or eventually a viaduct, should be formed to Batman's Hill, on the summit of which, conspicuous to the stranger coming up the river, might be erected a hall for the reception of the busts of Great Men. Towards the north-east, an avenue should conduct from the terrace-promenade to a pleasure ground or public park, on the pleasant wooded slopes between Melbourne and Flemington. In this park we might have a museum of statues, pictures, etc. ...

Modern critics shake their heads at the fact that the city was planned in such a way as to literally turn its back on its greatest natural asset, the Yarra River. With the advent of Southbank, they say, the planners' disregard of the river has finally been redressed. But there was an early intention that the township should occupy both sides of the river.

Initially the south side, opposite the settlement, was used almost solely for agricultural and grazing purposes. The river formed a natural obstacle to expansion of the settlement in that direction. Commuters crossed by boat or, at their peril, on foot across the rocks of the Falls or the crumbly dam wall that was later built there. By 1839, two punts and a ferry service were shuttling between the river banks. On the flat between the south bank of the Yarra and Emerald Hill (present-day South Melbourne) were the Brickfields. Here clay was quarried and bricks made, to meet the needs of the flourishing township. The Brickfields camp was intended to accommodate only the brickmakers, but others of the 'labouring class' were drawn to it because of the cheapness of living there, compared to within the town. The huts and tents were makeshift and life on the south bank was, from all accounts, pretty squalid. One writer gave the camp the classic tag of Victorian outrage, 'a nest of drunkenness and debauchery'; another styled the inhabitants 'a brood of the greatest scoundrels in the district'. It can well be imagined that the authorities viewed the Brickfields community with displeasure, as their ordered vision for the township's development would have sought to avoid the sordid aspects of cities like London where, in the previous century, 'A chain of smoking brick-kilns surrounded a great part of London and in the brickfields vagrants lived and slept, cooking their food at the kilns.'*

In late 1839, plans were afoot for the township to be extended across the river. Perhaps the authorities had plans for a second grid to mirror the first. Land speculation in the town was running at a high pitch and no doubt the government saw money to be made and a way of clearing out the Brickfields. On Christmas Eve 1839, the Yarra flooded. The brickmakers' camp was washed away, and with it plans for the town's southern expansion. In the words of a newspaper report early in the new year:

ocular demonstration has been obtained of the position in which parties foolish enough to build in such a situation would be

---

*   M. Dorothy George, *London Life in the Eighteenth Century*, Penguin, Harmondsworth, 1992, p. 105.

liable to be placed at certain seasons of the year. Since Tuesday
week nearly the whole of the land intended to be included in the
proposed extension of the township has been underwater.

And so the river remained the township's southern boundary.

The eastern boundary of Bearbrass was Spring Street, cutting across the rise of Eastern Hill. Early on, expansion took place in that direction, as the town's more aristocratic residents established country seats in (present-day) East Melbourne, Fitzroy and Richmond. Surveyor Hoddle proposed that the town's east–west streets be extended at their eastern end, but he was instructed that the town must terminate bluntly at Spring Street. In time, this allowed for the erection of Parliament House at the head of Bourke Street and the siting of the Treasury and its gardens.*

For all the prestige of the areas beyond the town to the east, that end of the township itself languished in the early years. The whole section east of Swanson Street was then designated Eastern Hill and was considered the town's back-blocks. The hill was covered with ragged gums, a popular source of firewood. William Westgarth wrote that, in 1841:

I used to traverse not a few dreary empty allotments in the hot
summer sun to reach the stores of my friend James Graham,
whose dwelling and business place in Russell, by Bourke street,
seemed then quite far out of the village ...

The township's principal chronicler, Garryowen (alias journalist Edmund Finn) put it more bluntly when he wrote of Eastern Hill:

---

* That part of Eastern Hill now occupied by the Fitzroy and Treasury gardens was known by the early settlers as the Manna Forest. The children of the town used to prize the abundant, honey-like sap (hence 'manna') produced by the white-trunked gums that grew there.

anyone who could think of investing there for anything other
than a dwelling, a timber yard, a brewery, or a house of prayer,
was booked as little less mad than a hare in the March season …

An Eastern Hill address may have spelt commercial suicide, but those who lived there thought it desirable to be at a respectable distance from the clamour at the town's western end. Socially, morally, and of course literally, they occupied the high ground.

Land sales: Hoddle gets a new hat

Towards the middle of 1837, gangs of convict labourers were put to the task of bringing Hoddle's grid to life. Armed with hatchets, they blazed trees to show the lines of streets and the position of allotments to be auctioned in the town's first land sale. Each of the grid's ten-acre blocks (except those reserved for government use) had been divided into twenty half-acre (2,000 square metre) allotments. One hundred allotments were offered for sale in June 1837.

John Batman would still have had the use of his legs in those days and could have strolled unaided to the survey paddock, at the south-west corner of Collins and William streets, to make his bids. The auction was held alfresco, with Hoddle as auctioneer, decked out in tall hat and standing on a tree stump to make himself seen. Hoddle made a neat commission from the day's sales: enough to pay for his two allotments in Elizabeth Street (one of which is now occupied by the State Bank building), with £3 12s 7d left over to buy a new hat.

True to form, Johnny Fawkner was the successful bidder for the first and second allotments under the hammer. The first, at the eastern corner of King and Flinders streets, cost him £32. During the land boom of 1839 – just two years later – the same land fetched £1,513.

Michael Pender paid only £19 for an allotment on the south side of Collins Street, east of Queen Street, upon which he built a hotel. When he finally sold it, forty years later, Pender received £33,000 for the property.

For £120, Henry Howey bought the block which today faces the town hall in Swanston Street and extends down Collins and Little Collins streets as far as Howey Place. By 1888, the estimated value of the land and its buildings was more than £1 million. However, Howey gained nothing by his canny bidding at the first land sale: within a year, he and his family were lost at sea. (Some years ago, an apparition clad entirely in white denim exposed himself to me in Howey Place. Could it have been the perverse spirit of Henry Howey, his fly buttons plucked by grazing sharks?)

John Batman paid some of the highest prices at the early land sales. These included £75 for the corner of Flinders and William streets, opposite the Customs House reserve, and £100 for the corner of Flinders and Swanston streets, occupied today by Young and Jackson's Hotel.

The second sale, of 65 allotments, was held in November of the same year, with auctions held roughly every six months thereafter, until the whole of the town grid had been offered for sale.

The makings of a 'large overgrown town'

By the fifth land sale, in April 1839, Bearbrass was experiencing a land boom, and many allotments purchased at earlier sales were being subdivided and re-sold for terrific profits. The resultant crowding prompted a squatter visiting the town to write:

> surely Melbourne will not be suffered to become a large
> overgrown town, in a hot country, without ample provision of
> spacious parks and squares, being made for its ornament, and
> for the healthful exercise and recreation of its outpouring, wall-
> pent, work-wearied people.

The 'coal pit' critic shared his concern.

> *Obviously the proper position for the Great Square of the city*
> *is at the intersection of Elizabeth-street and Collins-street.*
> *The rectangular block of ground bounded by Collins-street,*
> *Swanston-street, Bourke-street and Elizabeth-street, ought from*
> *the first to have been withheld from sale and left as an open plot.*

Not a chance. (Though he was right: it is the perfect place for a city square.) Apart from the authorities' equating a town square with rabble-rousing, the plain sum of the situation at Bearbrass was that land equalled money.

Land speculation was already having a dung beetle effect on the township, crumbling those substantial half-acres into ever smaller particles. It had originally been decreed that the 'little' streets running between the major thoroughfares of Collins and Bourke streets and the rest, were to be used solely as service lanes. The authorities had envisaged that purchasers would occupy the whole of their half-acre allotments, having the main streets as their frontages and using the between streets for rear access. For that reason, the back streets had been made only thirty-three feet (10 metres) wide, with no allowance for footpaths. The frantic subdivisions of the late 1830s led to the narrow streets in the heart of the township becoming lined with cottages, shops, workshops and other businesses; and, to service *them*, alleys and laneways were created ad hoc. So began the decay of Hoddle's pristine grid, as the streets took on a shape and a life of their own.

Great men and little streets

The main streets of Bearbrass never had a chance to assume their names *organically* – if they had you can bet that there would have been a Fawkner Street among them. But we might also have been endowed names like Sickle Street, Bullock-bog Road, Waterhole Road, and Stump Street, as well as the obvious Forest Street, Hill Street, Mill Street, Church Street, Docks Road and so on. When the Governor of

New South Wales, Sir Richard Bourke, visited the settlement in early 1837, he named the streets after the usual crowd of royalty, dignitaries and Great Men* – himself included. In years to come, no one was quite sure precisely which monarchs he had intended to honour and whose wife Elizabeth was. But nobody liked to ask.

Bourke did not even dignify the narrow thoroughfares between the east-west streets with names of their own. Because they were considered mere access lanes, their names simply echoed those of their 'parent' streets – Flinders Lane, Collins Lane, Bourke Lane, and so on. When, by 1843, they had grown into busy thoroughfares in their own right, they were renamed 'streets' by the town council and prefixed with the word 'Little'. Only Flinders Lane managed to defy the edict and has kept is original name to this day.

Not until 1847 were street signs introduced to the town:

Owing to the rapid increase in the town, and the inconvenience not infrequently experienced (more particularly by strangers) in ascertaining the names of the various streets, boards bearing the names of the principal streets are about being painted and placed at their various intersections.

But the first recorded street sign was erected not for the edification of visitors but for that of the town's own inhabitants back in the late 1830s, when the streets were still largely unformed. At the thickly treed eastern end of Bourke Street it was hard to distinguish the roadway from the bush that crowded it, so a resident in that part of town installed a board that announced THIS IS GREAT BOURKE STREET EAST.

The streets running from east to west were divided into eastern and western sections by Elizabeth Street. Collins Street East, for example, ran from Elizabeth to Spring Street, while Collins Street West extended in the other direction to Spencer Street. Street numbers do not appear

---

* Exhibition Street was originally named Stephen Street.

to have been in regular use until late in the 1840s, although, from the town's inception, Section 52 of the Police Act had ruled that:

> *Any person appointed by the Government may ... from time to time allot a number to each house, which number the occupier of every such house is required to have painted or affixed, in legible characters, upon the door of his house ...*

The naming of the town was yet another civilising act, and another Great Man was invoked.* There's an old saying to the effect that, by calling something by its proper name, you rob it of its 'dangerous magic'. Not so – all it took was a heavy shower of rain for there to be dangerous magic aplenty on the streets of Bearbrass.

---

*   Lord Melbourne, the then Prime Minister of England.

CHAPTER 3

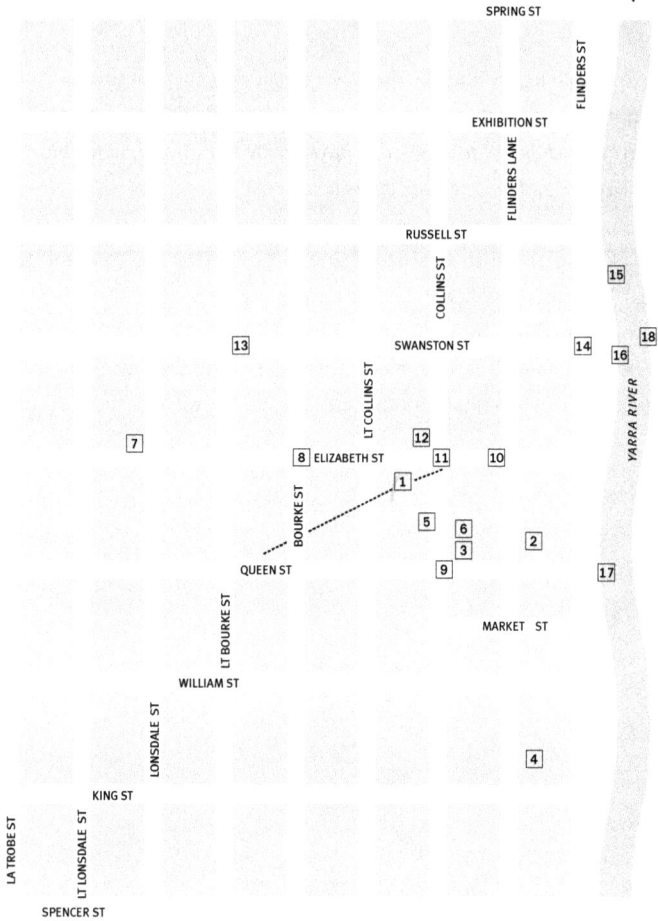

CHAPTER 3

Past Lives of City Streets

Capel's Entire ale rots new boots

Asked to imagine yourself at the corner of Elizabeth and Collins streets, you think of The Block – right? After all, that's the locale that is held up to (and tarted up for) Melburnians as the epicentre of nineteenth-century life in the city. But when you're done fancifying about the rustle of silk taffeta at the shopfronts and the twirling of parasols at the kerb and the swooping bows of tall-hatted toffs on parade, cross over Elizabeth Street.

There's public seating in the Elizabeth Street forecourt of the building at the corner, but this is no place to prop for lunch. Even on days when the town hall flag hangs limp, the gusts on this corner could snatch an exposed sandwich with the deftness of a Healesville Sanctuary emu. Just a little way down Collins Street, beside Henry Buck's, is a perpetually dark but sheltered laneway called Equitable Place. Here you'll find a number of places to eat and drink. Settle yourself in the window of one, shut your eyes, and picture this scene of yore.

∼

You can't see a thing. No moon. No street light. No bloody anything. It's late – must be after eleven – and it's black as a bloody coal hole. When's this? Must be August … no, wait … October, 1838. And you're sitting here … sitting? Half-buried, more like. How the hell did that happen? You were edging your way down the slope towards that damn gully (they call it a street – Elizabeth Street, would you believe?) and … then what? You must've slipped or … what's this? There's something hard against your shoulder. A rock? You reach back with one frozen hand. A bloody log. You must've tripped and now here you are, sunk past your knees in mud and soaked through.

It's not raining at the moment – hasn't done since late afternoon – but there's a stream of water trickling from somewhere to meet your hip where you're slewed on the ground, then using your thigh as a conduit to the trough of mud that's swallowed your boots. *Your new boots*! Damn this bloody town! Town? That's a joke. Not even a decent street. The *so-called* streets are poxed with logs, stumps, whole bloody trees – and mud! On that thought, you suddenly get your bearings (the constant trickle of water must be seeping into your bloodstream, diluting the brown ale). You're *in* the ditch of Elizabeth Street, or just on the edge of it. This is the spot where that stream from high up on the Bourke Street hill joins the main gully. You remember taking a long stride across it, higher up, on your way to Carr's public house earlier tonight. Damn Mick Carr! The others gathered themselves to leave about two hours ago and you were all set to leave with them. Tom Bullock had a fresh-killed lamb (from Batman's flock would be your guess, but Tom wasn't letting on) just boiled and was all for making a feast of it. He reckoned the girls'd be in it, too – Sarah, Mary and the other Mary. But Mick said to you, 'Hang about' – said there was something he wanted to show you – two half-hogsheads in the side parlour, got without duty off a ship just docked. The bungs were chattery and the contents would be half salt water, if you knew anything. You told him, 'Mick, you've been taken,' and he wasn't a happy man. Commiseration ran to a jug or three of Capel's Entire, after which Mick shooed you out, afraid that one of those half-wit constables might knock him up for serving after closing time.

Weaving north-east from Carr's, you didn't see a single bloody light. It was black as a boot all the way and, even before the tumble that landed you here, you'd barked your shins, smacked into a fence, startled a cow or two, and only a couple of times managed to make out blacker shapes in the blackness and skirt around them before impact. In fact, looking on the bright side, you can congratulate yourself for being roughly on course for Tom's place in Bourke Street East; if only you'd been a little higher up, or lower down even.

Minutes pass. You're aware of a warmer gush running the same course as the cold stream along your leg. Oh Jesus, it's the Capel's Entire coming back to haunt you. But the momentary warmth stirs you from your frozen stupor and you suddenly realise that Tom's is really just a short stagger away and, once across the gully, it's familiar territory. You picture that boiled haunch of lamb and the fireplace. Right, that's it. You've still got some feeling from the waist up, so you throw your shoulders back, twisting your hips down flat and shifting your upper leg slightly in the sucking mud. Now you throw your arms behind your head and, hooking your wrists over the log and using your elbows as levers, wrench your torso upwards and TTHHWUCK! your legs pull free of the mud. Panting, you heave yourself up into a sitting position, the small of your back hard against the log and your deadened legs splayed before you. While you catch your breath, you grope along your legs, making sure they really are there. Mud-caked trousers, heavy as wet canvas sails, cling to your numb knees and calves. Below that … *Jesus*! Wouldn't you bloody know it? Both feet lie bare, but for a slick muddy sheath. When the mud relinquished your lower legs, it kept your brand new boots as dues.

❦

The stream that claimed the boots originated on the north side of Bourke Street, just above Hardware Street, and meandered downhill to the south-east to join the main creek of Elizabeth Street at about the centre of Equitable Place. When the foundations for the Equitable Building were being excavated hereabouts in 1889, a box drain built in the late 1830s to carry the stream beneath the lane was dug up. The redgum planks were in a perfect state of preservation. Two metres away were found the remains of a pair of leather boots; curiously their well-preserved soles showed hardly any sign of wear.

Road-forming

When the streets were first laid out, it was generally believed that Flinders Lane would become the town's principal business thoroughfare. It's easy to see why when you look at Robert Russell's plan of the township in late 1836, before the advent of the streets. The buildings of the early settlers were mainly concentrated midway between the later lines of Collins and Flinders streets, overlooking the Falls and the basin of the Yarra. The popularity of this vicinity shows that, before street frontages were a consideration, the river was unquestionably the focus of the settlement. Convenience to the water and shipping was a high priority, but to build nearer the river than the later line of Flinders Lane was to risk flooding. The meandering east-west track, where it threaded through that most populated part of the pre-survey settlement, corresponded roughly with the subsequent line of Flinders Lane, with buildings dotted either side.

No sooner had the settlement been formalised by a survey and land sales, than Collins Street stole Flinders Lane's thunder – not surprising really, given that Collins Street had been allowed a breadth of ninety-nine feet to Flinders Lane's puny thirty-three.* In 1839,

---

* Even so, Garryowen wrote that in 1840 'Flinders Lane held the premier place in the small nobblerizing community' – that is, it could boast the greatest concentration of public houses in the township.

nearly all the town's shops were to be found in Collins Street and land auctioneers hailed it as 'the BEST STREET IN MELBOURNE, being the grand thoroughfare to and from the Country Districts' (two years later, it was 'the great outlet to the crack suburbs'). By 1840, Collins Street had won the popular appellation of 'the Regent street', which sounds pretty grand; but it would be a mistake to confuse the early Collins Street with the swank boulevard of the later Victorian period. Perhaps because of the heavy traffic it carried, Collins Street was outdone only by the notorious Elizabeth Street in attracting public ire at its atrocious condition.

Initially convict labour was used in forming the streets of the township. In the early 1840s, convicts were replaced by gangs of unemployed immigrants. Cranky road-users carped that five government road navvies did less work than one honest labourer back home in England. But imagine the task they faced east of Swanston Street, for instance, where the steep slope of Eastern Hill was thickly cloaked with huge gums, 'wild cherry' trees, and sheoaks. Road-making was not simply a matter of scraping a level ground surface and applying a crust of gravel. Journals kept by their overseers give an idea of the work that early road gangs were engaged in. During 1837–9, for instance, typical activities were: 'Falling and burning off trees in the streets', 'Stumping in Collins Street', and 'Filling up stump holes'. By these means, whole stands and forests of trees were reduced to stumps and thence to stump holes, and eventually – *very* eventually – transformed into macadamised roadways. The story of that transformation process is thick with mud, farce and danger.

Streetside amenities

The town allotments auctioned in 1837 were sold on condition that a structure be erected on each within a period of two years. By 1839, most of those allotments had been built on but, with roadways and footpaths still virtually nonexistent, land boundaries and street frontages were variously interpreted by land owners. Garryowen wrote:

Along the street line there was the greatest irregularity in the
manner in which the tenements were placed, some being in
accordance with the surveyed alignment, others several feet
back; and not a few built out on what could be only in courtesy
styled the footpath.

Where land in Collins Street still stood vacant in 1839, government
road gangs were employed to erect a two-rail fence, defining the street-
line. Early settler and historian, William Westgarth, appreciated the
need for such a fence on a rainy night in 1840.

We got into Collins-street but had much difficulty in keeping
its lines where there were not post-and-rail fences around the
vacant allotments … excepting the very centre [of town] there
were still wide intervals between the houses on either side of
Collins-street.

During building excavations more than sixty years later, James Whelan
(founder of Whelan the Wrecker) unearthed a section of the original Collins Street fence. He took it home to his Brunswick backyard,
where it was still in use as a sweet-pea trellis in 1932.

Cutting streets across the hill slopes of the town required extensive banking and excavating operations. The steep cliffs that sometimes resulted at the edge of roadways were supported by posts and
were supposed to be securely fenced with tea-tree. A report in the
Port Phillip Patriot in March 1840 alerted readers to 'the dangerous
state of the fence on the lower side of Collins-street at the corner of
Queen-street' and gives an idea of the hazards facing the Bearbrass
pedestrian, particularly by night:

There is a perpendicular fall of some six feet, with no sort of
fence to prevent the passenger from walking out over, and was it
not for the light afforded nightly by the lamps in the shop of Mr

Lazarus, we feel sure we should ere this have had to record some 'dreadful accident'.

Here it appears that the government was contravening its own regulation that any hole adjoining a street or public place should be enclosed and lit between sunset and sunrise. Moses Lazarus, who kept a jeweller's shop nearby, was under no obligation to keep his premises lit at night; only hotels (and later, theatres) were required by law to provide exterior lighting. Section 35 of the Police Act stipulated that a lamp with two burners must be kept 'constantly lighted and burning over the door' after dark. Publicans whose doorways were found unlit could be fined up to £5, unless it could be shown that accident or 'boisterous weather' had extinguished the lamp. Other extenuating circumstances were sometimes blamed, as in May 1840:

Mr Allington* was charged with allowing his lamp to go out on Thursday last at his public house, but it was proved to the satisfaction of the Bench that no good oil can be procured in Melbourne, and the case was dismissed upon Mr Allington promising to burn candles.

If the promise of good cheer and a sing-song were not enough to guarantee custom to the hotels and theatre, the lure of their compulsory street lamps ensured that their doorways became popular nocturnal meeting places. Throughout the 1840s it was a rare storekeeper who lit their premises after closing time, and the town council, chronically short of funds, was in no position to install public street lighting (think of the running costs – oil, wicks, lamp-lighters' wages).

John Sutch, years later, wrote of how he got himself 'bushed' whilst attempting the equivalent of a trip to the corner milk bar one dark night in 1838:

---

*   Probably William Allingham, licensee of the Ship Inn in Flinders Lane.

One night the writer went out to go to black-smith Rushton's
place, who lived near where the corner of Elizabeth and Little
Collins streets now is. I wanted to buy some butter off him. But
I never got there for, after a time, I found myself down by the
Yarra Scrub at the bottom of Elizabeth street. On my road home
I got into a post hole ... at the corner of Collins and Elizabeth
streets.

When parties of gentlefolk set off to musical soirées or fork suppers on moonless nights, a servant or one of the gentlemen would carry a lantern ahead of them. They kept to the middle of the roadway (or as close as they could judge it), partly for fear of being shanghaied by robbers lurking in the tea-tree scrub and behind fences, but mainly because even Collins Street was without a footpath until the mid-1840s.

Georgiana McCrae, who settled in Melbourne in 1841, recorded in her journal her first visit to acquaintances in Collins Street East: 'we went up the north side of Collins Street, without any sign of a pavement; only a rough road, with crooked gutters'. Those treacherous gutters were three to four feet deep and Robert Murray, a visitor to the town in that same year, suspected them to be of deliberate medico-athletic design. They were, he wrote, 'purposely neglected; in order to instruct the population in leaping during the day, and to furnish broken limbs by night for the advancement of medical science'.

Such footpaths as did exist during the early years of the township were provided by shopkeepers to give customers easy access to their stores. John Chisholm was a footpath pioneer in Bearbrass, having a paved pathway laid at the entrance to his grand Collins Street draper's store in 1839. Chisholm must have been a canny businessman. Imagine how alluring his flagged footpath – scrubbed and swept each morning by a shopboy – must have seemed to footsore Bearbrassians, their feet perpetually caked with mud or dust, their ankles ever on the turn. And if they paused to savour the clean, level ground at Chisholm's shopfront and their thoughts strayed to garters and gingham and Indian rubber braces, the flagging stones would soon have paid for themselves.

The stump-pocked streets of Bearbrass

In Collins Street itself at the time of Chisholm's footpath, trees were still being felled across the roadway and, for a long time after the logs were dragged away, their brutishly stubborn stumps held fast, constituting the town's chief traffic hazard. Rolf Boldrewood* told a tale of how a party of gentlefolk returning home from a ball, their carriage piloted along the lampless Collins Street by a 'gallant officer', came to grief on just such a stump:

> *The ladies were thrown out, the carriage thrown over, and the charioteer fractured. Paterfamilias, absent on business, marked his disapproval of the expedition by resolutely refraining from repairing the vehicle. For years it stood in the back yard with cracked panels, a monument of domestic miscalculation.*

William Westgarth wrote that 'Great gum-tree stumps were grievously prevalent' in the township of 1840, and the *Patriot*, in late 1841, complained that in Collins Street 'not a stump has been removed from Swanston Street upwards'. Swanston Street itself at that period was especially studded with the brutes, the town hall site remaining for a long time a knee-high forest of stumps.

Wherever possible, stumps were uprooted, leaving craters to be filled. If a stump put up too much resistance, it was burned out – or at least reduced to ground level. Thus 'there was still some holing and burning to be done' in Little Bourke Street in 1842, according to Martha Lonsdale. In 1845, the town council's public works committee

---

* The pen-name of Thomas Browne, who arrived in Melbourne as a young boy in 1840.

was formed and immediately set gangs to work clearing the remaining stumps from the streets. In three months, four hundred tree stumps were uprooted; an estimated one thousand still awaited grubbing.

One gigantic stump on the south edge of Collins Street, just east of Queen, held on defiantly for years. This truncated despot so tyrannised the street frontage of Michael Pender's allotment that when the Royal Hotel* was erected there in 1841, it had to be built skew-whiff – the mighty stump stood its ground.

In 1840, in places where entire trees still stood, laundresses suspended their washing lines from tree to tree across the streets. Garryowen gave a colourful account of their enterprise:

> Frequent accidents occurred through the fluttering and flapping of the white drapery so elevated, frightening horses and causing 'bolts' ... The washerwomen, and the half-dozen police then in existence, were on the best of terms and seemed to understand each other thoroughly; so the ladies were allowed to have a good deal their own way.

One of the central city's last remaining big trees was a giant redgum that encroached onto Elizabeth Street, alongside St Francis' Church. The tree projected into the street through a gap left in the church fence, and in the early 1840s it acted as church belfry, the bell hanging from one of its massive branches. The redgum landmark was finally felled in 1878 when St Francis' was extended, but a fragment of it survives in the sanctuary of St Patrick's Cathedral, in the shape of two episcopal chairs which were carved from its trunk.

---

* In 1842, the Royal Hotel acted as unofficial town hall; the inaugural town council met there to elect Henry Condell, a brewer, as mayor. There were suggestions that Condell's popularity with voters owed something to his largesse at the keg tap, come election time.

Bullocks and boggings

Beyond John Chisholm's footpath, the streets of Bearbrass in 1839 were a bootmaker's paradise. Their surfaces were still largely grassed, but turned to quagmires after rain. The *Herald* shared its readers' despair at the state of the unsurfaced roads in mid-winter, 1843:

> *The thoroughfares of Melbourne dignified by the names of streets, are worse than ever; they form one mass of liquid mud, varying from 3 inches to 3 feet deep.*

Collins Street carried mostly pedestrian traffic, as well as riders on horseback and an occasional dog-cart. Freight and heavy loads were generally pulled by bullocks rather than horses because of the rough terrain. In the township itself, much of the bullock traffic was confined to Flinders Lane and the docks area. In 1845, when Flinders Lane was finally banked, surfaced, guttered and footpathed, the *Patriot* referred to it as 'that "slough of despond" ... so long the terror of men, horses and bullocks'.

Georgiana McCrae's son, George Gordon McCrae, recalled from his childhood the spectacle of the bullock dray in the early township:

> *the drays with their longs strings of six, eight, and sometimes ten or more bullocks, kicked up a good deal on their way through the rough, rutty, and stump-studded streets. Then the oaths and objurgations of the drivers (to 'swear like a bullock-driver' was a household word) made the air horrid during the passage of the cavalcade ...*

Sometimes one bullock would come to a determined halt, settling down in the roadway and stalling the progress of the entire team. Faced with this situation, drivers possessed a catalogue of inducements to get the stubborn (or more than usually brutalised) bullock back on its feet. First came an unmerciful thrashing with the long handle of the driver's whip. If the beast of burden remained yet unmoved, its driver would loop its tail in two and twist until the bone broke with a sharp crack, to the applause of assembled bystanders. 'Few bullocks,' wrote McCrae, 'were found able to resist this gentle reminder.' The rare bullock that withstood the persuasiveness of the tail-twister would be finally prompted to its feet by having newspapers and twigs shoved beneath it and set alight.

The greatest hazard to the bullock dray's progress through the Bearbrass streets, however, was not the occasional refractory bullock, but the state of the streets themselves. Bullock boggings were commonplace. Thomas Strode, one of the town's early newspapermen, recalled:

> At almost every hour of the day may be viewed the interesting spectacle of drays being bogged in the muddy depths of Collins-street ... We remember on [one] occasion a dray of bullocks were so hopelessly imbedded in a hole in Elizabeth-street, that the animals were allowed to stifle in the mud, and its being nobody's duty to remove the nuisance, their remains with that of the dray, lie buried in that extemporary graveyard to the present day [1868].

Are the bullock bones and dray still mouldering beneath the tarmac and tram-lines, I wonder? That 'hole in Elizabeth Street' was probably at the Bourke Street intersection, near the erstwhile GPO. That corner and the intersection of Collins and Queen streets were the scenes of the town's most spectacular boggings. In July 1843, the *Patriot* reported that: 'At the junction of Collins and Queen-streets, there is a single hole deep enough to bury decently the whole corporation' – that is, the town council.

Elizabeth Street was, of course, the horror street of the infant metropolis. Westgarth regretted that a street had been made of 'this troublesome and unhealthy hollow', arguing that, instead, 'a reservation of the natural grass and gum trees' should have been left there and 'a succession of ornamental lakes and fishponds' created along the gully's course. The gully which formed the course of Elizabeth Street was often referred to as a creek, but it appears that, although the southern end had always been swampy, the running waterway came into being only after early attempts at drainage made the gully a conduit for stormwater channelled down the slopes on either side. A shower of rain caused a little rivulet to run along the centre of Elizabeth Street; a downpour swelled the rivulet into a 'brawling torrent'.

The only point at which Elizabeth Street could safely be crossed in bad weather was up at the high ground of Lonsdale Street. Following heavy rains in November 1839, a bogus advertisement appeared in the town's press seeking tenders for the establishment of a ferry service across Elizabeth Street. Years later, a man and his horse were drowned one night in Elizabeth Street, near the Bourke Street corner, and it was (only half-jokingly) proposed to the mayor that the town council should install life-buoys 'the whole length of the post office coast'.

Thomas Strode related the story of a man who, in 1838, was offered a half-acre allotment fronting Elizabeth Street, at the exact point where the stream from the Bourke Street hill met (present-day) Equitable Place. The asking price was a bargain-basement £36.

He replied that he would pay that price, provided the owner would present him with 36 pairs of stilts, 18 feet in height, for without them it would be impossible to gain access to the ground in winter ...

In the real estate business – then as now – it was a case of making an asset of an embuggerance. Thus we find auctioneer Charles Williams, in the winter of 1839, describing the situation of land for sale at the soggy south-east corner of Elizabeth and Collins streets as 'leading down to the approximate banks of the lovely Yarra'.

This lower end of Elizabeth Street had been deeply scoured out by the water that teemed from upstream and was popularly called the River Townend or the River Enscoe. Townend was a grocer whose mart stood at the south-west corner of Collins and Elizabeth streets from 1840 – the corner itself was known as Townend's Corner and was one of the town's boggiest. John Enscoe was a partner in a firm of Queen Street merchants and owed his link with the Elizabeth Street trough to his 'having nearly met a watery grave from a precipitate immersion therein', according to the *Patriot* in August 1840.

Enscoe wasn't the last to take an involuntary dip in the lapping waters of the Elizabeth Street ditch. In 1844, William Wentworth was swept into a flood-swelled drain whilst legging it across the inter-section of Elizabeth and Bourke streets on his way to the bank. He emerged gasping and minus his Orleans top-coat, the inside pocket of which had bulged with valuables destined for the bank vault. Despite a reportedly 'indefatigable' search by the town's street-keeper, Mr Wentworth never saw his blue coat or its contents again.

A daredevil butcher known as Joe the Fiddler attempted a crossing of Elizabeth Street at high tide in May 1848, his delivery cart loaded with choice cuts. A reporter from the *Patriot* was among the crowd that gathered to watch the sport:

> *On reaching the stream Joe resolutely took the deeps and waded through, notwithstanding the jokes of the by-standers, and encouraged by his success attempted the deeper waters on the opposite side. He got on admirably until he reached the middle of the current, where it was above his hips, and then the force of the floods carried him clean off his legs, rolling him over and over like a log; and hurried off the contents of his tray, to feed the fishes in the Yarra.*

A more-or-less permanent feature of the Bearbrass winter scene was Lake Cashmore, situated at the headwaters of the River Townend or

Enscoe – that is, at the intersection of Elizabeth and Collins streets. Lake Cashmore was the *aqua profunda* of Elizabeth Street and the most likely venue for unintentional aquatic displays. It derived its name from Michael Cashmore, an 'Israelitish' draper, whose General Silk and Haberdashery Emporium, built in 1840, overlooked it from the 'Block' corner (then Cashmore's Corner) – in fact, the waters of the stagnant pool reached to within a metre or so of his door.

Garryowen described Lake Cashmore as 'a formidable-looking water-hole … not sufficiently deep to drown a man, but quite sufficient to half do it'. John Quin tested its waters on the night of the winter solstice, 1841. Next day he fronted the court, where a *Herald* reporter witnessed the following exchange:

Bench – *Were you drunk?*
Quin – *Worse – oh, far worse, I was stupid.*
Constable – *I found him* swimming *in a hole in Collins-street, and drew him forth with a boat hook.*

Quin's saviour may have found it a welcome change to be on the blunt end of the boat hook, as constables and night-watchmen were more commonly the victims of Lake Cashmore's half-drowning propensities. A popular sport amongst larrikins and footpads of the town was to conceal themselves in the shadows and behind fences thereabouts, waiting to pounce on a patrolling lawman and turf him into the lake. This explains the ready availability of a boat hook.

Cashmore's was one of the township's most stylish stores,* but his floorboards must have looked like the players' race after a mud-bath at Windy Hill. Even supposing his doorway bristled with foot-scrapers, metal grilles and wire mats, mud must have found its way inside. Or did a clerk meet customers at the threshold, offering cloth slippers in

---

* During a coin shortage in the early '40s, Michael Cashmore's store was famed as the only place in Bearbrass that could give change for a £5 note.

exchange for their muddied footwear which was requested to be left on an oilskin mat by the door? Perhaps Cashmore even employed a boot-boy to scrape off the worst of the muck while shoppers browsed and bought. Even the complimentary-cloth-slippers scenario leaves muddy snail-trails across his floor and fixtures where the sodden hems of skirts and petticoats swished and dragged. Imagine the bargains to be had when low-lying bolts of muslin had to be sold off as shop-soiled.

Cashmore's customers had to be keen. 'Often to cross over from any portion of the now well-flagged and fashionable "Block",' wrote Garryowen, 'one required to be equipped in a pair of leggings or long mud-boots.' William Ames thought he was being most enterprising when he brought with him to the settlement in 1839 a number of large trunks full of women's cloth boots. Cloth boots, laced at the side, were all the rage in London at the time and Ames hoped to pay for his passage by selling them to the fashion-starved women of Bearbrass. He hadn't reckoned on the state of the streets. Even in summer months, cloth boots would have been an unwise choice for a shopping trip in town. The *Patriot* reported in January 1840 that government road gangs were working on Collins and Queen streets 'so that they may be rendered passable by the pedestrian without burying his leg in mud or water-holes'. Far from braving the mud and waterholes in cloth boots, a gentlewoman would borrow a pair of men's Wellington boots (in those days made of leather, not rubber) to wear over her best shoes for the walk to and from evening engagements. This small notice appeared in the *Patriot* in June 1840: FOUND – A WELLINGTON BOOT *in Little Collins-street – the owner may have the same on paying for this Advertisement.* Therein surely lies a tale – of a fork supper, a journey home by moonlight, a stump hole full of mud, a borrowed Wellington abandoned, and a cloth boot's ruination.

On the subject of mud, it remains only to relate the sorry story of Mr and Mrs Barney O'Leary and their triplets. In the winter of 1843, following a ceremony at St Francis' Church, the O'Learys and their guests celebrated the triplets' christening with a knees-up at Lynch's Rising Sun Hotel in Little Bourke Street. At closing time, the party piled into a hired open coach which lurched into Swanston Street and overturned, depositing its contents – triplets and all – in a pool of stinking slush.

Wet underfoot: the Yarra crossing

Flinders Street was formed on the flat along the riverfront – in fact, the street was known as The Flat in the early days. The roadway, on its southern side, lapsed into a marsh which deepened to become the river proper. In winter and wet weather, Flinders Street – its western end, at least – was almost lost to the Yarra. From Market Street westwards* Flinders Street was virtually the dockside, servicing shipping and the warehouses facing the river. When Charles La Trobe (Superintendent of Port Phillip and later the first Governor of Victoria) disembarked at Bearbrass in 1839, he had to wade through the Yarra shallows, negotiate the bullock-churned mud of the flat, and heave his sodden Wellingtons up the William Street hill to receive his official welcome.

Flinders Street ran along higher ground at its eastern end, with reeds and bushy scrub fringing its riverbank side. Early settler John Sutch recalled the non-view of the river in 1838: 'At this time the river Yarra was not visible to a person standing in Swanston-street, about where St Paul's Church now stands, owing to the dense tea-tree scrub ...'

Flinders Street was the springing-off point for travellers across the Yarra, heading for the Brickfields, Liardet's Beach (Port Melbourne), St Kilda, Brighton, and beyond. Serving the trans-Yarra traffic, as an extension of the Bearbrass streets, was a series of punts. First off the rank was the punt of Tom Watt, a builder who was hard on his servants, free with his fists, and fond of hanging out at Mrs Bowden's brothel in

---

* The rocky falls prevented ships from progressing further up the Yarra.

Williamstown. One of Watt's five daughters performed a champagne christening of the punt, imaginatively named *The Melbourne*, on Easter Sunday, 1838. Its departure point on the town side of the river was between Swanston and Russell streets, where a narrow trackway made of planks had been laid across the reedy swamp to the river bank. The punt could carry a bullock dray and its team, and the river-crossing was effected by a herculean punt-puller (or a horse) hauling on a rope tied to a tree on the opposite bank.

After a year, Watt's punt was joined on the river by a competitor, shuttling across from near the end of Elizabeth Street. Watt's response to the competition was to offer free beer for one day to all passengers using his punt. Unfortunately, as Watt later testified in court, 'The brick makers on the south side of the river ... took the utmost advantage of my liberality [and] crossed and re-crossed until they got drunk.' He was charged with having caused an 'outbreak against the quiet of the town' and had his punt licence revoked.

His licence was transferred to John Welsh, who established a punt at the point where Princes Bridge now crosses the river. Welsh once confided to a friend that he earned a clear £30 a week (a whole year's wages to most) from his punt business – which explains why Tom Watt had been so keen to keep his customers. In the early 1840s, punt passengers were slugged four shillings and sixpence each way, with double fares payable on Sundays. Aborigines and town councillors were carried free of charge.

An old Irishman named Paddy Byrne ran a passenger ferry service just above the Falls from about 1838. Garryowen recalled that Paddy would sometimes be 'asthmatically or rheumatically disposed', on which occasions his daughter, Polly, would instead skipper the ferry, 'with skill and liveliness'. Was old Paddy the same Patrick Byrne, I wonder, who was charged with being 'very drunk and riotous' at Smith's public house in 1838? Perhaps his occasional 'indisposition' owed something to an excessive dose of medicinal rum.

The Yarra's first bridge was a long time in the offing. It was

1846 before the first wooden construction of the Melbourne Bridge Company opened for business, crossing the river just upstream from the site of the later Princes Bridge. Patrick Doherty was bridgekeeper and toll-collector, and also acted as unofficial lifesaver. Bearbrassians were forever ending up in the Yarra – often intentionally, frequently at the behest of the demon rum, only rarely by accident. When Doherty died in 1851, aged just thirty-two, the inscription on his headstone, erected by public subscription, recorded that 'he saved eight persons from drowning in the Yarra'.

His employer also had reason to pay homage to Doherty's heroism, on another count. In 1849, Doherty fought off four armed ruffians who tried to rob him of the day's takings. Doherty was pistol-whipped but his attackers decamped leaving behind not only the toll-fees but 'a neatly-made pistol, of superior sort, with some initials erased, and a wig with long curls'.

As early as 1848, pedestrians had begun to make use of the spans of the unfinished Princes Bridge, as a way of avoiding Patrick Doherty's tolls. The stone bridge was completed in April 1850, but could not be opened to wheeled traffic until the road approaches at either end were brought up to scratch. Its official opening took place on 15 November 1850 as part of the Port Phillip District's separation celebrations. And Patrick Doherty was out of a job.

Good order on the streets

Section 15 of the Police Act spelt out some of the acts forbidden on the public streets of the township:

> *Any person beating carpets, flying kites, breaking, exercising, or exposing for sale any horse or horses, throwing rubbish, ashes, offal, &c., upon any carriage-way, foot-way, street, or public place ... or rolling, driving or placing upon any foot-way, any wagon, cart or other carriage, or any wheelbarrow,*

truck, hogshead, barrel, &c.; … shall forfeit not exceeding forty
shillings nor less than five shillings.

Needless to say, hogsheads *were* rolled in the streets and rubbish *was* thrown, empty liquor bottles and gobbets of steaming sheep entrails serving as the Bearbrass equivalent of today's McLitter. As Bearbrass grew, its government, town council and public institutions strove to ensure not only that the streets were in good order, but that there was good order on the streets.

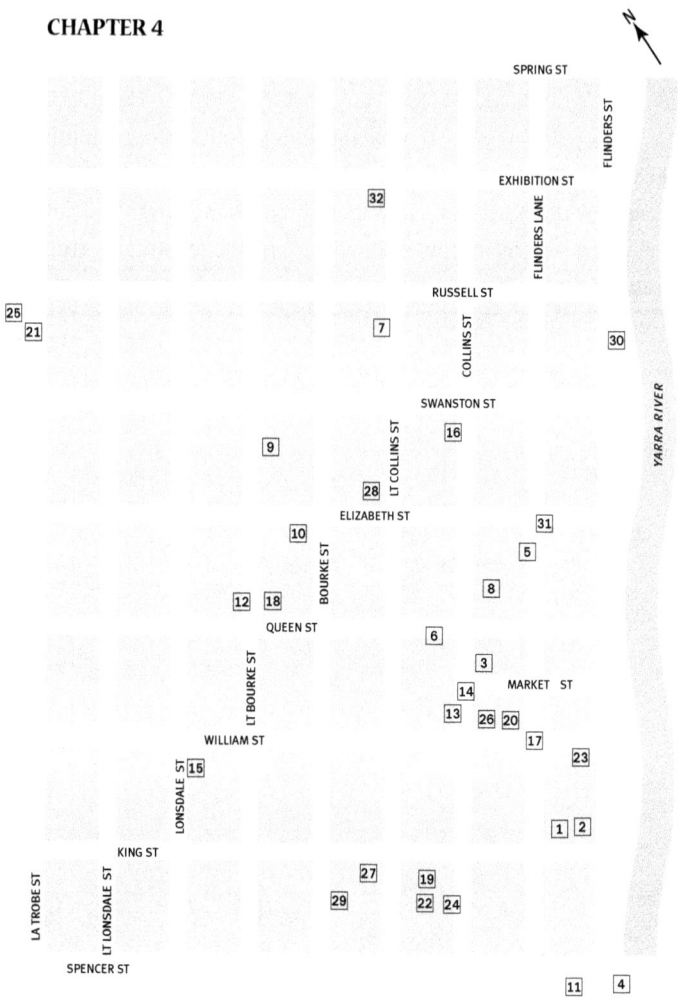

CHAPTER 4

N

SPRING ST

FLINDERS ST

EXHIBITION ST

32

FLINDERS LANE

RUSSELL ST

25
21

7

COLLINS ST

30

SWANSTON ST

YARRA RIVER

9

LT COLLINS ST

16

28

ELIZABETH ST

31

10

5

BOURKE ST

8

12 18

6

QUEEN ST

3

LT BOURKE ST

14   MARKET   ST

13

26 20

WILLIAM ST

17

LONSDALE ST 15

23

KING ST

1 2

LT LONSDALE ST

27

19

LA TROBE ST

29

22 24

SPENCER ST

11   4

1. John Moss's Ship Inn and brewery, scene of sundry brawls and collarings
2. Benjamin and Martha Baxter's cottage-cum-post office
3. The Melbourne Club house
4. Site of Craig and Broadfoot's duel
5. Oliver Adams's Crown Hotel, from which the 'excessively outrageous' Tom Grant was barred in 1837
6. Jemmy Connell's Highlandman Hotel, whose floorboards were splashed with Tom Fitzmaurice's blood in 1837
7. Waterloo Hotel, watering-hole of coffin-makers, 1846
8. Site of the disputed fence dividing Brentani and Simeon, 1847
9. Anne Naes' house, at the rear of Elephant and Castle Hotel, 1846
10. The rooms behind a shop where Ann Brown's husband beat her with an iron bar, 1843
11. John and Eliza Batman's house, from which their servant Elizabeth Pearce stole goods including a paper of pins and a hair comb in 1838
12. The house of a woman named Sutherland or 'Jenny McLeod', from whose dressing-table jewellery was alleged to have been stolen by an oysterman, 1845
13. The Lamb Inn, Fred Napper's undoing, 1841
14. The street near the market reserve where, in 1838, a man was arrested for 'making water' in view of a passing female
15. Tom Skilton pissed over Horatio Nelson Carrington's garden fence, 1842
16. Fleming's Edinburgh Castle Hotel, where Constable James Caulfield drank himself out of a job, 1838
17. Site of the 'chasm nearly brimful of thick slush', into which J.W. Hooson was chased by a bullock, 1842
18. The alley in which 'Dick' Swindell found her constable husband after he over-imbibed on his night patrol, 1848
19. The original police office, which doubled as a courtroom, 1836–8
20. The second police office-cum-court, originally built as the town's third gaol, 1838. Later afforded shelter to the district's first feral rabbits
21. Supreme Court, 1843, with gaol and bush at rear
22. The turf-and-thatch shepherd's hut that served as the first gaol, 1836–8
23. Second gaol, 1838, with Harper's and Yarra Yarra hotels adjacent
24. The fourth and last of the temporary gaols, 1840–44
25. The permanent gaol (now the Old Melbourne Gaol), 1844
26. The stocks, sited on the market reserve to ensure maximum humiliation
27. Convicts' barracks and tents, where Ann McNally fought off the scourger with a pair of tongs, 1837
28. The house in which Lizzie Wheeler and convict Tom Cohen were caught in flagrante delicto by Lizzie's husband, home early from a sea voyage, 1838
29. The scourger 'squatted in a den' on this site in the late 1830s
30. The government pound, in which wandering livestock were secured, late 1830s
31. William Wormsley's Fruit and Fish Mart, home to a spruiking rosella named Dickie
32. The Eastern Hill watchhouse, where unregistered dogs were slaughtered during the Canine War of the 1840s

CHAPTER 4
Law and Order

Round midnight in the nightclub precinct

If you're feeling game or frisky, you might like to pay a nocturnal visit to the city's nightclub precinct. It's at the western end of the city, centred on that stretch of King Street between Collins and Flinders streets. A decade ago, it was the Friday- and Saturday-night preserve of revved-up suburbanites. Two nights a week at least, this end of King Street was a motorcade of cruising V8s, their backseats occupied for the only time all week. The air was flammable with petrol fumes, aftershave and pizza farts, and bourbon-fuelled testosterone burned in a thousand pairs of Y-fronts.

Among the clubbers nowadays are almost as many backpackers as arrivés from the south-eastern arterial. And there's another element of change, summed up by a warning, SEXUALLY EXPLICIT ENTERTAINMENT MAY OFFEND, posted outside one of the new strain of clubs. Strip clubs have slunk down King Street, geared to girls' and lads' nights out and 'gentlemen's' lunches, and further sinking the locale into are-we-having-fun-yet? ickiness.

Take care, now. Watch out for that broken glass, tear your eyes away from that nipple-tickler, step round that pool of vomit … Better still, come back when it's daylight.

A choice part of town, it is – and so it ever was.

∽

On a late spring night in 1838, six of you are sitting around a packing-case table in the back room of John Moss's wattle-and-daub shanty, the Ship Inn, in Flinders Lane, just east of King Street. Jack Moss is one of the six, and there's two Toms, a Jemmy and yourself, besides Eddie Steel, the convict-flogger (and a convict himself), who's out of barracks after muster. You're at cards and Moss is winning, as usual – and totting up the rums on the slate beside him, he's winning on that score too. He answered a nightwatchman's knock just after the eleven o'clock call. One of the officious rozzers it was, a new one, and he wouldn't be side-stepped by the offer of a hand in the game or some liquid payola. Said he was wondering about the crack of light that showed under the loose-fitting window frame. But Moss, in flannel shirt and braces, said he was ready for bed and looked it. Then he plugged the tattling crack with a wad of rag and came back to the game. You haven't heard the midnight call, but it must be about that now and the game's close to breaking up for the night.

'That'll do me,' yawns one of the Toms. He's gone through all the brass that Moss advanced him.

'Yeh, me too,' says old Jemmy, easing the boot back onto his buniony right foot. 'The luck's with you arright, Jack. I'll square up when Cooney pays me for them pair of hogs next week.'

'Right enough,' nods Moss. Then – 'Here!' he hisses to you, just as you (in your innocence) make for the door through to the tap room. 'The back way. Just let me do this candle.' The others pull on their jackets, turning the collars up, and reach under seats for their hats.

'Right then, Jack.' Jemmy gives the cue to snuff out the candle and one of the Toms unbolts the back door. It opens with a minimum of scrape and, with soft grunt to your host, the five of you stump out into the yard and Moss eases the door shut behind you.

You stand still for a few moments, getting your night eyes and listening for the clanking step of the night constable. But nothing. Eddie scuttles off in the direction of the convict tents, a short but perilous distance away on the government block. Jemmy and the more sober of the Toms live up on Bourke Street.

'Wait about,' whispers the other Tom, 'I need a leak.'

'Be buggered,' Jemmy hisses back. 'We're off.' And, harking once again for noises of nightwatchmen, Jemmy and Bourke-Street Tom edge around the side of the inn and make for home. That leaves Tom-with-a-bladderful and yourself (also under the weather, it's true), skulking at Moss's back step.

At the rear of the Ship is Moss's brewery, where he turns out a decent ale from Yarra water. You and Tom make a latrine of the weatherboarded side wall of the brewery shed and, with the lightening of his bladder, Tom has an idea.

'I bet George'd like a drop of beer.'

'Eh?'

'George. Y'know, he's over in the logs.* This shed's packed with barrels of beer. Jack showed me once. I bet George'd like some.'

You're slow on the uptake. 'When he gets out, d'yer mean?'

'Nah, now – or in the morning, anyway. We could roll a barrel to the logs, don't yer reckon? It'd only be … what? A hundred yards? Then we could toss it over the wall into the yard and George could suck the skin off for breakfast.'

'How big d'yer say these barrels are?' you ask, as dubious as a drunk can get.

'Ohh … about so big.' Tom makes a broad circle with his arms

---

* 'Logs' is a convict-slang term for gaol, originating from the log huts that served as lock-ups in the early days of the Australian colonies. The gaol in which thirsty George was incarcerated was a brick store on the western corner of William and Flinders streets, which was used as a temporary gaol during 1838.

(having finished his business at the side of the shed and fastened his buttons in an approximate fashion).

'And how high's this fence?'

'Oh … about so high,' and he stands on tiptoe and stretches his arm up as high as he can.

'Yer bloody mad,' you say, shaking your head. 'We couldn't manage it. And anyhow, this shed of Jack's'll be locked – *and* he'd be none too pleased to find a barrel of his beer missing.'

'Heh! What he took from us tonight'd more than pay for a barrel of his shitty brew! And as for the lock … well, come and have a look.'

The entrance to the brewing shed is down towards the Flinders Street end of the block. There's a big pair of double doors, one of them inset with a smaller hatch. The padlock on the hatch looks puny.

'I could snap that with me teeth,' scoffs Tom.

As for you, you're feeling edgy. While the pair of you are pretty well sheltered from Flinders Street and the docks by tea-tree scrub, you're hard by Ben Baxter's cottage* and he's a cranky old specimen, sure to go hallooing for a constable if he hears so much as a twig break. (It's no fun for Ben and Martha Baxter and their two little girls, living back-on to the Ship Inn. Many's the night they've heard worse than a twig break – neck-breaking would be more like it.)

'Come on, Harry. Don't be soft. Wait here a mo'. I know just the trick.' Tom disappears around the side of the shed, and returns a minute or so later clutching a brickbat.† 'See! I thought so. Jack uses this to prop his back door open. Now just hold that lock out for us. That's it – like that.'

You hold the padlock out at the horizontal, but gingerly, with the very tips of your thumb and index finger. Tom brings the brickbat

---

* Ben Baxter rented this cottage from Johnny Fawkner. Recalled by one settler as a 'badly-ventilated two-roomed, brick-nogged cottage', it was described by Fawkner himself, when seeking a tenant, as 'A substantial Weatherboarded house'. Between 1837–9, Ben and Martha Baxter operated the town's first post office from the cottage's living room.

† A half or broken brick.

down with a mighty sweep – and misses the padlock entirely. Instead, it makes crashing contact with the heavy iron bolt below, and the brickbat crumbles into sandy clods.

'Bloody local bricks!' curses Tom. 'What we need's a decent lump of Sydney stone. Hang on – what about that back step of Jack's?'

'Oh, Jesus! Leave off!' You've had enough.

'No, no, wait ...' and Tom's off around the side of the shed again.

But you don't wait. You turn like a shot and elbow your way through the scrub towards Flinders Street.

By the time Tom reappears, panting and bent double with the weight of the bluestone door slab, you're halfway home. 'Bastard!' mutters Tom. He can't even lift the stone as high as the padlock, so he settles for kicking it instead. In no time – by the fourth kick – Jack Moss is pelting down the yard (though slowed down, it's true, by stumbling where his back step ought to be) and Ben Baxter's leaning over his back fence shouting, 'Oi! What's that damned racket!' Moss lunges at Tom and is dealing him a good pounding when Constable Mat Cantlon bursts through the tea-tree with handcuffs jingling and waddy rampant.

Ten minutes later in the cramped lock-up, George Penfold is woken by a poke in the ribs.

'Here, give us a bit of that blanket, will yer?'

'Tom! What are *you* doing here?'

'Well, see, I thought yer might like a drop of beer ...'

❧

In August 1835, the month in which the first white settlers staggered ashore at Bearbrass, the *Hobart Town Courier* expressed the fear that the Port Phillip District would be:

> *exempt from the control of Government as a receptacle for runaway convicts, and all other desperate characters, who would flock to Port Phillip, endangering the peace and prosperity of the colonists, becoming buccaneers, &c.*

Late the following year, the newly arrived Police Magistrate, William Lonsdale, seemed to confirm that fear, reporting to Governor Bourke that 'many of the lower order of people who had come over on adventure, were taking advantage of the absence of power to behave in a lawless and intimidatory manner'.

Lonsdale's use of the expression *'come over'* suggests that he referred to settlers from Van Diemen's Land. During the early days of the settlement, and particularly with the arrival of Sydney officialdom, there existed a spirited, if largely one-sided, rivalry between the Vandemonian 'Gumsuckers' and the 'Cornstalkers' from New South Wales. This rivalry was very likely the invention of (and certainly was perpetuated by) Johnny Fawkner, who viewed the Sydneyites as interlopers. The Sydneyites, for their part, took Lonsdale's line. The *Sydney Gazette*, in January 1837, characterised the Vandemonian settlers of Bearbrass as, for the most part, 'a drunken, worthless set, and a complete pest to the place'.

By February 1837, Lonsdale had somewhat modified his views on the culpability of the 'lower order of people' for the settlement's lawlessness. He wrote to Bourke that

> *Many of the servants are troublesome ill-disposed men and I regret in too many cases they have not good examples shown them from quarters where they should look for them.*

It was true: the 'higher order' was equally given to drinking and rowdy lawlessness. The younger squatters (and they were, almost exclusively, young) were a wild mob when they came to town. They formed the core of what became the Melbourne Club and were referred to by the press of the day as the 'gentlemen rowdies of the Waterford School'.* After a decent session of lubrication at their clubhouse, the

---

* The aristocratic excesses of the Marquis of Waterford being at that time proverbial.

Waterford-ish bucks of Bearbrass would take to the streets to heckle and bail up female pedestrians, scuttle the police (dunking the night-watchman in a waterhole, perhaps), smash shop windows, and even saw through verandah posts for a lark.

Another popular diversion among the 'higher orders', which fell somewhere between the categories of sport and theatre, was the staging of a duel – known as 'the usual alternative' to an apology, in the case of a dispute between ostensible gentlemen. One of the earliest Bearbrass duellists was Dr Barry Cotter, the settlement's first medico and a legendary drinker and gamester. As Garryowen wrote years later, there was a strong element of farce in the practice of duel-ling, Bearbrass-style:

> of the several duels fought ... in this colony, not one instance
> has ever occurred in which either challenger or challenged,
> or seconds,* ever drew blood from the other... one belligerent
> skinned one of his own toe-tops; another ignited his nether
> garments, and the coat and hat of others were perforated ...
> Furthermore, the Port Phillip duelling was impregnated with
> ... a desire on the part of the seconds, concurred in by some of
> the principals, to turn the affair into a joke – an Antipodean
> travestying quite foreign to the recognised style ...

Nonetheless, honour was avenged without bloodshed and the mutual sense of relief was generally such as to replace antagonism with bon-homie and back-slapping. In 1841, business partners Skene Craig and Alexander Broadfoot met in a duel at the foot of Batman's Hill. Historian Hugh McCrae summarised the proceedings thus: 'Craig missed Broadfoot, and Broadfoot missed Craig, whereupon they rushed forward to congratulate each other.'†

The people of the Kulin nation had their own system for settling

---

*   Each duellist had a sidekick, known as a 'second'.

†   *Georgiana's Journal, Melbourne 1841–1865*, ETT Imprint, 1992, p. 148.

disputes, which sometimes saw conflicts come to a head on the streets and outskirts of the town. In 1839, Aborigines met in battle at the northern end of town, beyond Lonsdale Street, on three occasions – in April, August and September. These were organised bouts in a running conflict between the different Kulin groups. A *Herald* report in April 1840 seems to describe a similar gathering of tribal groups in the town:

> *It was generally expected that a fight would take place on Wednesday night between the two native tribes at present parading our streets in a state of semi-nudity. Some spears were thrown, one of which struck and severely wounded one of the Melbourne blacks.*

In addition to the tribal clashes, fighting between Aborigines was sometimes engineered, as a kind of sport, by members of the town's larrikin element.

Brickbats and bottles: assault or 'fighting in the town'

Drunkenness appears to have been the common ingredient in most of the crimes and misdemeanours to attract the notice of the police and newspapers.* The crime of drunkenness itself I will look at in a later chapter – suffice it to say here that entire columns of tight-packed newsprint were crammed with listings of the previous day's offenders, whom Fawkner's newspaper gleefully branded 'lushingtons' or 'votaries of the jolly bacchus'. But in Bearbrass, as in the modern city, drunkenness was often far from jolly. 'Fighting in the town' (in effect, fighting in the street) was an offence on the police statute books and was a common outcome of too many rums or porters.

---

* Probably the next most common cause of appearance before the Police Magistrate was that of servants absconding from their masters before their contracts of employment had expired. These were free servants, not convicts, but the law came down heavily on them, as will be shown in the next chapter.

The drunken roars of one Tom Grant drew Constables Tomkin and Gomm to Oliver Adams's Crown Hotel one evening in March 1837. Grant was trying to force his way into Adams's public house, repeatedly charging the front door with his shoulder whilst Adams and a contingent of drinkers braced it from inside. The court next day heard evidence from the constables that, apart from being drunk, Grant 'was besides excessively outrageous' (that is, abusive) and was 'riotous, kicking and biting'. Eventually they had tied his feet and dragged him between them to the lock-up. Grant was imprisoned for a month.

Tom Fitzmaurice, a carpenter, awoke in the police lock-up one morning in July 1837, having been arrested the night before for fighting in the town with George Penfold. Two constables had arrived on the scene to find Fitzmaurice standing in the street with his shirt and jacket off (probably an offence in itself), bleeding and drunk. Penfold, the court heard, 'had been drunk in the town for two or three days past'. Both men were sentenced to four hours in the stocks. As the Bearbrass stocks immobilised only the legs of offenders, it is to be hoped that Fitzmaurice and Penfold were positioned beyond striking distance of one another.

Four months later, Tom Fitzmaurice was up on a charge of stealing tea, but went free after the case was dismissed. Soon after, he was on the receiving end of a fist thrown by his employer, Tom Watt, in the bar of Jemmy Connell's Highlandman Hotel in Queen Street, near the Little Collins corner. Tom Watt, you will remember, was a builder and went on to operate the first Yarra punt.

On a hot afternoon in February 1846, cabinetmaker Harry Dea knocked off early from the coffin he was working on and made for the Waterloo Hotel in Little Collins Street, to slake his sawdusty thirst with long pots of ale. Lurching out into the street some hours later, in company with John Quin (of puddle-swimming fame – see Chapter 3), Dea smacked straight into William Finn, who was making to enter the hostelry. 'Ere, wotchit!' protested Finn.

Sensing a challenge, the well-stoked Dea grabbed a fistful of Finn's waistcoat front and spat, 'Nah, *you* wotchit!', and, with his free hand, snatched the smoking pipe from between his teeth and jabbed it hard into Finn's left eye. Harry Dea got three months and William Finn got his waistcoat mended.

In January 1847, the *Herald* reported the arrest of a man named John McPherson on a charge of assault. No details of the offence were given, but the reporter noted that McPherson's reputation as 'a regular fighting man' had earned him the nickname 'Jack the Chicken'.

Tom Howard, a private in the 80th Regiment stationed at Bearbrass, was assaulted in a hotel – by the publican. John Moss, you will recall, ran a low dive called the Ship Inn in Flinders Lane. Howard, a regular customer, was deep in debt to Moss for gambling dues and had, moreover, been drinking on credit for almost two months. One day in August 1837, Moss grew weary of Howard's excuses for non-payment and, according to Howard's testimony in court, 'he abused me very much and took hold of me by the collar of my coat and shook me'. This grabbing by the collar (the origin, it seems of the verb *to collar*) was as common a fight tactic in the Bearbrass pub scene as it is in your average TV police drama today. (I had imagined this to be a mere piece of televisual choreography, devised to afford a close-up shot of both combatants, scowling.) Maybe gentlemen resorted to duels simply because their detachable collars made 'collaring' an impossibility.

Brickbats and empty glass or stoneware bottles were the most popular forms of missile or bludgeon among the brawling classes of Bearbrass. So real was the danger of flying brickbats or bottles that by the early 1840s the uniform of the Bearbrass police included a tall hat with a glazed leather crown atop upright iron bars, designed especially to deflect just such missiles.*

---

* The constabulary's heavy hats served another purpose. In Matthew Kneal's novel *Sweet Thames* (Black Swan Books, London, 1993), a London bobby of 1849 wore a hat of the same description. When asked about it, he explained: 'It's made to be strong enough to hold the full weight of a man, see. So if I come upon a wall I need to peer over, but that's too high, I can use my Chimney Pot as a step.'

A woman named Margaret Wilson was, on separate occasions, both flinger and flingee of brickbats. In September 1848, she was charged with assaulting her husband by throwing a brickbat at him. Three weeks later, she appeared in court to testify that she had herself been assaulted, by another woman. The *Patriot* reported:

> *She brought [into court] with her a bundle which she designated to the magistrate as a lot of 'combustibles' that had been used by her antagonist; the articles thus defined when opened were a knife, two half bricks, and a ginger beer bottle ...*

In early 1847, Charles Brentani, a watchmaker in Collins Street West, near Queen Street, had a fence erected around his yard following a rash of thefts from the rear of his premises. As his yard adjoined that of James Simeon, a slop seller (working men's draper), Brentani thought it only reasonable that Simeon should share the cost of the fence dividing the two properties. Not only did Simeon refuse to pay the one guinea asked of him, but he ordered his servant, Louis Alexander, to chop down the fence with an axe. Alexander set about the task with vigour and swung the axe at Brentani, slashing his trouser leg, when the watchmaker tried to save his fence. Mrs Brentani came to her husband's aid and was pelted with bottles and brickbats for her trouble.

Unrest between neighbours was by no means uncommon in Bearbrass. Judith Croaker was called 'a dirty Irish woman' by her neighbour Jane Gibson after the two had exhausted the topic of the weather one cloudless day in September 1837. During the fight that ensued, Croaker was struck on the side of the face with an earthenware jug hurled from Gibson's window. The court was unconvinced, however, that Gibson was the hurler and dismissed the charge of assault against her.

In July 1838, Catherine Doyle called on her neighbour, Jane Coghlan, for the loan of a cup of groats and a scrape of dripping. Well, one thing led to another: Coghlan accused Doyle of being a drunkard and a thief, upon which Doyle pulled off Coghlan's wig and shoved her so that she fell over a bucket. Doyle was charged with assault, but escaped conviction.

Anne Naes brought a charge of assault against Mat Cantlon, a former police constable, now (in April 1846) landlord of the Elephant and Castle public house. Naes lived at the rear of Cantlon's premises and claimed that she had been roused one night by knocking at her door and that, when she opened it, Cantlon knocked her to the ground with his whip. The *Herald*, in summarising the defendant's evidence, barracked shamelessly for Cantlon:

> *The woman, it appears, is of rather a questionable character,*
> *and had been at Mr Cantlon's on the night in question, with*
> *two men enjoying the pleasures of the bottle, and getting a little*
> *fuddled, commenced abusing Mrs Cantlon.*

Cantlon denied the assault and 'a respectable witness' was called to provide an alibi. The witness was not quite respectable enough to save Mat Cantlon from conviction, but the Bench imposed a paltry five-shilling fine, suggesting that the mud flung by the defence at Anne Naes must have stuck and dried.

No peace for the wicked: wife-beating

What is nowadays called domestic violence was in Bearbrass times given the plain name of 'wife-beating' – although the case of Margaret Wilson, above, suggests that husband-beating was not unheard of. The newspapers generally treated cases of wife-beating as either high comedy or high tragedy, apparently depending on the demeanour of the woman as she stood in the dock: the more feisty the accuser, the more the papers could be relied upon to camp it up.

The *Patriot*, in April 1839, reported on a case brought to court by C.S. Moore against her husband, whom she charged with beating her. 'After a short colloquy,' runs the report, 'she agreed to try her joy once more,' and the case was dismissed. Likewise in the case of The Queen v. Harris, in August 1847, an unelaborated Mr Harris made no attempt to deny the charge of wife-beating, but was let off, according to the *Herald* on the strength of his assurance that he would be 'more affectionate' to his spouse in future.

When Joseph Lacey faced the court in February 1841, charged with severely beating his wife, the *Herald* was roused to spirited editorialising:

> *This assassin-like conduct, we have reason to believe, is of too frequent occurrence in this town, and we are sure that every one who has the least feeling of a man about him, will cordially join with us in its suppression.*

(Still more so those who had the least feeling of a *woman* about them, one would suppose.) A year later, the same high-minded news organ was playing for laughs in covering the court appearance of an accused wife-beater:

> *A man by the name of Payne stood contrite at the bar of the court, charged with an assault by his better half who, rushing into the witness-box, pulled off a dirty cotton 'vipe', and [revealed] a black eye of more than ordinary dimensions ... The appearance of the orb, even after subtracting the dirt which formed the background, was certainly striking.*
> Bench – *Well, my good woman, speak out.*
> Woman – *Me husband's been punchin' of me.*
> Bench – *Well, what do you want to do?*
> Woman – *To swear the peace on him. I keeps a lodgin'-house, and works blessed hard. This feller goes a cuttin' it fat about the town, an' when he's tired o' that, comes home and insults my gentlemen lodgers, and winds up by pitchin' into his wife; he*

ain't no feelin' – your worships. I've guv that man six childer, but
it only makes him wus – nothin'll please the savage.
Bench – *Will you swear you are in fear of your life?*
Husband – *Your worship, she'd swear the hind legs off a*
bullock.

The boys in the newspaper office must have had a few laughs putting that report together. Never mind that the reader was left to wonder whether Mrs Payne really was in fear of her life – or indeed whether the saga was entirely a fabrication. Was the name Payne itself a pun? Add a laugh-track to that courtroom exchange and it could pass for a scene in one of the lamer sit-coms.

In November 1843, the *Herald* resumed its 'outraged citizen' tone in reporting the case of Ann Brown, who lived behind a shop opposite the post office and whose husband had beaten her with an iron bar. Trowelling on the pathos, the reporter described the woman's appearance in court:

> *with dishevelled hair streaming over her forehead, the features*
> *of her countenance completely obliterated by recent wounds,*
> *and obscured by clotted gore, her right eye apparently burst in*
> *its socket, and her cut and disfigured head enveloped in a dingy*
> *shawl of coarse manufacture, with a young baby about eight*
> *months old clinging to her breast …*

The case of a Mrs Finningan* was brought to public notice in 1839. According to the *Patriot*, 'this woman lately ran away from

---

*   Probably that name should read 'Finnegan' or 'Finnigan' (the spelling style of the *Patriot* – like that of Fawkner, its proprietor – was somewhat idiosyncratic.) There was an Owen Finnegan, a police constable, living in Bearbrass at that time; also John Finnigan, watch-house keeper. Perhaps Mrs 'Finningan' was the same person as Catherine Finigan who, in December 1842, requested that she be sent to Sydney, 'not knowing where I can this night get the shelter of a roof'.

her husband, it is said to cohabit with O'Riely.' Mrs Finningan now claimed that O'Riely* was threatening to kill her, to which the *Patriot* responded in unmistakable Fawkner style (random capitalisation and all): 'this makes true the Old saying, there is no peace for the wicked'. The court, for its part, clearly considered the woman's fear justified: her tormentor was ordered to put up a bond of £50 and two sureties of £25 each (£100 in all – a fortune!) as a guarantee that he would 'keep the peace', or else face prison.

Thomas Tyrrell, a private watchman on the Little Bourke Street beat, was in 1846 'ordered to enter into peace recognisances' after repeatedly beating his wife. Only a short time later, according to the *Herald*, he forfeited his bond and was brought back before the court, charged with 'most cruelly assaulting his wife by beating her on the head with bellows'. Likewise, Robert Graham was bound over to keep the peace towards his wife early in 1847. According to the *Herald's* coverage of his case:

> *The man it appears is a most disorderly fellow whenever he gets drunk, and is in the habit of burning his unfortunate wife's clothes while playing his pranks.*

The *Herald* failed to specify whether Graham torched his wife's clothes whilst she was in them, or whether he merely stoked the household grate with the contents of her wardrobe.

Without visible means of support: vagrancy

The fact that, in some cases, accused wife-beaters were bound over, to the tune of big money, to keep the peace towards their wives could be taken as a sign that the law was benevolent and regarded wife-beating as a serious crime. But the practice of sending the husband home with a vow of 'more affectionate' behaviour chiefly served the purpose of

---

* 'O'Riely' was in all likelihood Francis O'Reilly, who had been fined a couple of months earlier for threatening behaviour and drunkenness.

keeping the breadwinner in place. With her husband in gaol, a woman and her children might be safe from abuse but would have scarcely any means of supporting themselves. Heaven forbid that they should become a burden on the public purse! For the same reason, publicans were forbidden to sell liquor to any man whom it was deemed may 'by excessive drinking, so waste his estate, as thereby to expose himself, or his family to want, or greatly to injure his health'.

In January 1842, the *Patriot* reported that:

> *both the Chief and District Constables have been most active in apprehending and bringing before the Police Magistrate, under the Vagrant Act, all persons who loiter about the town without any visible means of support ...*

This rounding up of 'rogues and vagabonds' (as vagrants were also known) was taking place during a severe economic depression. During the month in which the above item appeared, the *Patriot* presented several vagrancy horror stories. One was that of a woman who, being unable to find domestic work in the town and having nowhere to live and nothing to eat, drowned herself in the Yarra. Another woman, the wife of a gaoled insolvent, intended to suicide by the same means. She began removing her clothes on the riverbank, weeping all the while, but her frightened child sounded the alarm. A Mrs Hilton, the wife of a Flinders Street publican gaoled for fraudulent debt, succeeding in drowning both herself and her baby in the river opposite her husband's former hotel. A tradesman, invalided by a badly ulcerated leg, was 'turned out of doors' by his landlord, who also impounded the man's tools of trade, when the lodger's inability to work prevented his paying the rent. He lived on the streets for some time, relying on occasional charity for food, until he died of 'apoplexy'. These cases the *Patriot* was able to report sympathetically in the same month it applauded the police for their energetic persecution of those without 'visible means of support'.

The following item from the *Herald* nearly a decade later shows the diligence of the constabulary undimmed:

> *A man named John Fitch was charged with having been found*
> *... lying in the public streets. Defendant stated that he was 87*
> *years of age last May, and obtained a livelihood by making*
> *skewers for the Melbourne butchers. Being now enfeebled he had*
> *sat down to rest when the constable came upon him, and took*
> *him into custody.*

Women without lawful means of support commonly resorted to prostitution as a desperate alternative to life and death on the streets. Often it proved no alternative at all, as in case of 'one of those misguided females', Janey Moor by name, who attempted suicide by swallowing poison in 1844. A later chapter will look at prostitution in Bearbrass in more detail.

The miscreant decamped: stealing and theft

We're all familiar with reminiscences of more innocent times, only a generation or two ago, when the citizens of our fair metropolis slept soundly in houses with doors unlatched and windows flung wide. Well, one report has it that as early as 1848* those who dwelt in and near the town kept their doors locked and bolted against thieving intruders. At the start of the following year, the *Herald* credited 'an experienced member of the Detective force' for the information that:

> *there are at present in Melbourne about 100 professional thieves*
> *of both sexes, and some 50 'outsiders', as they are technically*
> *styled – aiders and abettors, viz., the parties who receive the*

---

*   In fact, Johnny Fawkner fixed a lock to the front door of his hut in November 1835, when the settlement's population numbered only about thirty. This could be viewed as typical Fawkner-ish paranoia, but remember that his hut also operated as an unofficial inn and bottle shop.

*stolen swag, or watch for the others whilst they are perpetrating
outrages.*

Elizabeth Pearce was no professional thief; she was a professional
housekeeper, a servant of Eliza and John Batman. Acting without
the help of 'outsiders' she managed to steal, over a period of time, a
cornucopia of goods from her employers' house. Found in the hut
where she lived with her husband John, in February 1838, was the
following swag of items belonging to the Batmans: a silver pencil case,
two gold earrings, two silver clasps, a neck chain, a waist buckle, a
piece of linen for tablecloths, seven silk handkerchiefs, one silver
and two plated spoons, three drinking horns (silver mounted), two
striped sheets, two decanters, a tablecloth, a table cover, a fine piece
of linen, two pieces of calico, a sword belt, two books, one crepe
scarf, several pieces of lace and net work, six pairs of stockings, a
white pocket handkerchief, a pillowcase, a blanket, a piece of silk, a
paper of pins, the body and skirt of a child's dress, part of a merino
dress, some pieces of print fabric, a child's cap, a bag containing tape
and thread, several household utensils, glass and crockery, a hair
comb, a pair of boots, and 'some other small articles'. (How much
smaller could they have been than a paper of pins?) Also allegedly
stolen was £3 in a glove. Only the glove was found in the Pearces'
hut.

The glove-and-money combination again featured in a theft report
in December 1841. According to the *Patriot*, a woman was walking
near Benjamin Hancock's public house in Little Collins Street East
when 'some miscreant stopped here and forcibly took her reticule
[a drawstring bag] containing a pair of gloves and some silver, with
which he immediately decamped.'

Oysterman and fishmonger, Henry Clegge (or Clegg), was charged
in December 1845 with stealing jewellery from the dressing-table of
his neighbour in Little Bourke Street, a woman named Sutherland. In
reporting Clegge's arrest, the *Herald* did its utmost to cast aspersions

on his alleged victim. Not only was she 'better known as Jenny McLeod', but she lived 'not one hundred miles from the new theatre' (the Queens Theatre, on the south-west corner of Little Bourke and Queen streets). The implication was that she was a prostitute or – as bad – an actress, and thus fair game for burglars.

Not so fair game, apparently was the Aboriginal person from whom convict labourer, Michael Mathews, stole a handkerchief in April 1839. In fact, the record of Mathews' conviction does not actually specify theft: merely that the handkerchief was in his possession. The sentence of '25 lashes on the naked back' can therefore be taken as a reflection of either the harshness of convict discipline, the value of handkerchiefs, or the seriousness with which crimes against Aborigines were viewed – or all three. (An alternative explanation, of course, is that the magistrate's bunions were acting up that day.)

The tenderest and most vulnerable prey of the Bearbrass thieving community were the rural and pastoral workers who would come to town with their pockets full of cash only once or twice a year. In his exertions to slake his every thirst and appetite, the bush-worker was readily aided by publicans, prostitutes and many a fairweather drinking companion, all eager to unburden him of his wages.

Fred Napper arrived in town on Boxing Day morning, 1841, having just completed a stint of shepherding and shearing on an up-country pastoral run. He had £24 – six months' pay – in his pocket and made a beeline for the seedy Lamb Inn in Collins Street. Publican George Smith, himself an expert in the art of fleecing (his hotel was notorious as 'a roystering place for shepherds with cheques'), welcomed the dusty-throated shearer with rum and porter, and before long the bar was crowded with town types topping up their Christmas Day hangovers at Fred Napper's expense. Things got a bit hazy for a while after that, until Napper awoke on the Yarra bank in the late afternoon with a bad case of sunburn, empty pockets, and missing his silver watch besides.

Another hapless bushman was given a rude introduction to the big smoke on the very same day. According to the *Patriot*:

> *a person from the interior went into an eating-house in Little Bourke street, kept by a man named McGuinness, and during his stay there had his pocket picked of £17.*

Sailors were likewise susceptible to chicanery when they left their ships for a shore-leave spree. In 1843 a seaman named James Kenny accused Thomas Watson of stealing about £6 from the left-hand pocket of his vest. The *Patriot* detailed events leading up to the alleged crime:

> *while strolling along the margin of the Yarra, [Kenny] encountered Watson, shoeless, soapless and beerless; in fact he was the very picture of human misery on a tropical morning; taking pity upon the forlornness of his appearance, and observing by the frequent application of his hand to his throat, that the internal canal was dry and arid, he invited him to the Royal Highlander, and supplied his most pressing want with a pot of Condell's entire, which in a twinkling was flowing hissing down the heated cavity ...*

Kenny joined Watson in several repeat doses and, after a time, discovered his money gone. Watson denied the charge and was acquitted with a recommendation that he wash his face.

In June 1845, the *Herald* noted that Samuel Woulfe – whom it characterised as 'This famous clock-making-geological-itinerating alleged horse stealer' – had been remanded for seven days. A former watchmaker, he had been transported in 1838 and, as Samuel Wolfe, was appointed assistant lighthouse keeper at Shortland's Bluff (Queenscliff) in 1843. By 1845, his lighthouse duties had evidently given way to the 'itinerating' and horse-stealing phases of his career.

A gross offence against decency: indecent exposure

The West End Community Association complained to the City Council in 1993 that, when refused admittance to nightclubs, 'drunken men continuously exposed their genitals to passers by and urinated on cars, buildings and doorways.' In October 1838, not more than a shrill cooee away from today's nighclub precinct, Special Constable Henry Grimaldi was witness to an indiscretion of the same kind, but in broad daylight. In evidence against a defendant whose name has been lost to posterity, Grimaldi stated:

> I was on duty yesterday afternoon about 3 o'clock when I saw
> the prisoner in the public streets near the market reserve with
> his trousers down, making water in the open streets not near any
> shelter, a female was coming by and was in consequence of his
> indecent exposure obliged to turn back. The prisoner was drunk.

A year earlier, the town's gaoler had been dismissed after a drunken spree during which he 'exposed himself in the most indecent manner through the town'. Likewise, in May 1839, William Brazil ('a man of colour') was fined £5 for being drunk and 'exposing his person'.

The absence of public toilets – or any toilets – must have accounted in large part for the prevalence of indecent exposure charges in early Bearbrass, as must the fiddliness of fly buttons, particularly to the imprecise digits of the souse. Then as now though, there was always the hoon factor to consider. Tom Skilton and his mates, hoons every one, were cruising along Lonsdale Street shortly before dusk in the pre-V8 epoch of January 1842. No nightclubs, no Commodores with fat tyres and spoilers, not even a horse to ride furiously along the footpath – what was a hoon to do, with half a skinful and his bravado up?

As they drew level with the house of barrister Horatio Nelson Carrington, west of William Street, the lads spied Carrington and his family in the garden, tending their summer vegetable crop. Skilton nudged his mates and swaggered over to the gate. 'Oi, Mister

Carrin'ton!' he sang out. 'Need a hand with the waterin'?' and he commenced to unbutton his fly.

Carrington looked up. 'Clear off!' he shouted, waving a bunch of carrots.

But Skilton's chums egged him on. 'Garn, Tom, show 'em yer waterin' can!' 'Them roses look like they cud use a splash!'

Carrington grunted to his wife, who shooed the children towards the house. Skilton by this time had unleashed his wedding tackle and was pissing with aplomb over the middle rail of the three-rail fence that separated Carrington's garden from the street, smirking over his shoulder all the while.

'Right!' exploded Carrington. In four long strides he was at the fence, one swift hitch and he was over, and with a lunge he was at Skilton's throat. After a hearty collaring, during which Skilton's barrackers scarpered, Carrington commanded the lad to put his flies in order and then marched him off to the police office where he was charged with having 'deliberately committed a gross offence against decency'. Skilton's mates, who were known to Carrington, were rounded up and charged for their part in the outrage.

Able bodied and appears intelligent: the police

Garryowen described the early police force of Bearbrass as 'mostly a miserable set of broken-down cripples, with an "odd man" never in trouble occasionally amongst them'. Certainly they were not what you'd call a crack unit. Police Magistrate William Lonsdale had a difficult time finding suitable recruits – at least in the years before the unemployment of the early 1840s brought men clamouring for the job. Checking on the backgrounds of early recruits was not easy. Communication with Hobart and Sydney took time and Lonsdale more than once had signed a man up and credited him with a good character (on the man's own say-so) before word arrived from the Hobart or Sydney police that the new constable's career had hitherto been confined to the *other* side of the law.

Lonsdale would advise the Colonial Secretary of each new police appointment, including in his notification a description of the man. George Vinge he described as: 'about 29 years of age. Condition, free [i.e., not a convict]. Previous occupation, general servant. Character, good. He is able bodied. Reads and writes.' As to the character of James Caulfield, a former groom, Lonsdale could only ascertain that he had been 'steady whilst in the town'. Regrettably, Caulfield's steadiness did not last: within three weeks of his appointment he was found drunk and disorderly at Fleming's public house and was dismissed from the police force.

John Doyle was a military pensioner who had served as a constable in Van Diemen's Land and Lonsdale could find 'nothing objectionable in his character'. George Lee, an ex-convict labourer aged about twenty-six, was appointed in March 1839 despite the fact that his character was 'not much known'. The appointment of Lee is indicative of the scarcity of suitable police recruits at the end of the 1830s. Until about mid-1838, Lonsdale had striven to appoint only recruits of proven good character and reasonable intelligence, who were able bodied, and could read or write (or preferably both). From that time, Lonsdale's selection criteria disintegrated to the point where he was virtually reduced to recruiting the inmates of the lock-up.

In his notifications to head office in Sydney, Lonsdale did not automatically characterise every police recruit as 'intelligent'. In fact, after 1838, he seems to have abandoned the criterion of intelligence altogether. Until then, most appointees were given the notation 'able bodied and intelligent' or 'able bodied and *appears* intelligent'; however, a small number of them Lonsdale could credit only with being 'able bodied'. William Wright, Chief Constable from August 1838, was one such appointee.

Wright replaced the town's first Chief Constable, Henry Batman, whom Lonsdale had dismissed for accepting a bribe. Wright had been overseer of water works and a district constable in Hobart and came highly recommended, as 'active, intelligent, and trustworthy, with a thorough knowledge of men and things!' But though, in his standard memorandum to the Colonial Secretary, Lonsdale noted Wright's 'strong testimonials of character and ability', his summary of the new Chief Constable's qualities was otherwise limited to: 'He is able bodied. Reads and writes.' According to Lonsdale's usual criteria, Wright did not even *appear* intelligent. Perhaps Wright's appointment had been foisted upon Lonsdale who, as a result, was loath to acknowledge the man's abilities. Whatever the explanation, Lonsdale's omission sent the signal that he, for one, was not impressed.

Chief Constable Wright was commonly known as Tulip because of his distinctive 'uniform' of a green velveteen coat, cut away in front to reveal a scarlet vest with buttons strained almost to popping. The effect of garish full-bloom was topped off by what Garryowen described as a 'big, bulbous, carbuncly face'. The lesser constables presented a far more shabby appearance.

The uniform of the Bearbrass police was slow to take shape. Initially, the constable merely augmented his civilian clothes with a few accessories: around the waist was worn a thick leather belt from which hung a wooden truncheon ('half waddy and half bludgeon', according to Garryowen) and a set of handcuffs; the ubiquitous cabbage-tree hat was printed with the word POLICE, for the benefit of those who could read. A full uniform was introduced in 1840, featuring dark blue trousers and jacket, with pewter buttons and a red stripe around the wrist, and a yellow vest. Also part of the uniform was the brickbat-and-bottle-proof hat described earlier. Hugh McCrae's description evokes the extraordinary appearance of the Bearbrass constables of the 1840s:

> *These men looked pachydermatous in bulky uniforms, especially during winter-time, when they wore 'Long Tom' overcoats reaching to the heels of their Wellington boots. We can imagine their appearance through a Yarra fog, with lanterns strapped*

to their waists, feeling for their batons down the legs of their
*trousers, and ready to spring enormous rattles ... ***

Those rattles served as communication and alarm, in the absence of two-way radio or mobile phone, for constables on the night-watch. A greatly enlarged version of a (now) old-fashioned toy, the rattles took the form of a revolving clacker attached to a handle. When the handle was swung in a circular motion, the clacker spun about, kicking up a fearsome din.

James Rogers had plenty of cause to sound the revolving clacker during his twelve-month stint as a Bearbrass constable during 1837–8. First he was clouted by Patrick Mahony, who was drunk in the town and using indecent language near Moss's Ship Inn. Next, Peter Riley managed to strike Constable Rogers whilst 'lying drunk in the town'. Timothy Hall, running riot in Michael Carr's public house, collared poor Rogers when the constable tried to apprehend him. And John Tomlinson, also drunk and broadcasting abuse through the streets, clobbered both Constables Rogers and Freestun before the pair were able to subdue him with handcuffs and baton blows. Soon after this last incident, James Rogers threw in the towel.

David Magee must have been a bad 'un to have warranted turning out of John Moss's scurrilous Ship Inn in August 1837. He flung a threat back at Moss and at Henry Batman (then Chief Constable) who did the actual ousting, as he pushed his way into the tea-tree scrub that skirted the pub – 'I'll put a couple of balls through you buggers tonight!' Some time later, as Henry Batman accepted Moss's gratitude in gill measures at the bar, Magee reappeared in the doorway with a gun. 'Now, you buggers,' he bellowed, 'I'll give it to you!' But before he could take aim, several drinkers set upon him and wrested the weapon away. Magee broke loose and holed up in his hut with another gun and axe, bawling threats through the flimsy walls until eventually he tired and

---

* *Georgiana's Journal*, p.106.

was overpowered by police. In his defence, Magee stated that he was very drunk, a plea not likely to attract mercy. He was gaoled.

Constable John Mooney was the victim of assault twice in a single week in May 1841. On Thursday he was 'pounded' by William Hawkins in Flinders Street. According to the *Herald*, Hawkins sought to justify his actions by saying that 'he was carrying out the meaning of the adage, "bray a fool in a mortar"'.* The following day, John Caton beat Mooney with the constable's own baton. In committing Caton to trial, Magistrate James Simpson thundered that he was determined to put a stop to 'this description of outrage'.

A different description of outrage – that of police brutality and corruption – was less commonly reported in the press or set down in public records. A fleeting reference in the *Patriot* in February 1840 gives the impression that, far from being unheard of, unlawful behaviour by police was rife:

> *we have well authenticated statements before us of instances*
> *of excessive brutality and misconduct on the part of the peace*
> *officers – peace officers did we call them? … In nine cases out of*
> *ten they are the* peace breakers.

A few months later, the editor of the *Gazette*, George Arden, mounted a campaign against police brutality, asserting that 'their arrogance and presumption have increased beyond all reasonable limits' and condemning the force's stock in trade of 'fraud, bribery, corruption, oppression, intimidation, and perjury'.

Bearbrass constables were paid, in 1839, two shillings and threepence a day, in addition to a military food ration. At that time, a labourer's wage was about three shillings a day. Police wages, though, were supplemented by a fifty per cent commission on all fines

---

*   The upshot being that Hawkins meant to knock some sense into Mooney, bray meaning to crush or pound, as with mortar and pestle.

resulting from arrests. In the case of drunkenness convictions alone, this would have amounted to no small beer. Drunkenness laws were vigorously applied and with fines starting at five shillings for an initial conviction and increasing by the same amount at each subsequent conviction (fines of fifty shillings – ie. tenth convictions – were not uncommon), this was a beaut little earner for the diligent – or over-diligent – constable. Fawkner gloated, in concluding an 1839 listing of drunkenness convictions in the *Patriot*: 'Oh! ... how rich our young Queen will soon get at this rate.' Ditto the constabulary.

The most famed of Bearbrass constables was John William Hooson, a former soldier and one of the original police contingent to arrive from Sydney with Lonsdale in 1836. His police career was short-lived (he was dismissed for taking bribes), but he remained for years the town's foremost figure of fun. Described by Garryowen as 'an old half-cranky customer', Hooson's eccentricities earned him the nickname of 'Blatherskyte' or 'Sir Blatherum'. The *Herald* said of him in 1842 that he had 'all the noise without the use of a child's rattle'. W.F.E. (Frank) Liardet, an early settler and artist, insisted that Hooson had had 'a portion of his cranium shot away in the Peninsula War' and was thus 'a shingle-short'.

Hooson was notorious as street-keeper for the town council in the early 1840s, in which role one of his duties was to act as a kind of Bearbrass equivalent to that most hated of modern-day municipal officers, the parking inspector. He was also responsible for issuing licences to sell goods in the streets. In November 1843, a popular target for pistol practice was afforded by a portrait of Hooson, one in a series of 'Popular Portraits of personages possessing considerable local notoriety' produced by Collins Street stationer, Fred Pittman. According to the *Patriot*, the portrait was remarkably lifelike: 'It would require no stretch of fancy to imagine Mr Hooson, as represented, upon the eve of pouncing on an unregistered cart, respecting which he is especially vigilant.'

Hooson was dismissed as street-keeper in 1844 for keeping money paid to him by a fishmonger for a street-vending licence. He lived out the remainder of his years (he died in 1852) as a comic-pathetic character on the Bearbrass scene, drinking excessively, badgering the authorities for the job he felt was owed him, and roaming the streets to air his grievances in mutters and shouts. For short periods, he occupied the positions of poundkeeper and bailiff, but he was forever in trouble – overstepping his authority, neglecting his duties, or simply making a nuisance of himself.

But for all his buffoonery, Hooson possessed an impetuous sense of gallantry that saw him intercede in one instance, in support of C.A. Robertson, an Israelite missionary ('One of those itinerant preachers … with a very long and imposing white beard'), who was being shouted down by a rowdy crowd in the marketplace. Robertson had made a pulpit of a beer cask one Sunday afternoon in February 1844, but his spirited sermonising drew no converts, only a gaggle of drunken hecklers. According to an eyewitness from the *Herald*:

> *the appearance of Hooson, the street keeper, in a very loquacious mood, turned the groans and hisses into something worse …*
> *[but] Hooson exerted his well known power of oratory to secure the beer cask man a patient hearing …*

My favourite Hooson story, though, concerns his role in the inauguration parade of the first town council in December 1842. Hooson took it upon himself to act as marshall or conductor, marching at the head of the procession, followed by dignitaries, police, and 'Men, Women, Children, and dogs promiscuously'. Thoroughly in his element, Hooson semaphored as he marched, with a roughly fashioned flag of red-dyed calico on a short stick. But here … let Garryowen take over the story – he tells it with the relish it deserves.

> *Near William Street, a man was driving a bullock past St James' Church on his way to the slaughterhouses. The bullock was*

> *attracted to Hooson's red banner, and chased him. There was*
> *then at the junction of William and Little Flinders Streets, near*
> *the Custom House Reserve, a chasm nearly brimful of thick*
> *slush, and Hooson plunged headlong into this.*

The bullock took off in the direction of the river and the procession raised a cheer (whether for Hooson or the bull is hard to say) and swung right up Collins Street to wait on Superintendent La Trobe in his office on Batman's Hill. Hooson retrieved his muddy flag but could not retrieve his dignity, and so he left them to it and straggled home.

Another marvellous yarn of Garryowen's concerns Charlie Swindell, a police sergeant of the mid-1840s. The story goes that Swindell was married to 'a smart, stout stump of an immigrant girl, about his own height and make, whose lively proclivities on the voyage out procured for her the sobriquet of "Dick"'. Swindell's night patrols were punctuated by frequent stops at public houses which, with swigs from a flask betweentimes, would render him incapable of standing, let along swinging his truncheon, by midway through his shift. His trusty wife Dick would track him down to where he was slumped in an alleyway (his favourite was off Little Bourke Street, up near Queen), then dress herself in his uniform and carry on patrolling in his stead. (Presumably she covered the denuded Charlie with a blanket and made a bundle of her clothing for a pillow.) Dick had no cause to fear that any of the half dozen or so other police whom she might meet on the night-watch would blow the whistle on her deception; like her husband, they were either absent from their posts or insensibly drunk, or both. Eventually, however, she was unlucky enough to meet the Chief Constable, who, by the dim light of her lantern, recognised Dick and charged her with impersonating a police officer. Charlie Swindell was charged with neglect of duty; but for his thoughtful wife's blanket, he might have faced a further charge of indecent exposure.

Wanted men

Whether police sought a known villain or were simply rounding up the usual suspects following a crime, in the early 1840s their investigations usually began and ended with a search of the huts near the corner of Brunswick and Moor streets in Fitzroy and the brickfields on the south side of the Yarra. In cases where these criminal enclaves failed to yield up the culprit, a wider search would be instigated and a description of the suspect circulated to other districts. In November 1838, Thomas Hobbler (a.k.a. Flooden), an escaped Van Diemen's Land convict accused of cattle stealing and 'other serious offences', broke out of the Bearbrass gaol 'by making an aperture through the wall of the building' and was believed to have fled the town. Police issued this description of the fugitive:

> *Height: 5 ft 6 in*
> *Age: about 40 years*
> *Complexion: swarthy*
> *Hair: dark*
> *General Remarks: round shouldered, has an effeminate voice and smiling look, rather small mouth. Had on when he absconded – fustian shooting jacket and trousers, dark waistcoat and dirty straw hat.*

Hobbler was recaptured on the road to Yass and, in seeking to confirm the captive's identity, Police Magistrate Lonsdale stressed to Yass police that 'Hobbler has a peculiar expression of countenance and a small, peculiar voice'. After a further escape from the mounted police, Hobbler was once again recaptured and escorted under close guard to Sydney.

As in the case of Hobbler, the mouth of the fugitive Cold Chop Murderer,* William Morris, warranted special mention in the

---

* The case of the Cold Chop Murderer is detailed in Chapter 6.

description issued by police in February 1839. As well as his sun-bleached flushing jacket, Morris's 'rather pouting' upper lip was singled out as noteworthy.

The following notice appeared in the *Herald* in December 1840:

FIVE POUNDS REWARD. *Absconded from the hired service of Mrs Scott, taking with him a Grey Horse and some money, John Hayes, real name Stephen Little, complexion dark, marked with small pox, about 5 ft 6 in high,* S. Little *in blue jagged letters on the right arm, and walks lame; had on when he left a blue jacket, dark drab trowsers, and black hat.*

To the modern eye, accustomed to photographs or sophisticated computer images of crime suspects, these descriptions are remarkable for their precise detailing of physical characteristics and attire. More vague was the description of Henry Smiley, a sailor who escaped from gaol in August 1837, whilst awaiting trial for the theft of quantities of flour and tea, a keg of oatmeal, a one-gallon jar of gin, and an axe from a ship in port. Smiley was described as follows:

Age: 32
Height: 5 feet 7½ inches
Make: active
Complexion: dark, swarthy
Hair: black
Eyes: dark
Trade: seaman
County: Waterford
Marks: none

This word-sketch of Smiley contrasts markedly with that of the horse that he stole from the survey party in making good his escape. The equine abductee leaps to life in the circulated description:

*colour, chestnut; height, nearly 15 hands; tail short; legs of a
light colour; off eye, nearly blind; white spots under the saddle;
about eight years.*

It is interesting that, in compiling this otherwise comprehensive
description, the police neglected to classify the horse as mare, stal-
lion or gelding. Nonetheless, a half-blind chestnut horse or Smiley's
'active' make must have rung a bell with somebody, for the two were
apprehended heading north within a week of their descriptions being
posted.

The usual reward, in 1840, for the apprehension of a wanted
felon was £25 or, should the apprehender be a convict, a conditional
pardon.

As good as a play

The town's first legal action took place in May 1836, when a panel of
three arbitrators was assembled to settle a series of disputes between
those warring neighbours, Johnny Fawkner and Henry Batman. For
damaging Fawkner's fence and allowing his dogs to maul a calf and
kill rabbits belonging to Fawkner, Henry Batman was fined fifty-five
shillings, to which the arbitrators added, 'We cannot omit remarking
that there has been a forbearance on the part of Mr Fawkner ...' (A
degree of forbearance? Now *there's* a triumph for those who would
champion Johnny Fawkner.)

The legal business of the settlement was at first performed by John
McNall, a butcher who had previously worked as a lawyer's clerk in
Van Diemen's Land. William Meek, the settlement's first qualified
lawyer, arrived in 1838, allowing McNall to dedicate himself full-time
to the trade of butchering. Meek is said to have 'lived above the mild-
ness of his name', a claim supported by his role as 'second' in a duel
between Dr Barry Cotter and newspaper editor George Arden soon
after his arrival at Bearbrass. Among the legal men soon to appear on
the Bearbrass scene was the young barrister, Redmond Barry (later Sir

Redmond), who for a time lived and worked in a back room of J.W.
Hooson's cottage in Collins Street.

Until 1841, Bearbrass had only a police court, which heard and
sentenced minor charges; those accused of serious offences were sent
to Sydney for trial. In 1841, a bench of the Supreme Court was established in the town and a resident judge appointed. His name was John
Walpole Willis and he was thrust upon Bearbrass having already irked
beyond endurance the powers-that-be in Sydney and, prior to that, in
Canada. His brilliance and wit were undeniable – it was his temper
that was the problem. Garryowen wrote:

> *Such was his irascibility and so often was the Court the arena*
> *of unseemly squabbles that people who had no business there*
> *attended to see 'the fun', for, as there was no theatre in town,*
> *Judge Willis was reckoned to be 'as good as a play' …*

Willis's unpopularity with his social equals was perhaps due not just
to his temper, but to the fact that it was *they* – the upper classes – who
were most commonly the object of his scorn. He had about him a
humaneness that was unfashionable, even unsavoury, for the times.
As examples, convict discipline softened somewhat under his juris-
diction, and on New Year's Day 1842 'the whole of the prisoners at
present confined in Her Majesty's jail at Melbourne, were regaled with
roast beef and plum pudding, at the expense of His Honor Mr Justice
Willis'.

Contrast with that gesture of Willis's the practices of a police magistrate of the same period, Major G.F. B. St John. In lieu of sentences,
he exacted bribes. Mainly these took the form of foodstuffs and liquor
– presumably so that he could consume the evidence. Johnny Fawkner
listed St John's most common demands as 'from the half-dozen eggs,
or the pound of butter, up to a cow or calf, horses, grog, wines, champagne, brandy, and gin'.

Another corker amongst the magistracy was William Hull who,

in addition to his duties as police magistrate, ran a wholesale wine and spirit business in Flinders Lane. Garryowen recalled him as being 'given to the expression of somewhat peculiar opinions from the Bench'. In June 1844, Hull was called upon to preside over a case against a 'band of rowdies' who, led by a publican named Phillip Anderson, had broken up a temperance meeting the night before. Addressing the meeting had been Mrs Joseph Dalgarno and, rather than deal with the charges against the rowdies, Magistrate Hull censured Mrs Dalgarno in court, quoting the New Testament teaching that 'A woman should never speak before men.' The charges against Anderson and his fellow rowdies were dismissed.

Court cases were originally heard in the police office, situated on the government block, at the far western end of the town. A low, sloping structure built of sods, it was described as 'a great curiosity'. When the court was in session, an old packing case served as the magistrate's bench, with empty beer kegs as seats. That it was cramped goes without saying. In 1838, the police office moved to a new weatherboard building on the market reserve and it was there, in March 1840, that Frank Tomlins was convicted on the evidence of two Chinese men. As their 'heathen' status rendered them ineligible to swear an oath on the Bible, the two witnesses instead followed 'the Chinese formula ... of smashing two China plates with a stick of the stolen property' before giving evidence. China plates, indeed – were they having the court on?

From the mid-1840s, the Supreme Court was situated in Russell Street, near the corner of La Trobe Street. Garryowen recalled how, when the court was first built, it was considered to be 'quite out of town':

> *I remember when jurymen and suitors, during the adjournment*
> *of the court, instead of poking themselves into some*
> *neighbouring tavern ... used to betake themselves to the 'bush' at*
> *the rear of the gaol ...*

Before the '40s were out, jurors and legal folk would 'betake' themselves instead to the Supreme Court Hotel* on the corner diagonally opposite. An 1849 advertisement boasted of its 'seven Lofty Sleeping Apartments' from which guests could enjoy splendid views of 'Mount Macedon, Station Peak, St Kilda, Brighton, Plenty Ranges, Hobson's Bay, &c., &c., &c.'.

Two o'clock and all's well – and the gaol's burnt down

The gaol backing onto the bush in the mid-'40s was a part of what we now know as the Old Melbourne Gaol; at that time, it was very much the new gaol.

The first Bearbrass gaol was a converted shepherd's hut, built of turf with a rough thatched roof, on John Batman's sheep run to the east of Batman's Hill. William Lonsdale sequestered the hut as a government store and guardroom when he took charge of the settlement in September 1836. The town had yet to be surveyed but when the grid was in place the turf hut turned out to be set back from Collins Street, midway between King and Spencer streets. In time, other makeshift buildings and tents were haphazardly clustered in the vicinity of the store-cum-gaol, forming a compound known as the government camp. Once squared and given boundaries by the street grid, the camp became known as the government block.

The damp, flimsy cell on the government block was incinerated in April 1838, when two Kulin men called Bunja Logan and Jin Jin were being held on a charge of stealing potatoes from a settler's garden. Logan plucked a reed from the roof thatch and, lighting it from the flame of the guard's candle, used it as a taper to set the roof ablaze. The dry thatch went up like the proverbial packet of crackers and Logan made his leap to freedom. His cellmate clambered after him but was recaptured a short distance away. The burning of the gaol afterwards became a standing joke at the expense of constables on

---

*   Demolished in 1990.

the night-watch. They used to call the hours during the night – 'Two o'clock and all's well' – and some joker would invariably sing out in response, 'Two o'clock and all's well – and the gaol's burnt down!'

The gaol was torched only eighteen months after it was first put to use; yet the man whose candle Bunja Logan used as a lucifer was the fourth to hold the job of gaoler (or turnkey) – and to lose it. The first gaoler was sacked for being drunk on duty; the second, J.W. Hooson, released a prisoner in return for a bribe; the third disgraced himself on the day he was appointed; and the fourth snoozed while the gaol caught fire.

James Waller was the third appointed gaoler, the one dismissed before his duties even commenced. Applying to Lonsdale in October 1837, Waller vowed to bring to the post 'my utmost exertions, vigilance, sobriety and integrity'. Lonsdale was impressed and in due course the position was Waller's. In early December, however, Lonsdale informed the Sydney authorities that Waller's appointment had been rescinded.

> I have been prevented from placing James Waller in charge of the gaol of this town ... for on the day I told him of his appointment and immediately after making me the most positive assurance of being most particular in his conduct and attentive to his duties, he went to the lowest public house in the town ... [and] he not only got drunk but exposed himself in the most indecent manner through the town, and was in a state of intoxication for some days after.

Former constable George Vinge became turnkey in August 1839, but threw the job in after only four months, citing insufficient pay as the cause of his resignation. His wage was two shillings and ninepence per day, but he claimed that the job set him back fifteen shillings a week in expenses, 'not including washing or wearing apparel'. He told Superintendent La Trobe that this put his wage at 'far below that of a common labourer'.

After the burning of the first gaol, a brick store-room set back from the western corner of William and Flinders streets was rented for use as a temporary gaol, in mid-1838. Garryowen described it as 'more like a stable with a hay-loft overhead' with a step-ladder used for access to the second storey. A yard at the rear of the gaol was enclosed by a high tea-tree fence, this slender screen being all that separated the gaol yard from two public houses immediately adjacent. George Wintle, turnkey of the temporary gaol, complained that despite the posting of a sentry in the yard, 'the prisoners can easily elude his vigilance'. By what means, I wonder? With a share of rum and porter from the prisoners' sorties over the fence, or with a fistful of coins?

Before the year's end, Lonsdale was concerned that the gaol 'is in an extremely insecure state and is not adapted for the safe custody even of fines, much less of desperate felons bent on escape'. He proposed that the owner of the building should line the room used as a cell with 'strong boards, secured by iron fastenings outside' and also 'render the loft above fit for the confinement of females'. But the owner, in return for the modifications, demanded a much higher rent, so Lonsdale instead determined that a new temporary gaol (later to serve as watch-house) should be built adjoining the new police office and hospital on the nearby market reserve.

The new building was completed in December 1838 and was used as the town's gaol – to the extreme sufferance of its overcrowded inmates – until yet another, more substantial temporary lock-up was ready for occupation in early 1840. Situated on Collins Street, forward of the site of the original turf lock-up, the fourth temporary gaol was in use until the permanent one in Russell Street was completed in 1844.

The prominence (now hard to imagine) of the hulking bluestone structure on the Russell Street hill overlooking the township was an embarrassment to a community in the throes of the colonial cringe from convictism. That the first prominently sited public building should be a prison ...! The worst fears of respectable visitors and immigrants approaching by ship would, it was felt, be confirmed in their first glimpse of the town. How thankful affronted townsfolk must have been for the partial cloak of bush that fringed the new gaol.

Infinitely more dreaded

The Russell Street hill was known in the '40s as Tyburn Hill, after its namesake place of execution in London. The settlement's first hangings took place there in 1842, when the gaol on the hill was under construction.

Picture the scene in January 1842 when two Van Diemen's Land Aborigines named 'Bob' and 'Jack' were hanged for murdering two whalers at Western Port. They had been held in the temporary gaol in Collins Street and were conveyed through the streets to the top of the Russell Street hill, where the shell of the new gaol stood. The condemned pair sat on their coffins aboard a horse-drawn cart, which moved at a sombre pace so that the hangman, walking behind, and the crowd of onlookers – women and children among them – forming a procession behind him, could keep up. Still more spectators gathered on the hill itself. According to the *Patriot's* man on the spot: 'The tops of the trees adjacent to the place of execution were crowded with the Aborigines of the Yarra Yarra tribe.' On the throw of the lever, the fidgety crowd erupted into jubilant shouts and cat-calls. But Bob and Jack were still alive. John Davies, a first-time hangman, had botched the job, making the ropes too short, so that when the platform fell away the condemned men failed to drop, but were left dangling. They flailed violently as they died by slow strangulation. This was a spectacle that onlookers had not reckoned on. The crowd quickly broke up – mothers slapping their ghoulish, reluctant children homeward – and only a rum-hardened handful waited around to see Bob and Jack finished off.

The busy market square was the venue for the form of punishment in which creating a spectacle was the whole point. From early in Lonsdale's administration, wooden stocks were employed for the public humiliation of minor offenders (usually drunks) who were unable to pay their fines. Occupants of the stocks were seated on a low wooden bench, their legs stretched out before them at the same height and clasped by the ankles when the stocks were closed. Just think how their legs and backs must have ached! Two hours in the stocks was usual for a conviction of drunkenness; for being drunk and fighting in the town, Tom Fitzmaurice and George Penfold each spent four hours in the stocks. Women were required to have only one leg secured, halving the discomfort but not the indignity. Following a period during which the town was without stocks and non-payers instead served a spell in the lock-up, a new set of stocks was erected in 1846. The *Patriot* observed that 'This mode of punishment appears to be infinitely more dreaded than the old system of twenty-four hour incarceration.'

A treadmill came into service in 1842, as a punishing form of exercise for hard-labourers during period when poor weather or other circumstances kept them indoors. Designed for use by ten men at a time, the barrel of the treadmill would revolve as the men treaded its steps. Heaven help the short-legged or unfit among them. The *Herald* was present at the machine's first operation, when 'on its being mounted by ten lazy rascals, suddenly – by the weight of their sins or carcases, we don't know which – broke the barrel of the mill right in two pieces'. Modifications were made and the 'shin-scraper' was soon back in business, but it was to be dogged with breakdowns throughout its career. In November 1843, two youths, James Black and Abner Bett, were convicted of attempting 'a burglarious entrance into the shop of Herbert, the watch-maker, in Swanston-street, by removing the brickwork with a chisel' and were sentenced to spells on the treadmill for a term of six months. The treadmill was, understandably, a hated form of punishment.

From 1837, transported convicts were employed in the town on public works and as assigned servants. They were subject to the strictest of regulations. Whether housed in barracks on the government block or on the properties of their masters, convicts were not permitted to be out after sunset or six p.m., whichever was earlier. If found at large after that time without a written pass, a convict was automatically guilty of disorderly conduct, and flogged.

Convicts were the exclusive conferees of the scourger's lash. In the disarray of the early settlement and with their barracks little more than tents, the Bearbrass convicts were forever 'absconding' – sneaking out after muster for a drink or in quest of the opposite sex – and the lash-happy police magistrates were ever ready to sool the scourger onto them. Fifty lashes was the usual sentence for a first absconding offence; only occasionally was a reprimand or ten days' bread and water deemed sufficient punishment – usually where an assignee had clearly been misused by his master. Repeat offenders were not only flogged but were put to work on an iron gang for twelve months.

When Will Tobin was caught after muster at Jemmy Connell's Highlandman Hotel in Queen Street, he claimed that he was selling wooden toys which he whittled in barracks at night and had left a selection for Connell's young daughter to choose from. 'Fifty lashes,' intoned the magistrate, without looking up. 'Next!' Tom Cohen was found in bed, in broad daylight, with Lizzie Wheeler of Little Collins Street, by her sea captain husband, Bill. Both were drunk on beer. This time the magistrate looked up. Lizzie Wheeler, eh? 'Fifty lashes. Next!'

Constable Patrick McKeever took the stand. 'Yesterday morning,' he told the court, 'I met the prisoner William Hand in the town with a jug, and when asking him what he had in it he replied, "What the bloody hell is that to you?"'

'Hm, indecent language,' muttered the magistrate into his cuff. 'Fifty lashes ...' – he turned to the clerk – 'and make that *on the breech*.* Next!'

Charles Wincherer, overseer at C.H. Ebden's station, brought John

---

*   That is, the buttocks. The lash was usually applied to the upper back and shoulders.

McCluskey before the court, claiming that McCluskey was shirking his duties by pretending to be ill. Dr Patrick Cussen, the government surgeon, had examined McCluskey and told the court that there was nothing the matter with him. 'Nothing that fifty lashes won't fix, at any rate,' the magistrate sniggered, and McCluskey's pallor bleached from grey to white. 'Next!'

Martin Hizzentottle, from the road gang, was charged with refusing to obey orders. The Overseer of Roads described Hizzentottle's general conduct as 'irregular and bad'. 'Fifty lashes,' said His Honour, 'and the Court will adjourn for dinner.'

First off the rank in the afternoon session was the case of Thomas Pitman. The Overseer of Roads once again took the stand. At the end of the day's work, he told the court, he had ordered the convicts in his charge to gather up the tools, to which Pitman had exclaimed, 'By God, it's time to gather up the tools.'

'Twelve lashes' – amazing, isn't it, the difference a bellyful of game pie and Geneva can make? – 'Next!'

Benjamin Baxter told His Honour of his outrage at finding his two assigned servants, Joseph Richardson and Hanson Haworth, still asleep in their hut at the brickfield at seven-thirty a.m. 'They ought to have their breakfasts and be ready for work at six o'clock,' boomed Baxter.

'Quite right,' agreed the magistrate. 'Fifty lashes ... ah, there's *two* of the lazy wretches – make it twenty-five apiece. Next!' And so it went on.

A master had the power to appeal against his assigned servant's sentence, although instances of this actually happening were rare. In May 1838, Chief Constable Henry Batman found John Reeves, a convict servant, drunk in the hut of Tom Howard, and Reeves was sentenced to receive fifty lashes. Reeves was 'forgiven', however, following an appeal by his master (whom the records neglect to name).

In the late '30s, the scourger 'squatted in a den' where St Augustine's Church now stands, on the south side of Bourke Street, between King and Spencer streets. The distasteful position of scourger was filled by a succession of convicts. The first incumbent, Edward Steel, was paid one shilling and ninepence a day in his first year of duty, and two shillings and threepence a day thereafter. But the work could be relentless: in the week leading up to Christmas 1837, Steel was a full six days at the lash.

To wind down after an arduous day's flogging, Steel drank heavily (a funny thing, given that serving liquor to convicts was strictly forbidden), gambled (he lost his clothes to another prisoner and was docked a month's pay when caught), and went about 'alarming' women. Ann McNally, an assigned servant of Surveyor D'Arcy (also resident on the government block), was awoken by a noise in her tent one night in 1837. She sat up and saw Steel shaking the box in which her possessions were kept. McNally told the court, 'I was very much alarmed and threatened him with a pair of tongs,' upon which Steel fled the tent. Found guilty of disorderly conduct, the scourger forfeited ten days' pay. He was lucky to have avoided the flick of the lash himself.

The relative lenience of the penalty served on Steel suggests that there was hardly a legion of would-be scourgers waiting in the wings. Not surprising, really. Apart from most men's revulsion for the task itself, the incumbent scourger had to wear the active hatred of his fellow convicts.

Furious riders and killer dray wheels

As the 1840s wore on, the streets of the town grew ever busier. With traffic still largely unregulated, the pedestrians, horses, carts and drays thronging the town centre relied on common sense and luck to avoid contretemps. Inevitably, though, common sense sometimes took a holiday or luck wore thin. The former was very definitely the case when Thomas Price indulged in a spot of pavement riding in November 1847. In the words of the *Patriot*:

*About noon on Thursday, the peaceful siesta of the inhabitants of
Elizabeth-street was disturbed by the sound of trampling of, as
it appeared, a mob of horses, but which, on observation, turned
out to issue from one individual yclept Thomas Price, who was
performing sundry gyrations* à cheval *on the pavement, with
an obvious desire to enter a furniture shop there and display his
equestrianism among the chairs and tables.*

It was rare though for an instance of horseback tomfoolery to be
treated so lightly by the press. Accounts of children being trampled
by horses or crushed under cart wheels were an almost daily feature
in the late '40s. Eliza Courtney – 'whose moral character, it was
whispered, would not bear the strictest scrutiny' – was charged with
furiously riding (the equivalent of reckless driving today) through
the streets of the town in September 1846. She was very drunk and
unable to control the horse, whose hoof, in a very close call, grazed
the toe-top of a girl crossing the street with her mother. In a single
day in March 1848, two children were killed in traffic accidents. Little
Johnny Mullins, the son of a woodcutter, was crushed beneath the
horse and dray of a waterman in Little Bourke Street, while a girl aged
about nine was ridden over in King Street.

The *Herald*, in October 1846, reported the tragic case of Marion
and William Riece, a mother and son who were killed when run over
by a dray wheel. An inquest was held at which a verdict of accidental
death was returned and 'two deodands of 6d. levied on the wheel of
the dray'. This deodand business is an interesting thing. A deodand
(from the Latin *deodandum*, 'that must be given to God') was a token
payment representing the object that had been directly responsible
for a person's death. The idea was that the deodand would be put
to charitable use, effectively squaring things with the Almighty. The
levying of deodands dated back to early English law and the practice
ceased after 1846, the year of the Rieces' death. The shilling levied on
the wheel of the dray that killed the pair was indeed a token offer-

ing, but would have been exacted from the dray driver, William Riece senior, the victims' husband and father, whom the coroner must have figured had already paid dearly.

Livestock law and order

Every newspaper carried columns of Impounded Livestock notices, which described – somewhat in the manner of wanted felons – stray cattle, sheep and horses held in the government pound. These examples are from a July 1843 edition of the *Patriot*:

> *A red or yellow cow, white belly, slit in left ear, illegible off side near the shoulder.*
>
> *A red steer, open horns, a piece off both ears, illegible resembling k within a circle off side, near the shoulder.*
>
> *A black working bullock, black tip cock horns, small white spot on flank, supposed rt off side, near the shoulder.*

Animals would be released to their owners from the pound – originally in Flinders Street, between Swanston and Russell – upon payment of a fee.

In cases where wandering livestock posed a public nuisance, owners were charged and subject to fines. In 1838, the police magistrate heard that John Cronan 'did allow an entire horse of inferior breed to go at large in the town'. The charge was dropped on the condition that Cronan 'shall cause the horse to be cut without delay'. Apart from the menace posed to well-bred mares, it can be imagined that the presence of riderless horses – entire or otherwise – within the town was none too safe for the human occupants.

At large and menacing the townsfolk in February 1841 were 'Swine of all descriptions, shapes and sizes'. The *Patriot* related the following porcine atrocities:

*Not long since, a child was dreadfully mangled by a ferocious
sow in Little Flinders Street, and more recently a child has had
its ear torn off by a pig at Newtown [Fitzroy] ...*

John Wright, in June 1845, was charged with allowing a bullock to
stray in Bourke Street, another in Flinders Street, and five pigs in King
Street – someone had left the gate open. He pleaded guilty to the
charges, but 'bringing under the notice of the tender age of the pigs,
which were only suckers, he was only fined 20s and 10s costs.' Ohhh
... those five little piggies were too young to know they erred.

Just beginning its career of pestilence in Port Phillip was the rabbit.
You will recall that Henry Batman's dogs had killed rabbits belonging
to Fawkner way back in early 1836. But Fawkner – soon to be instru-
mental in the founding of the Acclimatisation Society – brought in
replacements. By 1846, market stalls were selling rabbits for stews
and escapees from the hutches were breeding under the police office
near by.

There are not too many instances to be found of townsfolk adopt-
ing native wildlife as pets. Cockatoos and rosellas were the excep-
tions, and an advertisement would occasionally appear in the lost
section of the newspaper classifieds seeking the return of a valued
feathered friend. William Wormsley ran a Fruit and Fish Mart at the
corner of Flinders Lane and Elizabeth Street and, in October 1841,
offered a £1 reward for the return of his 'Rosella Parrot' named Dickie.
Wormsley had been coaching Dickie to squawk "Errin's! Mack'rel!',
with a fair degree of success. But his efforts were offset by those of
the neighbourhood lads who would sing out 'Stinkin' fish!' every time
they passed. Sure enough, the day came when Dickie muttered indis-
tinctly, "Errin's! Mack'rel!' followed, clear as a bell, by a shriek of,
'STINKIN' FISH!'

The *Patriot*, in May 1845, reported that a charge of cockatoo-steal-
ing had been levelled against one William Potter. The charge was dismissed, however, after the bird's owner admitted that it was neither

caged nor tethered, thereby giving credence to Potter's claim that 'it hopped (not the twig) but upon his shoulder'.

The Canine War

Throughout the '40s, Bearbrass residents daily faced 'the danger of being torn down and perhaps devoured alive, to appease the craving appetites of the numerous half-starved and savage dogs which infest the town'. In June 1842, Tom Connor was fined thirty shillings for keeping an unregistered dog, which, according to the *Herald*, was 'an animal of large dimensions and most savage disposition, to the great terror and injury of all Her Majesty's quiet subjects in Little Bourke-street'.

Members of the police force were authorised to kill unregistered dogs – not just authorised, but rewarded to the tune of a half-crown (2s 6d) for each dog killed. To collect their half-crown bounty, constables were required to furnish proof of the deed, to satisfy the clerks of the Police Revenue office. Rather than have dog-killers heave in carcasses and whack them down on the polished counter-top, it was decided that the dog's tail would do nicely. Here then was another beaut little earner for the constabulary. In fact, to the end of November, policemen had presented close to £50 worth of dogs' tails for the year 1843 – in other words, in eleven months, nearly four hundred dogs had been destroyed.

Needless to say, the system was open to abuse, with some constables over-keen to collect the bounty. The proper procedure was to check a dog's registration and, in the case of an unregistered hound, take it to the Eastern Hill watch-house ('the usual place of massacre') where it was killed by a waddy blow to the skull. When the dog was dead, its tail was severed and taken as proof to the cashier. Instances abounded though, of constables using their truncheons to bludgeon any dog they encountered in the town, snipping off its tail with a pocket knife, and tossing the animal – perhaps still half-alive – into the river or up an alleyway. John Ewart, a gentleman, complained to the

Chief Constable in November 1843 that Nelson, his golden retriever and companion of eleven years' standing, had been destroyed, despite being properly registered. He had found Nelson dead and minus his tail at the Eastern Hill watch-house; the tail lay on a table near by, wrapped up in a handkerchief.

Perhaps as a result of overzealousness on the part of the police, or because the Police Revenue coffers were running low, in July 1845 an order was issued that the constabulary was to cease slaughtering dogs within the town ('except those belonging to the natives') until further notice. The amnesty was short-lived. By the end of December, the dog menace was again out of control. The *Herald* bemoaned 'the intolerable number of dogs at present infesting every street and alley in Melbourne':

> *The nuisance is bad enough by day, but parties obliged to be out by night are exposed to no little trouble and danger – a half-a-dozen curs snarling and biting at their heels. An accident of a serious nature occurred in Little Flinders-street on Friday. A boy, about eight years of age, happened to be engaged in some amusement, when a large dog made at him, biting at his face and mangling both cheeks in a shocking manner.*

In the New Year, the dog-slayers were back at work with such a vengeance that, by March, the *Herald* had dubbed the slaughter 'The Canine War' and had switched its allegiance to the dogs:

> *This* brutish *devastation is still progressing rapidly under the conquering baton of little Sergeant Swindell and Co. On Saturday this active dog-killer received a certificate from the Clerk of the Bench, for fifteen half-crowns, so many severed tails being forthcoming.*

Fifteen half-crowns – that meant Swindell had collected bounties to the value of £1 17s 6d on top of his week's wages of a little more than £1. It's easy to see why police were tempted to sever tails first and ask questions later.

The Canine War was still in progress in mid-1848 – in fact it had escalated, with the town's civilian population now also eligible to claim the half-crown bounty. In June, an unsuspecting mutt wandered into a sausage vendor's shop and exited soon after without its tail. A reporter from the *Patriot* was buying a pound of breakfast sausages when:

> The 'brute' ... *seized the poor animal by the tail, which, with a single blow of his knife, he severed close to the buttock. The liberated culprit ran away howling with pain, leaving his unmanly tormenter to make, if his conscience allows him, the sum of two and sixpence by his exploit.*

Evidently though, there was some doubt in the reporter's mind as to whether it really was the bounty that the sausage man was after – perhaps he planned a new line in gourmet sausages – as the *Patriot* report concluded with a warning: 'The inhabitants will do well to beware how they purchase sausages at his shop, at least for some days to come.'

The all-in spree of dog-killing inevitably got out of hand and was called to a halt late in 1848. In February the following year, however, the Mayor of the town again gave 'the fatal order', this time confining the task to the constabulary. On the eve of the slaughter season, the *Herald* reported that the constables were preparing their nooses and waddies, and that 'Constable Bryan Carr's redoubtable metallic glove is newly fitted up for hard work'. And so, in spasms, the Canine War continued, and Bearbrass dogs dozed twitchily, in dread of the bounty-hunters.

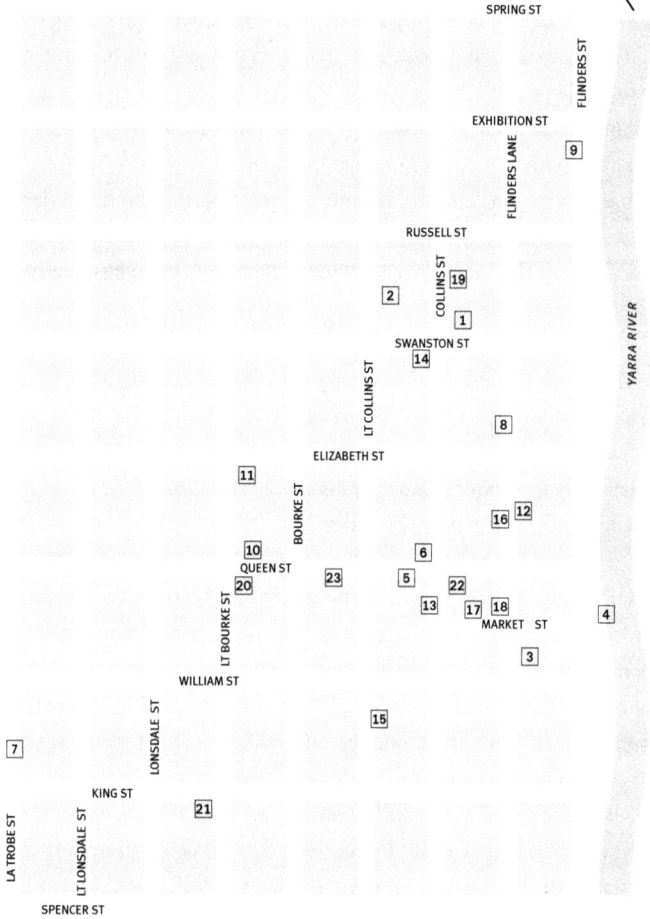

1. Thomas Napier's house and shop, now the Regent Theatre
2. Samuel Crook's cabinet-making and coffin factory
3. Birthplace of John Melbourne Gilbert, first white child born at Port Phillip, December 1835
4. Baptist immersion ceremonies, 1840s
5. Jem Connell's public house, where Tom Watt half-throttled a carpenter, 1838
6. Dr Barry Cotter's chemist shop, whence his housemaid took her leave 'in a clandestine manner'
7. Government relief workers' stop-work rally, 1842
8. Mrs Brown, dressmaker, late of Llandaff and Dublin
9. Yarro Cottage, home of the Welsh family, 1839
10. Mrs Joseph Aberline's 'Tuscan Straw Bonnet establishment', 1838
11. Mrs Weatherly, straw bonnet maker
12. The Adelphi Hotel, of 'noisy repute', where Frank Dutton's velvet-collared coat and Cumberland cap went missing in 1840
13. Thorpe's drapers shop, purveyors of Prince Albert Doeskin trousers
14. Donaldson and Munro, drapers – in 1841 the easternmost shop in Collins Street
15. John Lamb, Bearbrass's first barber, 1838
16. Henry Milbourne, hairdresser and wig-maker to the gentry, 1841
17. John McEchnie, the town's first tobacconist and snuff dealer, 1839
18. John Blanch's 'Sporting Emporium', scene of a gunpowder mishap, 1839
19. Premises of James Dick, tobacconist and illegal distiller – also his wife Meg, a dressmaker with royal credentials, 1839
20. The Queen's Theatre, from which William Dana was expelled for smoking, 1846
21. Mr Bland, portrait painter, 1848
22. Johnny Fawkner's original newspaper office, 1838
23. Printing office of the Port Phillip Gazette, where Thomas Strode worked up a whitlow in 1839

CHAPTER 5

Bearbrass People

Maid-of-all-work to a Particular Baptist

In the last thirty years of the twentieth century, the Regent Theatre swung from the brink of demolition to near-deification. These days it's re-prettified and back earning its keep. The Regent Theatre stands, of course, in Collins Street (the Regent Street of Bearbrass), a little way uphill from Swanston Street and the diminished City Square. Stand beneath the canopy that overhangs the wide footpath out front and tilt back your head. The effect of the decorative pressed metal lining, nippled with light bulbs, is somehow mesmeric, like the galactic ceiling of a planetarium. Take a seat outside the slot-in-the-wall café next door, or, even better, on the steps of the austere Baptist Church, not far up the hill and opposite. The proximity of this church gives echo to a slice of Bearbrass life in these parts – in fact, in 'a tolerably capacious building' known as Napier's Rooms, on the site of the Regent Theatre – in October 1840.

You're squatting before the hearth on a three-legged stool, skirt and petticoats hitched above your knees, relishing the warmth on shins that never see the light of day. A mighty pot of soup is on the simmer and, with a tin spoon, you idly poke the sheep's head that keeps bobbing to the surface. The missus doesn't approve of sheep's heads in her kitchen. Only fit for heathens, she reckons.

'Shanks will do nicely, thank you, Sarah,' she said tartly. 'It's not as if we can't afford them.'

But what does *she* know? Nothing's as good as a sheep's head for flavouring a soup just right. And young Thomas and Will love to chase about the yard with the skull on the end of a stick, once it's finished with.

Steps approach the kitchen door and you leap up, scuttling the stool and dropping the spoon with a clatter on the flagged floor. The doorknob turns and somebody pushes ineffectually from the other side.

'Sarah! Are you there? Open the door!' Crikey, it's Mr Napier.

You pull away the chair that's jammed under the doorknob and Thomas Napier senior falls into the kitchen.

'Sorry, sir, I …' you begin, but he blusters, 'What's happening? What was that chair doing there?'

'It's to keep Martha out, sir. See, I'm making soup' – you wave a hand in the direction of the fireplace – 'and there was that little girl of the McKenzies' fell into a pot just the same the other day and was scalded to death. Just the age of Martha, she was, and I thought …'

Napier clucks his tongue. 'That's right. Poor child. And she hadn't been saved, I suppose.'

'No, killed her straight out, I heard.'

'No, I mean *saved*. Those McKenzies – Presbyterians, aren't they?'

'Couldn't say, sir. I suppose …'

He presses his lips together in distaste and shakes his head. 'Poor child,' he says again.

Thomas Napier is a Baptist – not just a Baptist but one of them as calls themselves Particular Baptists. And it's a good name for him: particular. Particular about everything, he is. Him and his wife. It's not just sheep's heads, it's the state of things. Cleanliness. You saw the way he took in the fatty splash where the spoon had dropped on the flagging, even as he lamented over the McKenzie girl. Pots, vases, bedheads, doorknobs, windows – all have to be scoured and polished and wiped just so. And they get specially worked up about the undersides of things: mattresses, tabletops, doormats, things that no one ever sees.

'God sees,' is what the missus replied when you meekly asked whether it was really necessary to scrub the soles of the family's shoes every night.

And whose job is it to keep all those upsides and undersides clean? Yours, of course. The maid-of-all-work. Seven months you've been here and you're indentured for a year. Five months to go. Only a half-day off a week, one bath a fortnight if you're lucky (evidently they're not too concerned about the state of your underside, although they let you know smart enough if your apron's grimy or there's any hint of sweat about you), your bed's in a lean-to off the kitchen, and they watch your morals into the bargain.

'Who was that young woman Mrs Crook saw you with, Sarah?' asked the missus when you returned from your first afternoon off. 'She doesn't sound at all the type you ought to be keeping company with.'

Gawd help you if they find out about Patrick. And then there's the business of baptism. They want you to be baptised – 'saved', as Mr Napier calls it. You told them you were christened as a baby, but they reckon that doesn't count.

'Papist sham!' says Mr Napier. 'How can a baby confess repentance? And a trickle of water on the brow? That's not baptism. Full immersion! That's what it takes to drown the sins, the moral filth.'

But you've told them no, you've got your own religion. Napier snorted something about 'Geoghegan's scabby flock' but left it alone. Until the Reverend Mouritz arrived. He's the first real Baptist minister the town has had; before he arrived three months ago the services were held by lay preachers like Napier.

Reverend Mouritz stayed with the Napiers for his first two weeks in town and it was a fortnight too long for you. When you took tea to the sitting-room on the afternoon he arrived, he fixed you with a look of cold, black damnation and demanded, 'Has this girl repented?', as though you had SINNER branded across your apron front.

Mr Napier bowed his head in shame for you and said, 'No, I'm afraid not. We have spoken to her about it, Reverend, but … she's a papist.'

'Ha! All the more reason!' And Mouritz started in on you, his voice booming off the sitting-room walls as he showed off his preaching style for the first time in Bearbrass. He ended with what sounded like a threat – 'You *shall* repent!' – before sinking his teeth into a gingernut with a crack like a penny-bunger going off. His congregation looked impressed. You left the tea tray and fled.

It turned out not to be a one-off performance, but one that he reprises, with relish, every time he claps eyes on you. Never mind that Mouritz, with his black-cloaked immersion ceremonies in the bay out past Liardet's,* is the laughing stock of the town's unbelievers; close to, it's harder to see the joke.

Now here's Thomas Napier standing over you in the kitchen while you swab up the soup spill with a rag.

'Sarah, we have decided that you *must* be baptised. While you remain in our house as a sinner, unrepentant, you expose us all – Mrs Napier, our children – to your sins and their ordure.' Their *what*? 'You must show your repentance to the Lord. On Sunday, after services, we shall hold our first immersion ceremony at the Falls. Mrs Napier will explain the procedure, what you will be required to wear …'

'I won't,' you say, still kneeling, head down and breathing hard with anger.

'Father Geoghegan will not …'

---

* Liardet's Beach, as Port Melbourne was then known. In fact, the baptism ceremonies were held at Albert Park beach, near where Victoria Avenue meets Beaconsfield Parade.

'It's nothing to do with Father Geoghegan. I just don't think it's proper.'

'*I* have been baptised, Mrs Napier has been baptised. Are you saying that *we* are improper?'

'No, sir. It's just ... I don't hold with the idea of stripping off to my ... well, stripping off and bathing in public.' You're standing now, but with head still bowed and wringing the rag in your hands uneasily.

'*Bathing*! You liken it to that lewd exhibition? Baptism is a ceremony of confession, of repentance to the Lord. Nothing could be more modest than the gowns of our postulants: coarse black linen, securely fastened ...'

'But in the middle of town! With all them people watching – and laughing.' Patrick and his cronies, Lizzie ... You shudder. And if you didn't die of embarrassment, the stiff shroud would probably drag you under and drown you in the Yarra. 'No, Mr Napier,' you tell him, 'I won't do it.'

Napier pulls in a sharp breath through his nostrils. 'Sarah,' he says fiercely, 'I remind you that you are living in *my* house, as *my* servant ...'

Your head snaps up then and you meet his eyes for the first time. 'I'll leave, then.' Your voice is tight and measured like a whip-crack.

'You're indentured to me,' he retorts, as if that seals it.

'To *work* for you, not to take on your barmy religion or make a public bloody spectacle of myself!'

'Profanity! I won't have profanity in my house! Reverend Mouritz has your measure all right. He says that you're ripe ... no, *putrid* with sin. "That girl is *putrid* with sin!" he says.'

'Putrid, am I? Well, he'd know about that, wouldn't he? Preaching church in an undertaker's.* You're barmy, the lot of you. I'm not

---

* Baptist services were, by this time, held on the premises of Samuel Crook's cabinet- and coffin-making business, opposite the Napiers in Collins Street. Crook's building was set back from Collins Street, so that it stood on ground now occupied by the Victoria Hotel, at the rear of the Town Hall in Little Collins Street.

stopping here no longer. I work damn hard – you and your bloody undersides – and all the thanks I get is being called a putrid sinner by some mad old bugger of a parson.'

Napier is near-apoplectic by the end of this speech and his pinching fingers have hold of your upper arm, propelling you towards the back door. You catch him a flick under the ear with the wet rag as he shoves you down the step.

'Go then,' he hisses, 'but I'll put a warrant out for you. I'll tell them you refused to work, that you left without consent.'

That means gaol – if they catch you. But your Patrick's a constable. He'll help you get clear of the town and the law. They're always needing housemaids in the bush.

You gallop down the yard, not concerned about leaving your trunk behind – Lizzie'll fix you up with some clothes – or finding work without references, just glad to be shut of that bloody madhouse. As you duck under the top rail of the fence, you look back and Napier's still standing at the kitchen doorway, watching.

'Don't forget that soup's on the hob,' you sing out. 'Oh, and tell the missus the sheep head's for her!'

Mrs Macdonald does her bit

The white population of Bearbrass in 1840 was approaching 4,500. In the whole of Port Phillip, there were seven males to every three females. Women were especially scarce in the bush, so that in Bearbrass Sarah Caraboyne and her sisters probably found themselves outnumbered by men by a ratio of 2:1. In 1851, when the number of town dwellers had swelled to over 23,000, the population of the new colony of Victoria was still sixty per cent male. (Soon after, of course, a tidal wave of whiskery-faced, trouser-legged gold diggers would engulf the place, throwing the figures right out.)

Back in 1835, Bearbrass's European population of about fifty adventurous souls was increased by one when Mary Gilbert gave birth to a son on December 29. Johnny Fawkner recorded the event in his journal the following day:

> *The Boy Born Yesterday Evening is to be called James Port Philip*
> *Gilbert being the Son of Mary and James Gilbert, who came*
> *from Launceston in my Employ.*

In fact, when the boy was christened his name had been amended to John Melbourne* Gilbert, his first name presumably in honour of Fawkner, who had declared that the lad would be granted fifty acres of land in Port Phillip and a town allotment. Fawkner actually had his men mark out a town plot in the boy's name, but the official town survey later nullified all existing claims and young Johnny Gilbert ended up with nothing.

The Macdonalds of Darebin Creek, out Northcote way, certainly did their bit to ensure that Bearbrass flourished. In December 1841, Mrs Macdonald gave birth to triplets, having produced twins only a year earlier. The *Patriot* extolled her fecundity:

> *... if all goes well she is yet likely to present [her husband] with*
> *many similar gifts on each return of the season. Such a woman*
> *is truly a crown to her husband and her people.*

As to the character of the Bearbrass population, not only was it predominantly masculine, it was youthful. Squatter Edward Curr recalled of the early '40s that, 'In those days anyone over thirty was spoken of as old So-and-so.' Another writer noted that 'no deformity or old age, no decay' was apparent on the streets of early Bearbrass.

Add alcohol to the cocktail of youth and masculinity and you'd have had a high-spirited, ribald population, forever within a lucifer's

---

* Another whose name paid tribute to the new settlement was George Yarra Bilston, born the following year.

strike of violence. Sarah Caraboyne would have known well enough to skirt around certain parts of town on her afternoons off; even then, she'd probably have been waylaid and propositioned a dozen times on her way to meet her policeman beau. Just imagine the boisterous heckling to which the Reverend Mouritz's postulants were subjected as they were immersed at the Yarra falls in the sight of not only God but a fair-sized contingent of Bearbrass bodgies.

Manifestly wanting in staying-power

While the settler population of Bearbrass multiplied, the district's Aboriginal inhabitants were gradually excluded from the town. From the outset, it was determined that peaceable methods should be used to acquire land from the local Aborigines, and settlers were forbidden to use 'improper or unnecessary' violence against them. Beyond the town, atrocities were committed on both sides, but in Bearbrass itself reported instances of inter-racial violence were minimal. Nonetheless disease, alcohol, and other by-products of 'civilisation' had the – desired? – effect of culling the Aboriginal population in the vicinity of the town.

Until the early '40s, Aborigines were commonly seen in the township. This was in spite of attempts to lure them to a mission station on the site of today's Botanic Gardens, where they could receive instruction in the theoretical, moral and spiritual aspects of European civilisation. Under the guidance of George Langhorne, an Anglican missionary, Aboriginal children were induced to submit to school lessons, whilst adults received rations of food and soap in return for a few hours' labour each day. The mission, which started in early 1837, was not a success. In seeking to persuade Aborigines to remain at the mission, Langhorne failed to recognise the importance of their traditional patterns of movement. When the mission wound up in 1839, assistant missionary John Smith turned to innkeeping instead, with more tangible benefits – to himself, at any rate.

Garryowen recalled that in 1840 Bearbrass, 'At almost every turn, one met with the Aborigines, in twos and threes and half-dozens.' Edward Curr saw them too, but best remembered the 'strange effect' of hearing their 'shrill voices and strange tongues' in the street. By this time, their traditional garb of nakedness or a possumskin cloak was giving way to woollen blankets and cast-off clothes given them by the government and settlers. From their camps on the outskirts of the town, the Aborigines would bring in 'brooms' of tea-tree which they bartered for bread. Newspaperman Thomas Strode recollected that 'a black lubra ... would "run up" a tree in front of your residence in any part of the town, and lop off branches sufficient for a month's supply of firewood'. In payment they would ask for tobacco ('bacca'), bread or meat. G.G. McCrae, who arrived in Melbourne as a boy in 1841, later wrote that his family had found the Aborigines unsatisfactory as a source of cheap labour:

> Not positively lazy, but manifestly wanting in staying-power.
> Holding a horse, pulling on a rope, in punt or ferry, or anything
> in the shape of light work, they would undertake with alacrity
> and zest ... Hard work, such as digging potatoes, was scarcely
> in their line.

The townsfolk found the Aborigines of use, not only as kindling-pickers, but as a source of amusement. The ratbag element of the town would ply the Aborigines with grog and incite them to fight one another, all in the name of a bit of sporting fun.

By the early '40s, Aborigines seen in the town were often the worst-for-wear for grog and, with their traditional food sources disappearing as the town spread, many were reduced to begging for food. These factors fuelled the settlers' perception of the Aborigines as a degenerate race. Historian William Westgarth listed the reasons for their eventual banishment from the township as: 'their non-conformity in attire – to speak in a decent way – their temptation from offers of drink by thoughtless colonists, and their inveterate begging ...'

The ruthless expansion of the gold-rush years would almost finish the work begun by the Bearbrass settlers: in the twenty-seven years following Batman's penetration of Port Phillip, the population of two of the three clan groups whose lands encompassed the township had withered from an estimated 207 to only 28. McCrae had been right: they had indeed proved to be 'manifestly wanting in staying-power'.

Summot for his pains

The Bearbrass aristocracy would have had you believe that they had to grovel at the feet of their servants and tradespeople. They bemoaned the fact that a shortage of labour (except during the depression years of the early '40s) meant that the labouring classes of Port Phillip could command not only higher wages than their counterparts elsewhere in the colonies, but – in theory, at least – a degree of respect from their employers. Henry Meyrick, a wealthy squatter, remarked that 'The more poverty-stricken they are in England, in exactly the same ratio, the more bounceable are they when they come out here.' If they didn't exactly fear an inversion of the social order, there seems to have been a common perception amongst the masters of the township that the labouring classes were getting above their station.

In early 1836, the alarm went out that 'persons' servants are leaving them, and declaring themselves independent of their masters'. The embryonic state of the settlement, where no one could rightly claim ownership of the land, made for a situation something like the mythical 'level playing-field' spun by economists in more recent times. Servants had as much – or as little – right as their employers to mark out a plot of ground and call it their own. Johnny Fawkner not only granted an allotment to the infant Johnny Gilbert, but did likewise for each of his servants. But the ingress of government officials from Sydney stitched the frontier town up tight with statutes and street plans, so that there could be no question of the step up from servitude to the propertied classes being so casually trod.

Amongst the baggage brought to the district by the Sydney

authorities was the NSW Masters and Servants Act, the provisions of which gave lie to the notion that Port Phillip servants had the upper hand over their masters. The Act required that a contract be signed by both parties when a servant was employed, setting out the period to be served, duties to be performed, and other terms and conditions of employment. This might sound fair enough, but such contracts were heavily loaded in favour of the master: the servant had to be satisfied with the promise of payment at the end of the period, provided the conditions of the contract – 'and every of them' – had been fulfilled.

Should a master at any time become dissatisfied with a servant's performance, he could claim breach of agreement and have the servant fined or gaoled. For instance, when Henry Batman claimed in May 1837 that John Stewart, a sawyer employed by him, had failed to cut sufficient timber and 'would idle about the place', Stewart was imprisoned for a month. Likewise, shoemaker Thomas Hendrick was charged by his employer with failing to complete enough work, and was gaoled for two weeks. Sarah Caraboyne, employed as a general house servant by Arundel Wrighte Esq. in 1837, was imprisoned for three weeks and forfeited wages due to her because she refused to scour out an iron boiler on a 40°C day.

If a servant, on the other hand, had a complaint against a master, the Act offered virtually no means of redress; in any event, magistrates could generally be relied upon to side with masters where such cases did reach court. The alternatives open to dissatisfied or ill-treated servants were to abscond or refuse to work. Both actions attracted stiff penalties under the Masters and Servants Act, but were nonetheless frequently resorted to as preferable to suffering in silence.

Tom Watt, the punt-owner and builder, had a poor record (or, some might say, bad luck) as an employer. During 1838 alone, he had three servants abscond – or, in the words of the Act, 'leave his employ without permission'. First to spit the dummy was Tom Fitzmaurice, who left after only two months' service. When Watt caught up with him in Connell's public house, he threw Fitzmaurice to the ground, then kicked and half-throttled him. Watt was sentenced to a month's imprisonment for the assault, the same sentence being meted out to Fitzmaurice for absconding. In April, Watt brought another servant, William Hutchinson, before the magistrate for absconding. Watt testified that his servant was abusive and 'told me he would go where he liked in spite of me', and Hutchinson was sent to gaol for three months. A third servant, Thomas Schofield, pleaded guilty to a charge of absconding in September and was let off lightly, being only required to pay costs of 2s 10d.

The severity of some of the sentences levelled against servants – involving imprisonment with hard labour and forfeiture of up to an entire year's wages – indicates the absoluteness with which the law-making, servant-hiring colonial Establishment regarded the authority of the master and the submission of the servant. Possibly the cruellest aspect of the penalties handed out under the Act though, was that a master could insist that a servant return, even after payment of a fine or a term in gaol, to serve out the remainder of their contract. Even six months in prison did not exempt prisoners from having to return to situations that they had found insufferable, unless their employers made it known that they were not wanted. William Cane, for example, spent two months in prison after refusing to obey the orders of his employer, Thomas Glass. Upon his release from prison, Cane refused to return to Glass's service and was sentenced to a further two months, with hard labour. Considering that Glass had described Cane, in the first instance, as insolent and lazy, there can have been no other reason for insisting on his servant's return than to jerk his leash a second time and leave no doubt as to who was boss. After working eleven months of his twelve-month contract with Johnny Fawkner, Edward Smith, a bricklayer, refused to lay another brick, telling Fawkner that 'he would rather stay in gaol the remainder of the time he had to serve me than complete his engagement'. The magistrate obliged and Fawkner let him go.

In the case of Jane Stanbury, general house servant to Dr Barry

Cotter, a back-down circumvented the cruel sequence of imprisonment and recall. She had absconded from Cotter's service, taking her
possessions from his house 'in a clandestine manner' and was sentenced to two weeks in gaol; but upon her promising to 'do her duty',
the sentence was dropped and she returned to the doctor's house to
serve out her term.

Throughout the '40s, tradespeople and female servants were in
short supply. Of the former, Thomas Strode wrote that 'a sober and
steady workman ... possesses at once the means of becoming not only
independent but wealthy,' adding, ' – that is to say according to his
station in life.' In 1839, a notice had been placed anonymously in the
Gazette threatening, 'he wot hires to any settler under forty pounds a
year will get summot for his pains'. This smells like a hoax by a dis-
gruntled member of the employer class, bent on reinforcing the idea
of the Bearbrass labouring classes as extortionists.

In 1846, Bearbrass merchant James Graham, who acted as an agent
for his rural customer, wrote to a squatter:

> *I am afraid there will be no chance of your getting a single
> female servant from here ... Single women are now coolly
> and modestly asking £23 per annum! while able-bodied hard-
> working men can be had for from £20 to £22 a year ...*

A year later, the asking price had leapt to £28 a year in the neighbourhood of the town and 'at a little distance', £30.

You will notice Graham's use of the term *single* female. Married
female servants were more readily available, but their children were
considered a burden by employers. Witness the following extract from
a letter written by Graham to William Campbell of Port Fairy in 1844.
On Campbell's behalf, Graham had hired Adam and Isabella Marr as
general servants for an initial period of six months. Graham wrote
that he knew Adam Marr to be 'a very honest hardworking man', and
went on:

The woman seems also strong and active. The only drawback
against them is their having three children but I understand
that they do not require the attentions of their mother so very
much as to prevent her going through ordinary work ... I have
endeavoured to counter-balance the number of children by giving
them a very low rate of wages, £20 a year and only double
rations ... I have bound them down tight I think in every respect
... Their passage per the cutter Domain, *£4, I have paid for you,*
one half of which is to be deducted from their wages.

This means that, at best, the Marrs would receive £8 for their six
months' work and would be issued only two adult rations to feed their
family of five. As a single woman, Isabella Marr could have earned
more than that on her own.

During the depression of 1841–3, non-payment of their servants'
wages was commonly the first cost-cutting measure resorted to by
masters facing insolvency. Servants 'faithfully, honestly and justly'
performed the terms of their contracts, observing every 'wheresoever'
and 'whencesoever', only to have their masters claim hardship when
the time came to settle up. The *Herald* reported the plight of unpaid
servants in August 1841:

Every day the Police Office is full of hired servants applying for
summonses for non-payment of wages. It is abominable to see
the masters, when brought up to answer the charges, resorting
to every subterfuge to deprive their servants of their hard-earned
wages.

When a Dr Langford of Russell Street 'bolted' (ie., disappeared without
paying his creditors) early in the depression, his servant asked the
Police Magistrate if he could seize the furniture left behind in the
doctor's house, in lieu of eight weeks' wages owed to him. His request
was refused, other creditors being given priority.

Even in the event that payment was forthcoming, wages took a nosedive during the depression. John Thorne, John Watt and David Anderson petitioned the Colonial Secretary from Bearbrass in March 1842, claiming that:

> *the wages allowed, though sufficient to procure food, are quite inadequate to meet the enormous House rents or obtain the least Medicine, or Medical Advice ...*

Unemployment was high during those years and, more than ever, the master called the tune. Even cash-strapped employers must have derived satisfaction from knowing that, for the time being at least, the so-called labouring 'aristocracy' had been humbled.

Johnny Raws

The initial labour shortage at Port Phillip was due to the fact that wage-earners were generally unable to afford the expensive passage to the new district from Sydney or Van Diemen's Land. Half the proceeds of Crown land sales in Bearbrass was spent on an immigration scheme aimed at enticing labour to Port Phillip. When the first shipload of government immigrants arrived in January 1839, prospective employers were dismayed to find that its cargo comprised mainly the least desirable class of employees: married men and women encumbered with young children. On one hand, the authorities were keen to attract married immigrants, considering that they represented a steadying influence on the rackety settlement; on the other, their dependants were potentially a burden on employers and the government.

The 'Johnny Raws' or new chums, as immigrants were called, were drawn by offers of free passage to Port Phillip. Private ship charterers were paid a bounty by the government for the import of labour from Britain – £19 for each adult landed at Bearbrass. Unscrupulous shipping agents lured tradespeople and servants onto the bounty ships with cross-fingered promised of certain prosperity awaiting them at Port Phillip. Those who succumbed to the agents' wooing were soon disabused of their illusions: conditions on board the bounty ships were so awful that nearly ten per cent of immigrants died on the voyage out. Rations were meagre, sanitation appalling, and the crowding on board unimaginable. With bounties payable only on adult immigrants, the ship charterers cared little about the survival of the small children who accounted for the majority of deaths at sea. On board government ships, an average six per cent of immigrants died on the voyage.

Immigration to Port Phillip hit its stride in 1841, only to coincide with the onset of the economic depression and the backhanded slap of unemployment. Immigrants who had been led to believe that they could name their own wage in Bearbrass could find no work and no wage to give a name to. What is more, they were the target of animosity from workers thrown out of work by the effects of the depression, but who blamed their plight on the influx of immigrants. Garryowen put the immigrants' hardship down to laziness. He believed that there were plenty of jobs:

> *if they would only go a few miles into the country to get them; but they would not. They loafed and prowled about the Immigrants' Depot and at every tavern door the men sponged for a 'nobbler' whenever they could get it …*

As the numbers of unemployed and homeless immigrants grew, their camp was relocated from the government block to the south bank of the Yarra.* Unmarried female immigrants were accommodated separately in a rented store-house, which was denounced by the government medical officer as 'a Brothel on a large scale'.

The pitiful situation of many immigrants led, in time, to the for-

---

* Where, ten years later, another canvas town – of diggers bound for the goldfields – would flourish.

mation of charities and the initiation of government relief works, such as the building of a road between Bearbrass and Sandridge (Port Melbourne) and gravel-raising near the West Melbourne or Batman Swamp. When the government announced a two-shilling reduction in the wage paid to relief workers (or 'Navvies') in June 1842, a general strike was called. The newspapers reviled the strikers as:

the corps of bogtrotters … principally, indeed almost entirely
from the South of Ireland, and as utterly useless for any
supposable species of farm labour as can well be imagined.

Striking workers from the Sandridge road marched on the township, crossing the Yarra by the half-completed breakwater at the Falls and gathering up their comrades from that site, whence they headed, some two hundred strong, towards Flagstaff Hill. At the head of their procession they bore, as an emblem, a loaf of bread spiked on a long tea-tree pole. As the marchers approached the Flagstaff, they were met by Major St John, a police magistrate and renowned taker of bribes, on horseback. St John scorned the mob, declaring that their actions would achieve nothing and were unlawful, to boot. His order that they return to work was met with hoots of derision and defiance and, from one man close by the Major in the jostling crowd, the battle-cry that 'it was better to fight and die than live and starve'. According to Garryowen, the fellow was about to strike St John – a foreigner to starvation – with 'a big cudgel' when the Major wheeled his horse around and struck out with the handle of his riding whip, 'flooring' his would-be assailant. 'After this,' wrote Garryowen, 'the assembly quietly dispersed.' One wonders about the fate of the symbolic bread loaf – did it find its way, only slightly scuffed, onto Major St John's table as a sop to a light repast of salted sprats and vinegar?

The most debased and vilest dregs

If the luckless immigrants were 'bogtrotters' in the parlance of civic animosity, imagine the malevolence reserved for members of the convict class. In his inaugural letter home from the colonies in 1839, James Graham prefaced his first impressions with this comment:

It must be remembered what the generality of the white population of the Colony consist of, which is the most debased and vilest dregs of Great Britain and Ireland.

The Colonial Secretary was of like opinion and had directed, when Port Phillip was founded, that no convicts should be sent there. The early settlers, according to a speaker at an anti-transportation rally many years later, had come to the district 'under a distinct understanding that no convicts would be sent and that they were coming to a perfectly free and unpolluted Colony'. This ideal, however, soon fell victim to the district's labour shortage, with government and settlers alike being forced to concede that a convict servant was preferable to no servant. The honour of calling itself the first convict-free colony would belong to South Australia (whose population keep their State's badge of untaintedness brightly polished to this day).

The first thirty convicts arrived in Bearbrass from Sydney in September 1836, some for employment on government works, others for assignment to private employers. Small consignments of convicts arrived periodically thereafter, in response to requests from Police Magistrate Lonsdale: a blacksmith might be needed, or a baker, or a dozen labourers for the road gang. Before long, Lonsdale voiced a suspicion that the Sydney authorities were using Bearbrass as a sump for convicts who were 'incorrigible' and 'of the very worst character'. In later 1838, he told the Colonial Secretary that female convicts were proving 'troublesome' (in much the same way as single female immigrants were subsequently considered troublesome) and requested that no more be sent. At about the same time, with the government's immigration system set to increase the flow of non-convict labour, a directive came that no new convict servants would be made available to private employers at Port Phillip.

Transportation of convicts from Britain to New South Wales ceased in 1840. Because of the excess of labour caused by the economic depression and immigration, it was some years before Bearbrass felt the shortage of convict labour. By the end of 1843, the district had emerged from depression and, without a supply of cheap labour, vital public works were languishing and squatters crying out for servants. At the same time, British gaols and hulks were bulging with inmates. In 1844, a solution was presented: Port Phillip was deemed suitable as a place of rehabilitation for a class of convicts called exiles or 'Pentonvillains' (named after the model prison at Pentonville, from which some of them came). Categorised as being of 'the better class of prisoners', their good behaviour in prison had earned them free pardons. A free pardon was not quite what it appeared, however: the prisoner was freed from prison on the condition that they leave England (the exiles were all from English gaols) and not return until the term of their original sentence had expired.

Between 1844 and 1849, about 1,750 male exiles were transported to Port Phillip. Most served out their sentences in the employ of squatters, far from the town. However, some of those who remained in Bearbrass came under the notice of Dr James Clutterbuck, who condemned them (and exiles in general) as 'sunk in the lowest depths of vice and wickedness'. 'That,' says historian Michael Cannon, 'was a nineteenth-century way of saying that they were homosexuals.'* Dr Clutterbuck's estimation of the Pentonvillains gained popular acceptance and that slur, together with a growing public distaste for convictism in general, eventually led to a laden convict ship being turned away from Bearbrass in 1849. In August that year, a reported 1,500 citizens gathered at the

---

* Michael Cannon, *Old Melbourne town before the gold rush*, Loch Haven Books, Main Ridge, 1991, p. 28

Queen's Theatre Royal, on the south-west corner of Queen and Little Bourke streets, to protest against a continuation of convict transportation to Port Phillip. No more Pentonvillains were sent. Britain was left to find a new conduit for its prison overflow.

A correspondent to the *Gazette* in 1847 wrote that 'one half of our population are convicts' – in which category he included ex-convicts, as well as those still serving out sentences. 'Old lags' (as ex-convicts were called) were easy to spot on the streets of Bearbrass: their age betrayed them. Garryowen wrote:

> *at one time it would be something rare to find a resident over forty years of age who had not previously expiated some breach of the criminal law in chains, gang or prisons.*

Flash Maria and the contraband ladies

It was not uncommon for runaway convicts from Sydney and Van Diemen's Land to make their way to Port Phillip sporting a new name and (in the case of men, at least) a new configuration of facial hair. Where such an escape route was suspected, a detailed description of the fugitive would be despatched to Bearbrass so that the authorities there could be on the look-out.

In early 1839, eight men escaped from the wretched Port Arthur penal settlement in Van Diemen's Land. Police Magistrate Lonsdale was alerted to the likelihood that they were destined for Bearbrass when his Hobart counterpart, Joshua Sprode, notified him of the imminent departure for Port Phillip of a woman named Maria Oliver ('more generally known as "Flash Maria"'), who was known to be connected with one of the runaways. 'It is more than probable,' wrote Sprode, 'that if she is well watched some clue may be obtained of the runways in question.' The flamboyant Chief Constable of Bearbrass, 'Tulip' Wright, was assigned to do the watching. As he had formerly served in the Hobart constabulary, it was felt that he could not fail to recognise the notorious Flash Maria on sight. That is to suppose, of course, that she did not spot him first, the prow of his belly-swelled scarlet waistcoat being visible a good two town blocks away and preceding him around corners.

Making a more surreptitious entrance to the township than that of Flash Maria was the occasional 'contraband lady', a female transportee absconding from assigned service in Van Diemen's Land, who would be smuggled across Bass Strait in the hold of a cargo vessel, crammed into a beer cask with the bung-hole left open. Needless to say, contraband ladies pre-dated the crinoline; even a wide-brimmed bonnet would have been out of the question.

Vanity, fashion and slops

It is hard to say exactly how a contraband lady would have looked (other than crumpled and relieved, that is) when she emerged from her hiding place at the Yarra docks. Descriptions of the clothing worn by women at Bearbrass were seldom recorded for posterity. A crime report might mention the 'dingy shawl of coarse manufacture' worn by a battered wife, and the ballgowns of gentlewomen were guaranteed to receive the obsequious attentions of the newspapers; but writers and historians who recorded Bearbrass life invariably neglected to make mention of the way women dressed.

A likely explanation is that women did not observe a local dress code but, even in a frontier town like Bearbrass, dressed according to the accepted fashion of the times. Costume historians seem to agree that, in spite of scorching, isolated and makeshift conditions, Australian women of the Bearbrass period were well aware of and followed the changing fashions of Europe. Bearbrass drapers and haberdashers regularly advertised lists of their latest arrivals. Early in 1841, Donaldson and Munro, 'Scotch and Manchester Warehouse, Linen Drapers, Haberdashers, and Silk Mercers' of Collins Street East,* unpacked new stock which included:

---

* At the time, Donaldson and Munro's was the furthest shop east in Collins Street – on the north side, just west of Swanston Street.

An elegant and extensive assortment of Summer Shawls and
Norwich Turn-overs; Plain, check, and printed Muslin Dresses;
Elegant Mouselaine de Laine Dresses; Earlstone Ginghams;
Swiss-printed Chintzes; Superb Ayrshire needle-worked Muslin
Collars ...

And for those women who could afford to have clothes made to order, Bearbrass had its share of dressmakers. Advertisements boasting the patronage of the British nobility were deemed just the trick to attract the township's wealthier clientele. Mrs Brown, of No. 4 Little Flinders Street East, claimed to have formerly been dressmaker to the Countess of Llandaff and the ladies of the Court of Dublin, whilst, according to her published credentials, Mrs Margaret C. Dick of Collins Street had served under Mrs Williams, dressmaker and milliner to Queen Victoria.*

Dressmaking, whether professionally or for oneself, required a substantial outlay. This was due not (or not only), as you might expect, to the expense of the fabric and trimmings, but to the exorbitant price of needles and pins. In 1840, as much as sixpence might be paid for a single needle, and pins could cost halfpenny and a penny each. Presumably this was one reason why, when Mrs Paddy Welsh of Yarro Cottage, sought a housemaid and needlewoman in 1839, it was stipulated that 'her character must bear the strictest investigation'. What a responsibility that needlewoman would have to bear – all those precious pins and needles. One or two pinned each day to the hem of her petticoat would soon add up to a tidy sum. For how long would Mrs Welsh buy her story that, 'They must've fallen through the floorboards, mum'?

The clothes of working-class women echoed the fashions of

---

* Mrs Dick's tobacconist husband, James, was gaoled in 1841 for distilling spirits, in spite of his insistence that the peppermint-flavoured liquor was 'for family use' only. Perhaps his wife's royal connections paid off, as he was freed from prison by the personal order of the New South Wales Governor, Sir George Gipps.

women of means. That echo might have had a lag of some years, by which time fashions of a few seasons past would have been handed down through the ranks and modified for working wear. A woman who wore the same plain dress all week would probably have a best dress for Sunday wear. Over a period of years, this same best dress could be altered by its thrifty wearer in small ways – a new lace collar, a change of neckline, the addition of an Indian or paisley shawl – as a nod of recognition to changing fashions.

Another way of giving an old outfit a leg-up into the new season's fashion was by means of a bonnet, and the bonnet-makers and bonnet-sellers of Bearbrass were undoubtedly onto a winner. Tuscan straw bonnets, with a high rounded front, were all the rage in the township's early years, with the Dunstable and Leghorn styles running close behind in popularity. Mrs Joseph Aberline sold imported stock of straw and coloured silk bonnets at her 'Tuscan Straw Bonnet establishment' in Queen Street in 1838. Even a bonnet could be given several incarnations with the like of enterprising straw bonnet-maker Mrs Weatherly ready to alter them 'to the most fashionable shapes on the shortest notice'.

Children's clothing was generally just a scaled-down version of that worn by adults. But there is evidence that, by 1849, Bearbrass mothers were making greater allowance for the summer heat in the way they dressed their children, if not themselves. A *Herald* scribe disapproved:

> *It is unfortunately the fashion with many ladies at the present time, to let their children be exposed with bare neck, arms, and legs … In children, especially, the skin should be protected by a just and general clothing, light in summer, warm in winter, with flannel next the surface at all times.*

On the subject of men's apparel, Garryowen wrote that style of dress was an apparent 'line of demarcation' between free immigrants and

ex-convicts throughout the 1840s. Free men, he wrote, were distinguishable by their 'heterogenous garb':

the men's upper and nether garments of every known cut, fashion
and material – cloth, frieze and corduroy – and the headgear
either a felt hat or bell-topper, then stylishly known as the
'Caroline'. Their coats were mostly not over-long swallow-tailed,
and the would-be swellish portion went in for glaring brass
buttons.

Old lags, according to Garryowen, dressed with more uniformity, typ-
ically replacing their convict 'slops' with a cabbage-tree hat, a cloth
jacket, gaudy neckerchief or tie, and moleskin or drill trousers. In fact,
the outfit which Garryowen attributed to ex-convicts was common to
all men of the labouring classes, be they expiree or free immigrant, as
well as to a good many well-heeled squatters.

G.G. McCrae recalled that the Bearbrass gentleman of his 1840s
boyhood wore a figured or embroidered waistcoat beneath a short-
waisted coat with broad lapels, a high collar, and swallow tails swooping and dangling behind. The trousers were tight-fitting and strapped
down under the soles of square-toed boots. At the other end of the
ensemble soared an impressive belltopper hat, wrought of black
beaverskin. Mr Jephson Quarry, an Irish gentleman who arrived at
Bearbrass in 1841, was a fine specimen of the breed. With his black
hair and high cheekbones, he was described as 'a lady-chaser who
stalked his feminine game in a tall "Caroline" hat, a Willy-Wagtail
coat with brass buttons, flowered vests, and white trousers strapped
under Wellington boots'.* Squatter Edward Curr had observed quite
a different trend in 1839: 'that the time-honoured black hat and dark
clothes of the old country had given way to straw hats and white
suits'. Here it appears that Curr was describing his fellow squatters,

---

* *Georgiana's Journal*, p. 90.

who adopted and adapted the costume of the working man, recognising the practicality of pale, lightweight clothing in a hot, dusty land. And perhaps there was more to it than mere practicality: maybe the young squatter cultivated his rugged, outdoorsy image. His shirt was of blue woollen serge or cotton twill, depending on the season, his trousers were moleskin, his hat of woven cabbage-tree leaves, and he wore almost a quarter of a cow in leather: boots,* belt (with tobacco pouch suspended), holster, and spur-straps – some even had their trousers lined with the stuff.

A list of clothing stolen by runaway convicts from the hut of James Simpson, Esq. in March 1838 allows for a peep inside a gentleman-squatter's cedar trunk. Missing were:

> *[a] pair of drab trousers, blue dress coat, blue surtout coat, green round jacket, blue silk jacket, three shoes, one Cashmere waistcoat, one pair of white trousers, four cotton handkerchiefs, two silk pocket handkerchiefs, one pair of silk socks.*

Why *three* shoes, I wonder? Was one of the runaways an amputee, or did the third shoe play a part in a regular party turn of Simpson's? Or perhaps that 'three shoes' signified pairs, a distant precursor to the objectionable use of 'pant' to mean a pair of same.

Francis H. Dutton placed a notice in the *Herald* in July 1840, seeking:

> *The gentleman who by mistake took from the Adelphi Hotel, on the night of the Ball, a blue pilot cloth Top-coat, black velvet collar, check lining … Also, lost at the same time, a brown Cumberland cap.*

---

* By the 1840s, boots of kangaroo leather were also available.

This sounds a very informal kind of coat and headgear to have worn with formal dress. Perhaps Dutton was not a guest at the ball but merely a drinker at the bar of the Adelphi Hotel that night. And perhaps his check-lined coat and Cumberland cap were plucked from a peg in the hall by a young gentleman in evening dress, out for a lark after the tedium of the ball. Certainly some kind of hijinks is to be suspected because the Adelphi Hotel – on the south side of Flinders Lane, between Queen and Elizabeth streets – was said at that time to be 'approaching the Lamb Inn in noisy repute'. More will be told of the Lamb Inn in a later chapter – all that need be said here is that it was headquarters of the gentleman rowdies of the Waterford School.

This class of young gentleman would have been the very clientele targeted by A. Thorpe, Wholesale and Retail Draper, whose Collins Street premises stood opposite the Melbourne Club House. In 1841 Thorpe offered 'a splendid assortment of the most fashionable Goods ever imported to these Colonies'. His stock included 'rich Orleans and Crapes for Gentlemen's Coats', Cassimeres, Tweeds, Doeskins, Buckskins and 'the latest fashionable article for Trousers known as the Prince Albert Doeskin'. For just over £4, a gentleman could purchase Thorpe's 'very best wool-dyed' coat, 'lined with silk, &c.'; very best trousers ('not to be equalled') cost half that price. One pound would buy a Valencia or Toilinette waistcoat, whilst fancy waistcoats in 'Silk and Satin, plain and figured Velvets' (as worn by Jephson Quarry) cost nearer £2. Among the trimmings on offer to the Bearbrass dandy were fancy Spitalfields bandannas, black Brussels ducapes, satin handkerchiefs, and Indian rubber braces.

George Sinclair Brodie of Bourke Street catered to the other end of the menswear market in 1839. His stock-in-trade included Flushing jackets, pea and monkey jackets, youths' hair caps, Guernsey frocks, and plait, palm-leaf and drab hats. A Guernsey frock was a kind of loose-fitting, long-sleeved smock which hung to the knees and was traditionally worn by agricultural labourers. Johnny Fawkner had issued 'Gurnsey' frocks, in 1835, to his servants and to favoured Aborigines, 'Bait Banger', 'Dallah Kalkeith', and 'Boy'. In 1841, frocks and 'trowsers' made of duck (a heavy-weave cotton) were advertised as just the thing for sheep-shearing.

A heavy frock of duck or canvas and one of lighter cotton (or 'Parramatta', as the cloth produced at that place was called) were part of the yearly clothing ration for male convicts at Bearbrass in the 1830s. The remainder of the ration comprised trousers to match the two frocks, three striped shirts, three pairs of shoes, and a straw hat and a cap (or two caps).

The clothing issued to convicts was commonly referred to as 'slops'. In spite of how it sounds, this term was not just more of the usual disparagement slung at convicts; the same name was given to working clothes in general. The range of clothing categorised as slops in an advertisement for Benjamin's Cheapside House in 1844 would be worn with pride, and paid for handsomely, by Toorak bushmen today, and included:

> *pilot coats, woollen and cotton cord trousers, pilot cloth trousers, moleskin trousers of every shape and quality, blue cloth and moleskin jackets, plush sleeved vests, glazed hats, cabbage tree hats, regatta shirts, check shirts, blue twilled shirts.*

Slops came in two grades, common and best, so that an inventory of Johnny Fawkner's store in August 1836 included '12 Best Duck Frocks, 12 Common Duck Frocks, 9 Best Cord Jackets, 1 Common Cord Jacket', and so on. At the time of making the inventory, Fawkner issued old Jemmy Gumm (one of his servants) with a Best Moleskin Coat and five 'Striped 3/6 Shirts'.

The drapery business of Donaldson and Munro was passed a forged cheque by a customer in December 1841, and the description of the offender classified him as a slops-wearer:

Sallow complexion, rather hard-featured; height, from five feet ten inches to six feet, with a slight stoop; about twenty-four years of age; long sandy hair, with an uncombed wild appearance; had on dark drab moleskin trousers, blue flannel shirt, broad-brimmed straw hat, neither neckerchief nor jacket.

No mention was made of the goods paid for by the forged cheque. If they included a neckerchief, jacket and comb, the forger could easily have eluded detection, sitting stooped but otherwise unrecognisable in a public house at the other end of the township, his complexion heightened and features softened by rum.

Were flecked woollen trousers a sign of criminality or just favoured by lazy bachelors because they didn't show the dirt? 'Blue speckled trousers' were the most distinctive feature of a seaman named Edwin Robins who absconded from *Bright Planet*, a barque berthed at Bearbrass, with a coat-pocketful of passengers' jewellery in August 1840. James Eyles Mounsher, another speckled-trouser wearer, was sought for embezzlement of 'certain sums of money' from his employer, George D'Ailey Boursiquot, in 1847. Those 'certain sums' must have been considerable for Boursiquot offered a whopping twenty guineas reward for Mounsher's apprehension:

In height he is about 5 feet 8 inches, florid complexion, light hair, eyes, and very little eyebrow, rather bald, about 25 years of age, had on at the time he absconded a light tweed coat, pepper and salt trousers, and cabbage-tree hat.

The seemingly ubiquitous cabbage-tree hat was not to everyone's taste, a fact capitalised on by a Mr Johnston of Queen Street. In 1845, he opened a 'hat manufactory' producing a vast range of styles:

from the fantail of the dustman to the shovel hat of the church
dignitary, the intermediate grades including everything which
the head of man can desire in way of covering.

In the mid-'40s, William Howe set up a dyeing business in Collins Street. The staple of his trade was in the deadening of pale and coloured clothes for mourning. Howe took pride in his craft, concocting advertising doggerel that made the doings of his pigments and tinctures sound more like sorcery than a part of the death industry. In one burst of verse, he told of how his dyeing process:

... renders clothes what e'er their hue,
Grey, drab, or brown, or dusky blue,
A matchless black or perfect sable,
By process quite inimitable,
And 'ere the sun has twice gone down,
His first rate finish can be found.

Alongside his dyery, Howe operated the equivalent of a dry-cleaning plant where the likes of ladies' cloaks and riding habits, and doe and buckskin breeches were 'cleaned and finished up in true fashion'. In 1846, he moved to Queen Street, where his operations were enlarged to incorporate the improbable-sounding 'Imperial Leather Legging Warehouse and Shepherd's Life Protector, and Renovating Mart'.

Hairy mania

Embezzler James Mounsher seems to have been pretty light-on in the facial hair department, with his 'very little eyebrow' and no whiskers worth a mention. In the Bearbrass era, whiskers were thought to reveal a great deal about a man. On one of the labouring class, a full set of whiskers raised the suspicion that their wearer had something to hide: that he was an escaped convict or wanted felon. In December 1839, Lonsdale harboured just such a suspicion of a man named Joseph Sains (who also answered to the names John Ray and Kangaroo Jack). The police magistrate wrote to his Sydney counterpart that:

> *he has worn almost constantly since he has been in the district*
> *his beard, whiskers and moustaches unshaven, which in a man*
> *of this class can hardly have been for any other purpose than*
> *that of deception.*

At the other end of the social scale, Dr William Henry Campbell's whiskers almost cost him his professional reputation and livelihood. Arriving in 1841, he set up a medical practice in fashionable Newtown (Fitzroy) and, after a time, began to wonder why he had yet to see a single patient. Garryowen tells the story:

> *He had a black beard and moustache, and was informed that*
> *Melbournians distrusted people, especially professionals,*
> *with other than closely-shaved faces. Whiskers of moderate*
> *dimensions might be tolerated, but as far as any medical*
> *practitioners who sported a moustache … it was simply*
> *preposterous!*

Campbell shaved his moustache and his practice thrived. In fact, before long, he was known as 'the Handsome Doctor'.

Another whose whiskers brought him close to professional suicide was a solicitor whom the irascible Judge Willis threatened to have struck off if he continued to appear in court sporting a moustache.

The rule for the professional classes then seems to have been that side-whiskers and – at a pinch – an under-chin beard were acceptable, whilst a moustache was decidedly not. Besides obscuring the facial features – and the minute observations of mouth-shape and countenance evidenced in the descriptions of some wanted felons show a strong belief that the face held the key to the character (an 'open countenance', in Victorian times, was commonly cited as an attractive physical and moral characteristic) – there was the question of hygiene. Moustaches were very likely regarded as unsanitary: hoarders of snot, soup and spittle, incubators of virulent microbes. On the other hand, perhaps the moustache was simply unfashionable among the upper classes of the period, whose gauge of respectability, in facial hair as in all things, was the raw-faced British nobility.

The young squatters, on the other hand, tended to set their own, informal, rules of dress and grooming, and those extended to the matter of whiskers. According to Curr in 1839, squatters 'were distinguishable by their hirsute appearance'. The Hon. Robert Dundas Murray, visiting the district in 1841, noted that they wore 'moustaches and beards of Turkish luxuriance' which (mixing his ethnic analogies) he said made some of the squatters look 'more like Italian brigands than clean faced Englishmen'. William Westgarth continued the Continental theme. 'This hairy mania is very contagious,' he wrote in a letter home at Christmas 1840:

> *A stranger in town would think he had found himself in some French or Italian town, from the foreign hairy appearance of the persons he meets.*

Johnny Fawkner, writing in the *Patriot* in March 1839, plainly found the 'hairy mania' hilarious. He and Eliza had been 'Perambulating Town on Thursday last' when:

> *passing down Queen-street, we were seriously startled ... by the hideous appearance of some sort of hairy monster on horseback, what added to the Alarm was, the cadaverous and unearthly cast of that part of its face which was not covered with long, mangy hair. It was dressed as a man, in a fancy coat and tassel, jacket, trousers, and, wonderful to relate, it wore spectacles.*

Ten years on, with Bearbrass less a frontier town and more a provincial capital, His Worship the Mayor gave the order that members of the police force were to be clean-shaven and keep their heads 'barbarised' in a tidy manner. There were any number of barbers in the town, prepared not only to shave and clip but to fashion elaborate hairpieces for clients whose scalps required addition rather than subtraction of follicle-fillers.

John Lamb was the town's first barber, setting up shop in 1838 in the section of Little Collins Street later called Chancery Lane.* In 1841, Henry Milbourne operated a hairdressing business nearly opposite the Adelphi Hotel in Flinders Lane, making 'Wigs, Fronts, and Ringlets' to order and offering a private room for hair-cutting. Milbourne would wait on gentlemen at their own residences, saving them the trouble of negotiating the bullock furrows of Flinders Lane. The town's most popular barber of the '40s was George Cooper, a big fellow with a baritone who, when he wasn't barbarising, performed on stage at the Victoria Theatre. Garryowen described Cooper as possessing 'small dramatic ability, overlaid by a tremendous quantity of assurance' – desirable qualities, surely, in a man who made his living with a cut-throat razor.

Calling himself a 'Peruquier', Samuel Croft made perukes (wigs with dangling curls) and scalps (toupés) 'of the most undeniable fit'. Wigs of the curly kind were worn by men and women alike, and were by no means confined to the moneyed classes. You may recall that when neighbours Catherine Doyle and Jane Coghlan fell to blows, Coghlan's wig was the first casualty. And when bridge-keeper Patrick Doherty fought off four armed robbers, he was left clutching a gingery, long-curled peruke. The police investigating that incident may well have paid a call on Samuel Croft, producing the hairpiece for identification. Was it one of his made-to-order jobs or an off-the-rack Portuguese import?

---

* Lamb soon gave up hairdressing in favour of hotel-keeping, and was later fined for sly-grog selling.

The Aborigines of Bearbrass dressed their hair and bodies with animal fat coloured with red ochre. Reverend William Waterfield, the town's first Congregational minister, observed a group around a campfire one evening:

There was a saucepan with some pieces of fat boiling in it and after taking out the fat and eating it, they first dipped their fingers in the saucepan and rubbed it on their bodies and hair of the head, and then drank the rest.

Both men and women wore headbands of netted thread, also coated with red ochre and sometimes dressed with a long, drooping feather. More commonly, a white clay tobacco pipe would be tucked beneath the band, just forward of the wearer's ear.

Smoking

Among Bearbrass men, smoking was almost universal – a pipe for the working man, a cigar for the gent. The cheroot – a slim cigar, the closest relation to the modern-day cigarette – crossed class boundaries. John McEchnie was the town's first tobacconist, selling makings to the smoking man, and fancy snuff besides. His shop in Market Street opened in September 1839, but less than three months later McEchnie's entire stock went simultaneously up in smoke and his young son was killed when the gunsmith's shop next door exploded. John Blanch's Sporting Emporium was flattened on the afternoon of 17 December when a customer who had first called at McEchnie's absentmindedly flicked cigar ash into a barrel of gunpowder. The two-storey shop was packed with the stuff (the government having refused Blanch's requests that a powder magazine be built for its safe storage) and the resulting explosion was like an apocalypse. Garryowen described it:

For a few moments there was the deep sound of a distant storm
as the expanding air struggled in the lower apartments –
another minute and it burst through the upper storey, and with a
crash equal to the loudest thunder, carried away in a huge mass
of smoke and fragments the roof, rafters, and walls.

John Blanch was horribly injured but lingered, fully conscious, until ten the next morning. His wife Sarah, aged only twenty-two, was killed outright ('dragged from amidst the charred and smoking ruins the body of a female, her whole form scorched and withered, denuded of every particle of clothing except the fragment of a shoe that remained on the right foot'), as was the cigar-toking customer. Young McEchnie, who was weighing tobacco at the counter of his father's shop when the Sporting Emporium went up, died from his injuries more than two weeks later. The three Blanch children – John Jnr, Ann, and Willie – had been walking at Flagstaff Hill with a maid-servant and were showered with debris from 'their once happy home' as they rounded the Collins Street corner on their return. A second customer in Blanch's shop survived, but had his skin so scorched as to remove all trace of the smallpox scars which his face had borne since childhood.

From that same year, 1839, James Dick (sometime distiller of pep-permint liqueur and husband of dressmaker Meg) had his tobacco-nist shop in a wooden hut – the grandly named Universal Emporium – in Collins Street, just east of where the Regent Theatre stands. In 1840, his advertised stock included 'Negrohead, Cavendish, and York Returns Tobacco, Taddy's Plain and fancy Snuffs, in three pound and half pound Jars, Real Planchados, Nos. 4 & 5 Superior Young Queen, Havanah & Chinsurah Cigars', as well as an assortment of plain and fancy pipes. The most commonly sought pipes were made of unglazed white clay and were so brittle as virtually to warrant the label 'dispos-able'. Plain clay pipes were very plain indeed, while the fancy designs into which their bowls and stems could be moulded ranged from the regal (the head of Queen Victoria) to the comical (a cat and fiddle) to the pornographic (a naked women in congress with a dog). In the most popular clay pipe design, an eagle's leg formed the stem, with its claw grasping the bowl.

'Bacca' was a currency in which Aborigines were frequently paid by settlers for their labour. The clay pipes in which they would smoke their wages could be worn ornamentally when not in use. Not only were they worn tucked into ochred headbands; sometimes the stem was poked through a hole in the septum of the nose, so that the clay pipe rode the top lip like the thin ghost of a moustache.

In the early, wild days of theatre performances at Bearbrass (see Chapter 8), the audience's smoking would produce a haze so dense that the stage could scarcely be discerned. A drive for respectability in the theatre resulted in a ban on smoking therein, a ban that was disregarded by (among others) William Dana, the fiery commander of the native police. When requested by the theatre's proprietor to extinguish his cigar, Dana replied, 'I'll see you hanged first,' upon which bouncers were summoned and he was strenuously shown the door. Outside in Queen Street, Dana vented his spleen at a man lounging – smoking, in fact – near the theatre's entrance. As luck would have it, the object of his foul-mouthing turned out to be the Chief Constable, and Dana was next day fined £2 for his outburst.

A true and faithful likeness

The art of photography arrived at Bearbrass in August 1845 with Mr G.B. Goodman, roving daguerreotypist. From premises in Flinders Lane, Goodman offered a portrait service that, with no sitting exceeding five seconds and the whole picture finished and delivered in four minutes, rivalled the speed of the modern-day photo booth. Goodman's advertisement described the process as 'the reflection of the figure itself fixed in a mirror', with the result 'a true and faithful likeness both of face, figure, dress, expression, &c., &c.; … in effect a SECOND-SELF'. A daguerreotype portrait cost a guinea (twenty-one shillings), which price included a handsome gilt and morocco frame.

Demand for Goodman's 'sun portraits' – as daguerreotypes were also known, bright sunlight being an essential ingredient in the process – kept him in Bearbrass until the year's end. In November, a consignment of larger photographic plates arrived from England, expanding Goodman's portrait repertoire to include groups, buildings, landscapes, horses, and prize bulls.

Sun-portraitist Douglas T. Kilburn set up shop in 1847. Like Mrs Dick, the dressmaker, Kilburn boasted a connection with royalty: his brother was Photographic Artist to the Queen. For all that, his starting price for portraits was a mere ten shillings – less than half Goodman's price, but still beyond the pockets of most common folk. Commencing sittings in the springtime ('as soon as the fine weather sets in'), he advised patrons that his studio, in 'Collins-lane, near Elizabeth-street', was fitted 'so as to soften the daylight and thus protect the sitter from the painful glare of the sunshine, and the publicity of the open court yard'.

Nearing the following winter's equinox, Kilburn would have been grateful for a little more of the sun's glare. The meagre winter sunlight reduced daily sitting times to, at best, four hours – from eleven a.m. to three p.m. – and many days saw not a single break in the cloud shrouding Bearbrass.

A portrait painter, the inauspiciously named Mr Bland, provided competition at the grander end of the market. In his Kelly's Cottage studio, on the corner of Little Bourke and King streets, Bland blended art and flattery year-round, heedless of the barometer reading.

The voice of the people

Portraitists and publicans, bonnet-makers and barbers, all employed the newspapers to spruik their wares. Bearbrass's three principal organs were the *Patriot*, the *Gazette*, and the *Herald*. But first came Fawkner's *Advertiser*. Its premier edition appeared on New Year's Day, 1838, handwritten in ink by Fawkner himself. Guests at his hotel could scan the foolscap pages gratis; for less-blessed mortals, the price was one shilling. An antiquated printing press* and type arrived in March to give Johnny's pen-hand a rest, but too few Bearbrassians were willing to pay the cover price of what was, as the name suggested, essentially an advertising rag, and the *Advertiser* expired before the end of April.

Later in 1838, the *Gazette* appeared. Its premises were in Queen Street, near Little Collins, and its editor was Thomas Strode, a Sydneysider. That proud Vandemonian, Johnny Fawkner, responded with the *Patriot* early in 1839, and a year later the *Herald*† joined the fray. During the early '40s, each of the three was published two days a week, giving Bearbrass a newspaper every day except Sunday. In their editorial leanings, the *Gazette* and *Herald* tended to be flunkies of the government administration and the squatters, while the *Patriot* advocated the interests of townsfolk and traders.

The stage was set for unfriendly competition, not just because of differing political allegiances, but because three newspapers in a frontier town had to fight dirty to survive. Besides, Fawkner loved a good stoush. In 1840 – when the bounds of decency were set by religious considerations rather than the Sex Discrimination Act and the Press Council – the *Gazette* characterised the *Patriot* as 'an old woman whose low and impudent vulgarity would do no disgrace to the forensic abilities of a Billingsgate fish-hag', and described its contents as 'the senseless tirades of a blathering old bitch'. In like vein, the *Patriot* labelled the *Herald* a 'dung-hill cock'.

According to the *Gazette's* Thomas Strode, Fawkner's share of the dirty tricks ran to more than invective. Strode alleged that Fawkner bribed the *Gazette's* compositor not to appear for work and, when

---

* Fawkner's printing press is in the collection of the Melbourne Museum, though not on display.

† The *Herald* survived Separation, gold rushes, depressions and wars, but could not survive Rupert Murdoch. The final *Herald* was published in 1991, a hundred and fifty-one years after the newspaper was founded. It is commemorated in one-half of the *Herald-Sun* title.

Strode had the man gaoled under the Masters and Servants Act, Fawkner kept the prisoner supplied with luxuries throughout his incarceration. While his compositor supped on game and enjoyed early nights in the lock-up, Strode was forced to set the type alone for six weeks, during which period he slept for only two hours a day and developed an abscess on his typesetting finger. 'On another occasion,' wrote Strode in his memoirs:

> *The lad engaged by the proprietors of the* Gazette *to deliver the newspaper to the subscribers was found lying on the causeway in close proximity to the public house kept by that 'hater of Sydneyites', insensibly drunk, the newspapers entrusted to his charge for delivery to the subscribers, in a pool of water, reduced to pulp and completely spoiled.*

In the mid-'40s, the *Gazette*, like its paperboy, dropped its bundle. The *Argus* had its genesis in 1846 and, like the *Patriot*, was more likely to champion the interests of the town-dweller and the working man than those of the Establishment. In fact, the *Argus* eventually absorbed the *Patriot* and with it Fawkner's motto – a quotation from John Knox: 'I am in the place where I am demanded by conscience the truth, and therefore the truth I speak, impugn it who list' – so that the spirit of the 'doubly convicted scoundrel' was borne on the *Argus*'s masthead far beyond his lifetime and ignominy.

Superintendent La Trobe was clearly fed-up with the feisty, bickering broadsheets when, in 1848, he summed up their distinguishing characteristics as 'ignorance, disregard of truth, and a reckless and studied spirit of misrepresentation, often amounting to the most malevolent libel'. Had he still been in town, the stormy Judge Willis of the Supreme Court would have hollered 'Amen!' Dismissed from his post in 1843, Willis had condemned Bearbrass as 'a miserable little town where everyone knows everyone's affairs and frequently knows more than the truth regarding them'.

CHAPTER 6

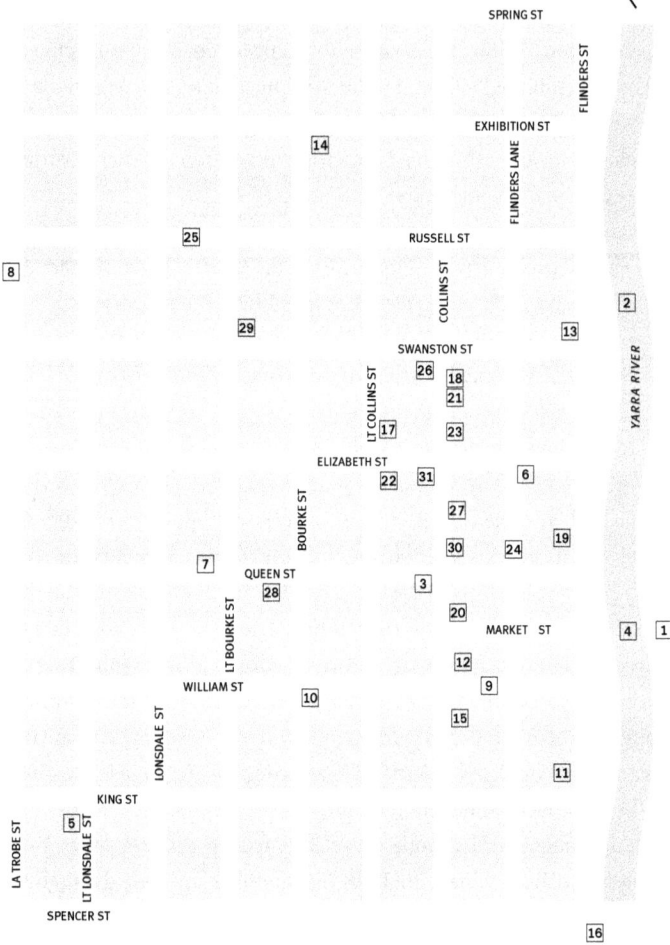

SPRING ST

FLINDERS ST

EXHIBITION ST

FLINDERS LANE

14

25

RUSSELL ST

8

COLLINS ST

2

29

13

YARRA RIVER

SWANSTON ST

26

18

LT COLLINS ST

21

17

23

ELIZABETH ST

22   31

6

BOURKE ST

27

30   24

19

7

QUEEN ST

28

3

20

LT BOURKE ST

MARKET   ST

12

4   1

WILLIAM ST

9

10

15

LONSDALE ST

11

KING ST

LA TROBE ST

5

LT LONSDALE ST

SPENCER ST

16

1. Johnny Fawkner's farm at Southbank
2. The spot where Fawkner's kangaroo dogs landed the settler's first 'boomer', August 1835
3. Mr and Mrs Howe, bakers specialising in game pies
4. John Batman Jnr drowned trying to land a schnapper at the falls, 1845
5. Georgiana McCrae's 'Argyle Cottage', an early kit-home brought to Bearbrass from Singapore
6. William Wormsley's Fruit and Fish Mart
7. The green-painted premises of Henry Clegg, fishmonger and oysterman
8. Bearbrass's best mushrooming spot
9. The house of Henry Batman, in whose kitchen garden Johnny Fawkner planted shallots
10. The Reverend Thompson's cabbage garden
11. The plot that nurtured Ben Baxter's monster turnip
12. The original market square (later the Western Market)
13. Hay and corn market, 1841
14. Eastern Market, from 1847
15. George Smith's garden, from which onions were stolen in 1836
16. John Batman's Tasmanian spuds drove convicts to thievery in 1837
17. Orchard and vineyard, late 1840s
18. John McNall, law clerk and butcher
19. John Tancred slaughtered two bullocks without a licence
20. The Melbourne Club, from whose kitchen Cassimere Frezygiviski stole dripping
21. The hut of John Gunn and Mary Dobson, where stolen mutton was found under a table
22. Adam Murray, sausage vendor
23. William Overton, baker and confectioner, supplier of 'comfits' to the Batman children
24. Tim Hurley, a baker, fell down in the street after drinking his master's takings at Carr's public house
25. Fred Cox hit a stump when delivering bread in a box-cart
26. William Nicholson's store, with its steam-powered coffee grinder
27. The Imperial Inn, where landlord Henry Baker imposed a levy on teetotal diners
28. Stephen Toogood's dining rooms and sly grog outlet
29. The London Eating and Boarding Establishment, where soup was always ready
30. The Royal Hotel offered real turtle soup
31. John Yewer's eating house, the soup specialists

CHAPTER 6

A Land of Chops and Steaks

Turnip precinct turned cappuccino precinct

In creating Southbank, the city planners at last embraced the muddy Yarra. They spanned it with a dog-legged footbridge, upstream from the former falls, and this is the most scenic approach to the warm-salad zone. Choose a Saturday afternoon for your visit. Cross Flinders Street at the foot of the Elizabeth Street ditch, then plunge down the stairs into the subway beneath Flinders Street station. Observe the 'Do Not Spit' signs on the white-tiled walls; save your sputum for Southbank. At the river end of the subway, take a few steps or the ramp and you're onto the bridge's timber decking with the brown river moving sluggishly beneath.

Now the key word for visitors to Southbank is *promenade*, so use your time on the footbridge to cultivate the right kind of look: think Cannes, give your hair a shampoo-ad swish and tilt your chin up like you might be someone famous. Assume the attitude. (But don't, whatever you do, walk into the pointy end of one of the handrails that jut out wherever the bridge takes a wriggle.) You're approaching the shopfront of the generic international city that has eaten the last of Bearbrass.

At the south end of the footbridge, you'll have to skirt around a flurry of Asian bridal parties taking photo calls. Oblige – with a mixture of worldly largesse and civic pride – the requests of tourists to photograph them against the murky Yarra backdrop. Then promenade your way to an outdoor table and be seated.

The noise of the place is astounding. Overlaying the din of music, voices and clashing crockery are bleating tourist ferries and the roar of diesels and freight wagons pulling through Flinders Street station. Gaggias keep up a constant guttural hiss, apparently sending hostile signals to the seagulls as they're uncharacteristically shy about snatching crumbs.

In the early days of Southbank – fifteen years ago – a pumped-up parliamentarian dubbed it 'the longest cappuccino precinct in the southern hemisphere'. I pondered that one for a while. What about Lygon Street's coffee strip, or Brunswick Street's? They'd be longer, surely. Then it came to me: of course – he meant *the river*. Myself, I'd have called the Yarra more *caffe latte*; but during the Moomba water-skiing, its surface all frothy with speedboat chop, perhaps then it does resemble nothing so much as a gigantic trough of cappuccino.

A hundred and seventy years ago, a parliamentarian-to-be, Johnny Fawkner, laid his own plans for the development of the Yarra bank. The river was brown then too, but no caffeinated analogy entered his head. Spuds and turnips were to be the main attractions of Fawkner's Southbank.

◌◌◌

It's the last day of November 1835. Your baby's only a month away, if that (a length of twine holds your skirt up; it's been two months or more since the hooks and eyes of the waistband met), and when Jem came in last night he told you, 'The boss wants you to help over the river tomorrow.' Seeing you about to gallumph, he said, 'Don't blame me, Mair. All hands on deck, he says. Including Mary, he says. He made a special point.'

'I'll see the missus about it. She'll say she needs me at the house.'

'Nah, she's coming over too. And she already spoke up for you, but he says if you can handle all that washing you shouldn't have any trouble chucking a few handfuls of seed about. Don't worry, the missus'll keep an eye on you.'

There was a pile of washing that you were supposed to be seeing to today, but Mrs F. said this morning, 'It can wait, Mary. I'll give you a hand with it tomorrow. Johnny wants to get the garden in today.' So across the river it was.

They took the horses over a week or more ago and ploughed it, almost right to the river. You watched them from the place on the opposite bank, upstream, where you do the washing for most of the settlement. The long grass that had dried from green to flax over the past month disappeared as the plough turned the black soil upper-most. Right at the river's edge grew a fringe of gums, mainly straggly but with a couple of beauties amongst them. They set fire to them late one afternoon. Sitting outside yours and Jem's hut, you watched them burn till bedtime, and in the morning they were gone. Mr F. was pleased with the job. 'It's looking good, boys,' he said.

Jem headed across with Billy and the boss (Charlie and Jack are camped over there in a tent) just after seven this morning. Then old Jemmy rowed back for you and the missus. It actually felt good to be on the water again. Old Jemmy's a good, smooth oarsman and there was only the slightest of currents. Even Mrs F., usually twitchy and full of nerves, relaxed for once and trailed a stick of dry grass over the boat's side. You reclined against a sack of seed potatoes and, after serving you a kick behind the ribs as Jemmy pushed off from the bank, the baby lay still and flattened itself into the rhythm of the boat.

Jem was away up the field making running repairs to the furrower, but he waved as old Jemmy handed you ashore on the south bank. Near by stood the brittle black fangs of the burned river gums. Jemmy hoisted the sack of spuds over his shoulder and led the way around the field's edge to Charlie and Jack's tent. Mr F, in rolled-back shirt sleeves and with a cheesecloth bandana round his head, was squatted on his haunches sorting seed into bags.

'Hello, m'dear,' he greeted Mrs F, looking up. Then, 'Mary,' he said, 'you can start with the damsons, I think.' Up towards that top corner. Charlie'll show you where we want them. Charlie!'

You made your way between and across the fresh furrows and Charlie showed you the spot to start pacing out the damson stones. Two rows over from you he was doing cherries, his lumpish frame made lumpier by the Guernsey frock he had on. (Jem refused to wear his, telling Mr F he couldn't work the horses in a frock; but he said to you, 'I'd look a fair cully in that, now wouldn't I?' and he hid it at the bottom of his trunk.)

The soil was a coarse, black, sandy loam. Fine dirt for spuds, your pa would say. When your damson stones were all gone Mr F gave you a bag of carrot seed and sent you down to sow it beside the radishes, which they'd put in a few days earlier and were already showing green. On the other side of the radish bed, Jem and Jack were doing drills for the spuds and making you laugh with a bawdy song about a barrow-girl, Covent Garden Bess. They'd just got to the 'Carrots-oh!' verse when the toe of your boot caught on something hard, sending you belly-first into the dirt.

'Jesus, Mary!' Jem scrambled through the radishes, but you were up on your knees before he reached you.

'I'm all right. Just help me up.' He took a hold of you under the armpits and hauled you up. 'No harm done ... oh, the seeds.' They'd spilled from the bag in a clump when you fell. Jem scooped them roughly up.

'Do you need a rest, Mair? There's Jack and Charlie's tent. Go on, I can finish this lot.'

'No, really, I'm all right,' you reassured him. 'I just tripped. There must've been something ...' and you poked the edge of the furrow with your toe, the same one that had tripped you. 'Here. What's this?'

It seemed to be a piece of iron, heavily rusted and clodded with black soil.

'Give us a look,' said Jem. He clouted it hard against the sole of his boot and most of the dirt fell away. 'It's a pot, a cooking pot! Here, Jack, what do you make of this?'

And Jem handed it to Jack, and Jack handed it to Charlie, and Charlie handed it to Mr F., who'd come over to see why you'd all stopped work. Then he showed it to Baitbanger and Dalla Kalkeith (also in their Guernsey frocks), who shook their heads. How had an iron pot come to be buried maybe eight inches underground, whence the plough had dragged it up only a week ago? Charlie was convinced that it meant the French had been here before you, while old Jemmy reckoned on it being the Spaniards. 'Could be gold underneath that rust,' he said. 'It's heavy enough.' As for Mr F., he just said, 'Buckley'll know.'

∾

Johnny Fawkner meant William Buckley (the 'Wild White Man'), who had escaped from the short-lived Sorrento convict settlement in 1803 and spent the intervening years with the Port Phillip Aborigines. Now in John Batman's employ at Bearbrass, he did indeed know the provenance of the iron pot. Having reached the south bank of the Yarra after their first night on the run, Buckley and his fellow fugitives had paused to rest and plan their next move. For the sake of speed they'd decided to lighten their loads, and an iron 'kettle' was among the items ditched in the scrub.

Fawkner secretly treasured Buckley's discarded pot. To him, it was a sign that he was irrefutably the founder of Bearbrass – that destiny had ordained it so. Here was a link between his earliest foot-fall at Port Phillip in 1803 (with his convict father at Sorrento) and his pioneering arrival at Bearbrass, thirty-two years later. He had his blacksmith clean up the pot as best he could – it was badly corroded

– then Fawkner kept it always in a private place of honour. When Eliza Fawkner found it in one of the large drawers of her husband's desk after his death in 1868, she recognised neither the pot nor its significance. She contemplated the grizzled iron relic for only a moment before consigning it to the dust cart and thence to a cesspit in the orchard.

Wild food

Before the sowing of even the radish crop that would greet Fawkner on his arrival, his forward party had lived on dried and preserved foods brought with them from Launceston, richly supplemented with fresh produce from the local native tuckshop. Fawkner had sent a pair of kangaroo dogs on the *Enterprise*, and on the day of the schooner's mooring at the Yarra falls they set after 'a fine boomer' close by the vessel on the northern river bank. The dogs pursued their startled prey through the Yarra scrub, finally driving it into the river a little upstream from where the Princes Bridge now crosses. Night was already falling, so the weary pioneers supped that night on chewy salt meat; but at noon next day they paused in their exploring and clearing and building for long enough to do justice to the boomer's haunch, roughly butchered by Jem and roasted by Mary over a tea-tree fire.

A new arrival of January 1836 remarked that 'the flesh of the kangaroo, with all the natural variety of wild fowl, was in abundant use', fresh mutton and beef still being very scarce. But the Bearbrass settlers seem not to have developed a permanent preference for marsupial flesh – after all, it was in the interests of the mutton-raising squatters that they should not. In the rivers, lagoons and swamps close to the township, the abundant fish and wildfowl were easy spoils for settlers with fishing lines, firearms, or an Aboriginal servant or two. Fawkner's journal of his early days at Bearbrass is full of references to local foodstuffs:

Novr. 17 Tuesday – I had 24 sand snipe made into Sea pie for dinner.

Wednesday 18 Novr. – Mr B. good success fishing caught plenty Bream.

Saturday 21 Novr. 1835 – Caught a Swan on the Lagoon in my land.

Sunday the 6th of December – Men out fishing and Shooting, no fish, Fowls, 2 Ducks 3 Teal 2 Widgeons 1 Pigeon and 1 Diver.

Tuesday the 22nd day of Decr. 1835 – Dined at Mr Batman's on a Roast Swan very good ... Preparing to go down to the river tomorrow to get Swans for Christmas.

The local game birds provided sport and dinner for early settlers, but seem not to have been commercially exploited to any degree. In 1841, Mrs Howe, a former Yorkshire housekeeper, now wife of a Queen Street baker, did a special line in game pies. Her 'big boy', after a morning's baking, would repair with fowling piece and gunny sack to the West Melbourne swamp. Unlucky spur-winged plover ended up in Mrs Howe's game pies which, in turn, ended up on the tables of the well-to-do, at seven shillings a pop.

Arriving at Bearbrass in March 1836, a squatter named David Fisher complained that he 'could get nothing to eat' at Fawkner's inn* and was therefore grateful for John Batman's offer of accommodation. As Batman's servants had been busy on the river that day, the family and their guest 'dined, supped, and next morning breakfasted on a schnapper fish and damper'.

The pinky-red schnapper were caught in the Yarra, as occasionally were herrings, massing below the Falls. The Batman family's partiality for schnapper proved fatal in 1845, when nine-year-old Johnny Batman drowned after slipping from the Falls' rocky ledge as he tried

---

* This in spite of the fact that, according to Garryowen, Fawkner had 'established a queer sort of table d'hôte (or, as he translated it, 'table hotty') for his guests'.

to land a big 'un. Later that same year, the *Patriot's* fishing correspondent remarked that:

> *Schnappers, weighing twenty-five pounds, are being hawked*
> *around the town at from ninepence to one shilling each. It is not*
> *considered any great feat to catch twelve dozen of herrings at*
> *the falls in the course of four hours and within like time to land*
> *from the Salt Water River, thirteen dozen of bream, weighing*
> *from one pound to one and a half pound each.*

Bream from the Salt Water (Maribyrnong) River was the first fish
Georgiana McCrae saw when she made her home in Little Lonsdale
Street West in 1841. A fisherman hawked his silvery catch through
the Bearbrass streets. A 'poor old man', John Blackmore, was 'pursu-
ing his humble vocation' as a fish-hawker in June 1844 when he was
hailed in Little Bourke Street by a Mrs Whelan, wanting a bream for
her husband's dinner. Blackmore set his basket down at her front door
and produced two fish for his consideration. 'Nay, nay, they're none
but tiddlers. It's a middlin'-sized one I'm wantin'.' Old Blackmore,
with arthritic fingers and a fisherman's patience, chose a heftier bream
from his basket and held it up by the tail for inspection. Mrs Whelan
squinted at it, flicking the hawker's wrist to make him turn the fish
around. 'How much?' she demanded. Blackmore named his price. Mrs
Whelan snorted. 'Fer a middlin' one like that?'

'Middlin'?' protested Blackmore. 'That there's a big 'un.'

'Big, you call it? *And* the eyes are cloudy. I'll give yer threepence
fer it.'

'Threepence! I wouldn't give you a tiddler for that!' retorted
Blackmore indignantly, and began packing his fish away.

' 'Ere, Peter!' called Mrs Whelan over her shoulder, and her big
builder husband appeared. 'This coster's tryin' ter diddle us.' Her shrill
tone had fetched the dog of the house to the door as well, its big black
head thrusting between her skirts and the door jamb.

'Go on, Jap,' bid its master, giving it a knee in the backside, 'clear that bloody old cove out of here.' The dog flew at Blackmore and caught him a bite above one knee and another on the wrist, before the old fellow managed to land it a blow on the head with the corner of his basket.

Peter Whelan was charged with suffering his dog to bite the fishmonger. Giving evidence in court, Blackmore claimed that two witnesses were passing in the street at the time of the attack – 'respectable gentlemen, one of whom the complainant said sells sausages'. Neither witness could be prevailed upon to give evidence (in the case of the sausage-vendor, professional rivalry was most likely to blame for his refusal, a fondness for dogs less so*), but a conviction was secured nonetheless and Whelan paid a stinging fine. He went right off fish after that.

Georgiana McCrae and her contemporaries could have found a full range of local fish at William Wormsley's Fruit and Fish Mart, down at the corner of Flinders Lane and Elizabeth Street. (Wormsley's spruiking rosella, you will recall, went missing – presumed stolen – from its perch outside the shop doorway in October 1841.) From the mid-'40s, Henry Clegg traded as a fishmonger and oysterman in Little Bourke Street – 'The house is painted green/It's easy to be seen/At the corner of Queen/And Little Bourke-street' ran his advertising jingle. Oysters were a cheap feed: at six shillings per bucketful, or about threepence a dozen, they were a favoured accompaniment to a pint of ale taken 'outdoors' from the Pastoral Hotel, on the corner opposite Clegg's.

Native plant foods seem to have been little utilised by the settlers. Most, like Fawkner, planted vegetable gardens and fruit trees as soon as they arrived. In the early years of the settlement, no one produced much in excess of their own requirements – or at least none that they were prepared to see convicts fed with. When, in 1837, some of the

---

* See 'The Canine War', Chapter 4.

convicts employed on public works were suffering from scurvy, Police Magistrate Lonsdale wrote to his Sydney superiors: 'I find it impossible to procure vegetables but I have made some of the men gather a wild plant which is a good substitute.' The only native yield of the Bearbrass soil that was popularly sought out for eating by the settlers was the mushroom. A favourite spot for mushrooming was the Russell Street hill, where, in the '40s, townsfolk could witness a hanging and scrounge a feed of mushrooms for tea, all in an afternoon.

Pot 8 Os and the great cabbage-compeller

Johnny Fawkner had at first established his garden and orchard on the town side of the river, on land claimed by John Batman and the Port Phillip Association. After a bit of a tussle Fawkner conceded, accepting £20 from the Association in compensation for his crops and fruit trees and laying out a more extensive 'farm' on the south bank, between the river and the marsh. Fawkner's crops included peas, French beans, radishes, potatoes (on at least one occasion spelt 'Pot 8 Os'!), cherries, damsons, apples, carrots, turnips, cauliflower, Savoy cabbages, curly parsley, Indian corn, pumpkins, melons, vegetable marrows, and cucumbers.

Fawkner had no garden at his house in the settlement, so he planted some 'Shalots' in the garden of his nearest neighbour, Henry Batman, the idea being that the cook could fetch them by the handful as they were needed. Even supposing the shallots survived the indiscriminate appetite of Batman's goat, it is unlikely that Fawkner enjoyed any of the harvest: by the time the crop was ready, he and Batman were on far-from-cordial terms.

At the south-west corner of Bourke and William streets in the early '40s was the substantial garden of the St James' Church clergyman, the Reverend Adam Compton Thompson – also known as 'the great cabbage-compeller'. His hobby was cabbage-growing and he devoted his garden to that vegetable alone. The first crop, in virgin soil, was a whopper, much remarked upon by the townsfolk, churchgoing and otherwise. Around mid-winter, when the crop was at its most luxuri-ant, three young gentlemen squatters in search of entertainment after closing-time wrenched the palings off a section of the cabbage garden fence. Towards dawn, Reverend Thompson was woken by the sounds of snorting and trampling. His beloved cabbages (except for three beauties bowled down the Bourke Street hill by the rowdies) had been laid to waste by the roving livestock of the town.

Benjamin Baxter, once he had given up postmastering, had the time to cultivate a fine cottage garden at the rear of his house in Flinders Street, near King Street. In February 1840, he harvested a turnip that was two feet (61 cm) in circumference. He credited his horticultural success to a combination of bullock manure (a few shovelfuls scraped from Flinders Street near the docks each day) and the yeasty slops from John Moss's brewery next door. A twenty-one inch (53 cm) long cucumber sounds fairly unremarkable to us who are accustomed to the gangly continental variety; but one such specimen created a sen-sation when exhibited at the Bearbrass market in 1842 by a gardener named Sullivan from Merri Creek. It was, marvelled the *Patriot* next day, 'raised without a particle of manure'.

Georgiana McCrae mixed in the same elevated circles as the bom-bastic Major G.F.B. St John. He appears to have taken a shine to her and, there being no Interflora outlet at Bearbrass, he expressed his admiration in vegetables. Georgiana wrote of one occasion, not long after her arrival in 1841, when:

> *I perceived Major St John riding across the flat towards 'Argyle Cottage' with what, at first sight, appeared to be a large green parrot held hawkwise on his wrist. On his arrival at the gate, the major flourished a fine full-grown Cos lettuce in his hand, exclaiming: 'One of the first of the kind raised in Port Phillip!'*

Bearing in mind Police Magistrate St John's alleged weakness for bribes of the comestible kind, one wonders which exonerated miscreant deserves credit as the district's cos lettuce pioneer.

It is plain to see why the Major would have welcomed offerings of fresh produce: in 1841, prices at the market were astronomical and the hoary vegetables brought over from Van Diemen's Land were not a patch on those grown locally. Potatoes at that time were sixpence and more a pound (roughly 500 g) and a very small cabbage cost almost a shilling. One begins to understand why the Reverend Thompson chose the hobby he did.

The market at which these over-priced vegetables were for sale was situated at the rear of the Customs House. Market Street, which forms the block's eastern boundary, was not allowed for in the original street plan, but was added once the market site was fixed upon. (Running from Collins to Flinders Street, midway between William and Queen streets, Market Street is the one irregularity in the town grid.) The market square was not put to its proper use until 1841, when post-and-chain fences were erected, enclosing the market and dividing it into sections. The first trading day was 15 December that year.

The appeal of an open-air market palled as the winter months approached, so rows of fairly ramshackle timber stalls were erected on the market square. By the late '40s, they were reduced to 'miserable hovels – calculated to throw a gloom over the choicest fruit and vegetables which could be produced'. They were replaced in 1849 by a brick market house – eight stalls in two rows facing one another and connected by a covered arcade. This was now called the Western Market, to distinguish it from another market at the town's eastern end. In 1841, a hay and corn market had been established in Flinders Street, on the present site of St Paul's Cathedral. This market moved to the eastern end of Bourke Street in 1847 and its wares diversified to include fruit and vegetables and other goods. The eastern end of town was still relatively out-of-the-way, and the Eastern Market was not an immediate success: in June 1848 'seldom a stray visitor' was to be seen there. Gradually, though, it gained ground on the Western Market, taking over the latter's custom altogether when it was gutted by fire in 1851, just as the gold rushes promised to make its stallholders richer than ordinarily overpriced vegetables ever could.*

Early on at Bearbrass, vegetable theft was commonplace. Thomas Halfpenny and William Harrison stole onions from the garden of publican George Smith in December 1836 and were fined £1 each, plus three shillings – the value of the onions. Bunja Logan and Jin Jin, who torched the lock-up in 1838, had been incarcerated there for stealing potatoes from a settler's garden. Convicts Robert Horne and Thomas Pittman were likewise charged with lifting potatoes from John Batman's garden in 1837; the meal cost them fifty lashes each. The stolen spuds were cooked for them and shared by John Cox, baker to the Bearbrass convicts and himself a convict. For him, the meal's bitter after-taste ran to twenty-five lashes.

By the mid-'40s, the township's vegetables were principally supplied by market gardeners out Brighton way and were brought to market by dray, via St Kilda Road and Balbirnie's wooden bridge. Johnny Fawkner by now held extensive acreage at Pascoe Vale (or Pascoeville), north of Melbourne, including a vast orchard. In 1846, he advertised the following apple tree varieties for sale: Nonpariel, Golden Knob, Loans Permain, Norfolk Beaufin, Kentish Broading, Beauty of Kent, Ribatone Pippin, Newton Pippin, Cockle Pippin, and Wellington Pippin. Apples, figs, and grapes were grown on land off Little Collins Street, at the rear of what is now the Block, in the late '40s. So fine was the quality of this fruit that John Carson, an early president of the Royal Horticultural Society (formed by Johnny

---

* The histories of these two markets, long and colourful though they are, fall outside my Bearbrass brief. But briefly … The Eastern Market burned down in 1855, but was rebuilt and, though largely eclipsed by the Queen Victoria Market after 1880, continued to trade until its demolition for the Southern Cross Hotel in 1960. The Western Market was rebuilt in 1856, but never regained its early prominence. In 1934 it was converted to a carpark and in 1960 it too was demolished.

Fawkner in 1848), took samples with him to England for examination by members of the Society's parent body in London.

A land of chops and steaks

Fourteen-year-old Thomas Browne arrived with his family from Sydney in 1840. Writing forty years later as Rolf Boldrewood, Browne recollected how Bearbrass had seemed like 'a land of chops and steaks' after Sydney, where a long drought had made meat a scarcity.

From the very first, Bearbrass settlers brought with them livestock to make food of. On her pioneering voyage, the *Enterprise* carried a crate of poultry and a sow with a litter, and within two months there were mobs of sheep and pigs, goats and milch cows aplenty grazing at the skirt of Batman's Hill. Until the town was laid out, John Batman's sheep run encompassed much of the western end of the settlement, and livestock being fattened for the table crowded onto town allotments (with increasingly squalid consequences) throughout the '40s.

Soon after his arrival, Lonsdale outlawed unlicensed slaughtering within the township proper. A killing-ground was established on swampy ground at the Yarra's edge, west of Batman's Hill, from whence the river's tidal flow carried the bulk of the slaughteryard filth out into the bay and beyond the townsfolk's care. John McNall (formerly a lawyer's clerk) arrived early and was the settlement's first butcher. In 1838 he set up permanent premises in Collins Street, just west of Swanston, at the rear of which he was licensed to carry out his slaughtering and butchering. Flocks awaited the cleaver on the ground adjoining, crowding for shade and shelter under a lone eucalypt and prevented by a post-and-rail fence from wandering onto the town's Regent Street or eating the neighbours' caulies. The vicinity of McNall's butchery was a favourite mustering place for the Aborigines. Just before nightfall, the butcher would clear out his shambles, tossing the unwanted sheep heads, chitterlings and numbles to the waiting figures and their dogs.

In competition with McNall from 1838 was the butchering

partnership of John Tancred and Patrick Smith. Tancred was in strife early on for slaughtering two bullocks (tough old meat, that) on land in Flinders Street, at the back of Carr's public house, that not being his licensed killing-place. In December 1838, Tancred claimed that wethers from his flock had been stolen by McNall and his servants. In court, Tancred enumerated other occasions when the rival butchers had disputed the ownership of sheep. In one instance, McNall had insisted that an animal of his had been slaughtered by Tancred, and attempted to enter Tancred's shambles to examine the fleece for its brand. According to Tancred's own testimony, 'I cautioned him not to interfere with the head or skins or any part of the *former sheep*.'

In the times of Bearbrass, 'former sheep' were more commonly mutton than lamb. Boiled mutton was the usual purpose to which a wether's haunch was put, and is what a Mr Webb would have had in mind when he advertised in 1839 for 'A Female Servant that can cook a plain joint'. Georgiana McCrae's household did business with a butcher named Henry Mortimer, whose cart called twice weekly with a side of mutton and a shin of beef for soup. Beef and mutton cost threepence ha'penny a pound, veal and pork fourpence. The driver of the butcher's cart would throw in, at no cost, a sheep's head and pluck – 'for the dogs' – and the McCraes' thrifty Scotch cook, Ellen, would prepare them 'Scots fashion' for her master. (A lodging-house keeper who prided herself on being a 'good-managing lady' reputedly victualled a houseful of lodgers for three days on a single bullock's head.) The threepence-ha'penny mutton carried so much fat that Ellen was able to string out the household budget still further by making candles for her own use and for the nursery. When Cassimere Frezygiviski, a ticket-of-leave man, had the same idea he was charged with theft for 'purloining' fat and dripping from the kitchen of the Melbourne Club where he worked as a cook.

A saucepan full of boiled mutton looked like being the means of nailing a bad 'un named John Gunn in January 1837. A neighbour of John McNall's in Collins Street, Gunn was charged with stealing a sheep from a flock in the Flinders Lane yard of Dr David Thompson, immediately behind Gunn's property. When Henry Batman (then District Constable) arrived to search Gunn's hut next day, he found Gunn and his de facto wife, Mary Dobson,* about to tuck into a hearty dinner. Batman tendered to the court as evidence three pounds of boiled mutton and some 'boiled flour' (probably dumplings) which had been cooked along with it, all still in the saucepan. Fawkner's servant, Mary Gilbert, appeared as a witness for the prosecution. She had been visiting Gunn's hut on the morning after the sheep's disappearance, she told the court, when her little son Johnny, still crawling, had pulled a cloth off a washing tub under the table. In replacing the cloth, she glanced into the tub and saw the mutton inside. Gunn was committed to stand trial in Sydney, but was granted bail after Police Magistrate Lonsdale expressed doubts about some of the evidence against the accused. (While Lonsdale condemned Gunn as 'a man of bad character', he had to concede that, 'Some of the witnesses are also bad characters ...') The sheep-stealing charge was later dropped, but after a string of minor convictions Gunn was charged two years later with involvement in a major theft and sent to Sydney for trial.

Shepherds were often accused of killing their masters' sheep for food. One such, David Cleary, a convict servant of squatter William Bowman, was charged with 'killing a lamb and boiling it in a pot' in September 1838. Cleary's claim that the lamb had been killed by native dogs won no favour with the magistrate, who committed him for trial in the Supreme Court. Sheep-stealing, it can be seen, was no trifling misdemeanour, no victimless crime: sheep were property, and property was All.

William Morris was a shepherds' cook with no culinary panache and a very short fuse. In February 1839, he served up a breakfast of

---

* Mary Dobson emerges as what used to be called a 'fallen woman'. 'I was brought up in the family of Mr Nidye in Van Diemen's Land,' she told the court, 'where I learnt to read, I was christened and I used to go to church.' With bowed head, she added, 'I have lately resided with John Gunn at Port Phillip.'

cold chops – well past their use-by date – to the two shepherds whose hut he shared. One of them, Tom Renton (alias Weugh), when he clapped eyes on the superannuated chops, declared them 'not fit for a dog to eat'. With a cry of, 'You buggers, I'll have you all! Morris seized a pistol and shot Renton dead on the spot. The other shepherd, John Summer, seemed unsurprised by Morris's actions, telling police, 'I have known Morris about 19 years. He never had a good character.'

With the depression of the early '40s came the establishment of boiling-down works on the Yarra and Maribyrnong rivers. Squatters unable to find a market for their wool turned to the business of exporting tallow, produced by 'boiling down' sheep to extract their fat. From just fifty tons in 1843, tallow exports increased to 430 tons the next year and to 4,500 tons (worth more than £130,000) by 1850. Until 1848 (when they were ordered downstream, past the Maribyrnong River mouth), boiling-down works – complete with their putrid stenches and unspeakable by-products – clustered on both sides of the Yarra below the Falls. Because the tallow industry was vital to the district's economy, and as the river above the Falls remained relatively unpolluted, the townsfolk were for a long time prepared to tolerate the execrable goings-on at their town's western periphery. Imagine though, the welcoming impression given visitors and new arrivals, whose vessels' approach to the town would have been through a river scummed with stinking greyish grease and sheep organs.

The townsfolk tolerated the boiling-down works for another reason. Only the fat was wanted by the tallow trade, and the unwanted meat could be bought very cheaply. Georgiana McCrae wrote that in 1843 'legs of mutton, denuded of fat, were to be had at the boiling-down works for 5s. the dozen'. Ship captains stocked up on the bargain-priced mutton, which was preserved by salting for long sea voyages. Mr McLure, tutor to the McCrae boys, had mixed feelings about the tasty soups that Ellen produced using mutton from the tallow works. Returning from a summer evening stroll amongst the sheoaks of Batman's Hill, he composed a poem on the Melbourne

Melting Establishment, whose works gurgled away at the foot of that eminence. It began: 'And now, on Yarra Banks, are seen/Deeds bloodier than e'er had been/At Linden, Prague, or Waterloo ...'

Occupying a marginally less gruesome branch of the dead animal trade was Adam Murray, a sausage vendor in Little Collins Street ('two doors from Elizabeth-street'). Armed with a machine guaranteed to fill sausages at the rate of 100 lbs (about 45 kg) an hour, Murray commenced business in December 1841. His sausages cost a shilling a pound for pork and eightpence for beef: three times more than butcher's cuts. But wait – these were no common barbecue spitfires, but Continental delicacies of regal origin. According to Murray's advertisements, they were 'prepared after directions given him at Berlin, by CONRAD AMMERSCHUBER, principal cook to the beloved King of Prussia'.* Was Murray the unnamed sausage-vending dog tail slasher who featured in Chapter 4? Probably not, since the dog lost its tail in 1848 and, with prices like his and a depression just around the corner, Murray's sausage-making days were almost certainly numbered.

No pudding after dinner

Meat featured prominently in the rations of servants and convicts. On 7 November 1835, Johnny Fawkner recorded in his journal: 'Gave Jas & Mary their first ration 17lbs Beef 17lbs Flour 5 Ounces Tea & 3½lbs of Sugar. Quart of Milk daily.'† The beef and flour would have been one week's ration; the tea and sugar probably had to last longer than that. Presumably the Gilberts' ration was supplemented with vegetables from Fawkner's garden and they could manage without salt because the beef, at this early stage of settlement, was the long-life,

---

*   Adam Murray either had some pretty impressive connections or was a master
      of self-promotion. When in the business of supplying shell lime to the building
      trade in 1840, he had claimed that his lime was manufactured 'after the directions
      of Signor Ancello Cornaro, modeller and plasterer to the King of Naples'.

†   Metric equivalents are: 7 kg each of beef and flour, 140 g of tea, 1.5 kg of sugar,
      and a little over a litre of milk.

salted stuff. Mary and Jem Gilbert's ration was roughly the same as that of convicts in the mid-1830s.

Tales abound of servants who were dissatisfied with the rations their masters gave them (or failed to give them); those who acted on their dissatisfaction were liable to be hammered by the Masters and Servants Act. John Donovan, a shepherd of Arundel Wrighte's in 1837, used 'some very gross expressions' to complain about his rations, then 'called his dog and went away'. He was gaoled for a month and may well have found the meals, if not the surroundings, a change for the better. Another shepherd, John McDonald, persistently neglected his flock for the sake of a hot meal. His employer, Charles Driver, told the Police Magistrate, 'he persists in coming home to his breakfast and dinner, leaving his flock alone … I have found him at least half a dozen times in his hut at dinner after I gave him directions not to do so.' After a month of confined dining at the Bearbrass lock-up, McDonald would have been glad to get back to a pocketful of cold chops and a half-loaf on the run.

Squatter Henry Meyrick complained in 1845 that, 'This Wiltshire scoundrel' (a servant of his) 'had precisely the same food as I eat myself,' and *still* wasn't satisfied. The 'scoundrel' condemned the bread as poor, the lamb as tough, the raisins weren't the seedless sort, and – most insufferable of all – 'there ain't no pudding after dinner'. Another squatter with property near Bearbrass told the *Patriot* in 1847 that, although amply supplied with milk, 'one of his men grumbled seriously at the hardship of having to drink his coffee *minus cream*'.

The Bearbrass bread jinx

Bearbrass bread was something of a tricksy commodity. In the case of Edward Davis, a convict servant of Charles Ebden's, getting the loaves home was the problem. In December 1838, he was sent from his master's residence in Collins Street West to buy bread from Overton's bakery in Collins Street East, and was next day found floating face-down in the Yarra, the four loaves gone as schnapper bait. An inquest heard that Davis was 'sober and not in the habit of drinking at any time'.

The same could not be said of Tim Hurley, a baker in John Batman's employ. Unlike Davis, Hurley started off with the loaves but failed to make it home with the money he was paid for them. One morning in November 1838, he set off from Batman's Hill with bread he had baked before dawn. Having delivered the lot and received payment, on Batman's behalf, of twenty shillings, 'I got drunk and spent some and believe I lost the remainder.' Batman's overseer found him insensible in Flinders Lane, a short distance from Carr's public house.

Mother Nature, rather than human nature, was to blame for yet another failed bread delivery in December 1841. On a delivery run for baker Fred Cox, a box-cart collided with a stump in Russell Street and overturned, trapping the driver and his load inside. When eventually the cart was righted, the squashed* and dusty loaves (it was December, thank goodness, and the roadway was largely free of mud) were sold on the spot at greatly reduced prices.

Cakes, comfits and coffee

William Overton – four of whose best wheaten loaves poor Edward Davis carried with him to the 'great divide' – advertised himself as a 'baker, confectioner, rusk and fancy biscuit maker'. He pioneered the confectionery trade in the town, commencing business in Collins Street, to the east of Elizabeth, in 1838. Before Overton 'titillated the palates of the fanciers of sweetmeats', they had had to make do with the stale, broken biscuits and rock-hard toffees on offer at the merchants' stores. After their father's death in 1839, John Batman's children (seven daughters and a son) consoled themselves with sugar buns and lollies from Overton's. In three months, they ran up a bill

---

* This accident (which, uncannily, occurred within a rasped cooee of today's Greek quarter) resulted in the appearance of the township's first flatbread. Unfortunately, it pre-dated the town's first souvlaki bar by about one hundred and twenty years.

of £144, to achieve which each Batman child must have consumed the equivalent of a box of Black Magic and a hummock of profiteroles every day.

By late 1840, Overton had competition. The *Patriot* rejoiced:

> *A few months since, confectioner's shops were 'like angel's visits, few and far between' … [but] week after week some new competitor for the patronage of the public started into the field, until at every corner cakes and comfits gladdened our eye.*

The advertised stock of Mrs Carroll, 'Melbourne Restaurant & Confectioner' – Indian preserves, orange chips, candied lemon, crystallised bananas, motto kisses, bon bons with conundrums, refined licorice, Italian licorice – gives an idea of what Bearbrass folk liked to suck on.

Mrs Carroll's store (which appears, despite its name, not to have been a restaurant in the modern sense) also specialised in imported savoury delicacies such as pickled mushrooms, Durham mustard, Labrador salmon, dried sprats, Lochfine salted herrings, best Indian curry powder, cayenne pepper, potted bloaters, 'sardeens', shred and pipe vermicelli, 'maccaroni', blanc mange, bottled fruits, jams, marmalades, preserved meats, Chili vinegar, raspberry vinegar, chutney, tomato sauce, preserved ginger, olives, capers, sauces, and pickles. A pickle drought in 1838 was broken when three cases of them arrived in a merchant's consignment from Launceston. Within three hours the lot were sold, at the gourmet price of seven shillings and sixpence for a small bottle.

Bearbrass tea-drinkers could choose from varieties including hyson skin, twankay, pouchong, souchong, gunpowder, orange pekoe, congen, and black leaf pekoe, all available by the ounce from the larger grocers. Coffee-drinkers, as yet ignorant of the cappuccino precinct in their midst, also had their cravings ably met by the town's grocers, who imported coffee beans raw and roasted them fresh daily.

William Nicholson had a store at the north-west corner of Collins and Swanston streets in the mid-'40s and did a big line in coffee. He roasted the beans early every morning, then left it to his shop-boy to grind them by hand as they were required. In mid-1845 Nicholson installed an elaborate device, powered by a one-horsepower steam engine, which both roasted and ground the beans. Here was novelty indeed for Bearbrass shoppers. Crowds gathered at the store's Swanston Street window to see 'the berry, the produce of Mocha and Java' reduced to ambrosial grit. The shop-boy rejoiced only briefly at his release from grinding duties: his principal employment now involved chopping wood and stoking the steam engine's boiler. But Nicholson's coffee sales soared – at least until the summer, when the steam engine heated the shop to over 45°C, spoiling stock and driving customers away. The hand-grinder was reinstated and the shop-boy – hair singed, apronfront perforated by flying sparks, and missing the tops of two fingers – was delighted.

Soup always ready

Not far from the coffee-coloured river itself, early risers in 1847 could find 'Comfort in the Morning' at John Holley's Flinders Lane eating house, where hot coffee was served from four to eight a.m. At Stoneham's Temperance Coffee House in Queen Street, a cup of coffee could be had 'at any hour', with breakfast, dinner, tea, or supper available 'at a minute's notice'. For those who liked to wash a meal down with something stronger than coffee, Henry Baker's Imperial Inn in Collins Street offered shilling meals: 'A hearty Breakfast at nine o'clock – 1/-; a substantial Dinner at two o'clock – 1/-; a comfortable Tea or supper at seven o'clock – 1/-.' But Baker appended a proviso: 'NB – 50% increase on the above charges to those individuals who practise teetotalism.'

Garryowen reckoned that the town's first public eating house independent of a hotel was opened by Richard Graham in Elizabeth Street in 1840, while his contemporary, Thomas Strode, identified the first 'dining rooms' as those of Stephen Toogood, 'in a brick house situated on the west side of Queen-street, between Bourke and Little Bourke Streets'. These establishments, like most that followed, offered accommodation as well as meals. This might sound innocuous enough, but sleeping apartments attached to eating houses were popularly perceived as little better than opium dens. Escaped convicts and runaway seamen would lie low there, having meals sent up until the heat was off or they could clear out to the bush, and the clattering cutlery of diners often masked the squeak of bedsprings as prostitutes turned tricks overhead. But the chief blemish on the good reputation of Bearbrass eating houses was the fact that many operated as sly grog shops, selling liquor (usually cheap and tainted stuff) without a licence. In August 1841, the town's new Chief Constable, Frederick Falkiner, was a wake-up to the vice behind the viands. He was, said the *Patriot*, 'indefatigable in his exertions to suppress the crying evil', springing raids on eating houses, willy-nilly. In one day, William Wood and Edward Griffiths, both proprietors of eateries in Little Bourke Street, and John Dykes of Collins Street were all charged and fined as sly-groggers. In 1845, pioneer victualler Stephen Toogood was likewise charged.

Despite the distractions offered by some eating houses, there were patrons who were simply after a good feed. It was to these discerning diners that Mr Powell Courtier directed advertisements for his London Eating and Boarding Establishment, at the corner of Swanston and Little Bourke streets, in 1848. Courtier trumpeted not just the nature and quality of his offerings, but also the unique manner in which they were prepared:

> *Fitted up with* STEAM APPARATUS, *on an Entirely New* SCIENTIFIC
> PRINCIPLE. *Whereby the Various Viands are prepared in a manner
> now adopted in the first-rate Hotels and Clubs in London.*
>
> *Hams, Fowls, Joints, &c., &c., for a Cold Collation, always
> ready. Hot Joints, Fowls and Fish, with every requisite for a*

plain dinner, or luxuries fit for the 'Gourmand', from 12 to 4 p.m., and suppers on the same scale from 6 to 12 a.m., daily. SOUPS ALWAYS READY. Oxtail, Mock Turtle, and Pea Soups, with Mutton, and other Pies, always Hot, and fit for immediate use.

Soup, then as now (unless it be truffle), made for a cheap, warming meal. The Royal Hotel in Collins Street matched Powell Courtier's mock turtle soup with 'a constant supply' of what its advertisements claimed was the real thing. In 1850, an advertisement for John Yewers' eating house, opposite the post office in Elizabeth Street, gave the impression that a bowl of soup was on a par with gold discovery as a cause for excitement. 'SOUP! SOUP! SOUP!!!' it bawled from the front page of the *Patriot*. Admittedly, soup *was* the highlight of Yewers' advertised fare, the rest amounting to mixed grills and meat pies.

Public house patrons, as the next chapter will show, needed little inducement to imbibe. But to maximise thirsts and bar takings, publicans would sometimes lay on complimentary snacks of the highly salted kind, a practice that continues to this day. In those far-off days before the advent of Burger Rings and nachos, drinkers were invited to dip into a cask of preserved herrings, glistening with oil and caked with salt. Delicious they were, and *so* moreish. One publican estimated that, in an evening, a cask of herrings costing fifteen shillings made him an extra £5 in ale sold. *And* his patrons thanked him for the free feed.

CHAPTER 7

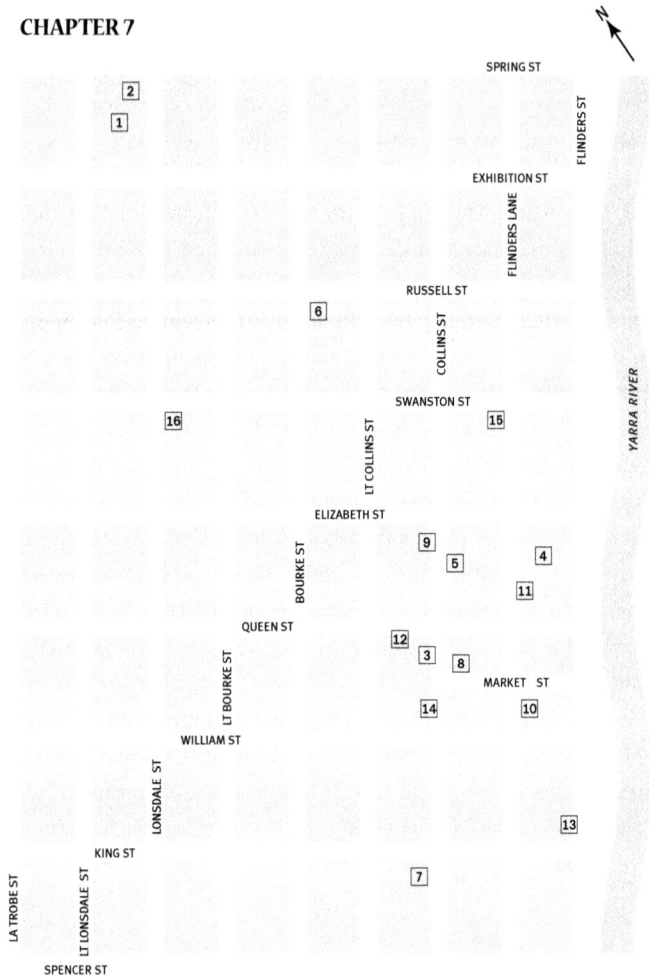

1. Leichardt Street

2. Mary Gilbert's bottle tree, the stump of which was finally grubbed out in 1988 to make way for the Casselden Place government offices

3. The drapery business of A.H. Hart, a 'dacent man' with a tough policy on shoplifters

4. John Mills's brewery, turning Yarra water into ale

5. The Imperial Inn's Henry Baker reckoned his ale as good as 'Liquid Food'

6. The store of merchant James Graham, scourge of the monkey-suckers

7. Lizzie Nash's sly grog shanty, 1838

8. Originally Fawkner's second hotel; from 1839, the unlicensed premises of the Melbourne Club, reputed in 1841 as little better than a gin shanty

9. The Edinburgh Castle Hotel served hearty mixed grills for breakfast

10. Fawkner's first hotel, 1835–7

11. Michael and Kitty Carr's Governor Bourke Hotel

12. Jemmy Connell's Highlandman Hotel

13. The Royal Highlander Hotel

14. The notorious Lamb Inn

15. Monahan's Queen's Arms Hotel, originally a Wesleyan chapel

16. The Caledonian Hotel, former palatial home of a Presbyterian minister

CHAPTER 7

The Colonial Vice

Bottle

There existed until recently, at the north-eastern corner of the town, an unsignposted lane called Leichardt Street.* Practically the entire cohort of alleyways bisecting the easternmost block between Lonsdale and Little Lonsdale streets has, in the past fifteen years, been stomped on and obliterated by office towers. Leichardt Street was one of the latest to go. Formerly one of the city's more unexploited and characterful quarters, this fag-end of Little Lonsdale Street has nothing much left to show of its old self. Wander there if you like; but you won't want to linger. The wind-tunnel that surges through this section of Little Lonsdale is strong enough to wrench a mod from a moped. There's hospitality to be found in the neighbourhood, though. For those seeking a taste of the erstwhile, racy 'Little Lon', the pub on the Spring Street corner still offers a traditional local

---

*   Named (though misspelt) for the explorer, Friedrich Leichhardt, who disappeared
      while attempting an east-west crossing of the continent in 1848, the year after
      this part of Bearbrass was subdivided and auctioned.

delicacy: steamed dim sims swimming in a saucer of port. Otherwise, there are imported ales to be had at the Exhibition Street corner, or coffee and cake in a food hall muralled with cavorting wenches.

In 1988, and again in 2002, Leichardt Street was the focus of major urban archaeological excavations, farewell gestures as the neighbourhood was progressively torn up. In amongst the brick foundations of the workers' cottages that had once lined the narrow lane were found clay pipes, fragments of dinnerware, broken glass by the bucketload, buttons, coins, needles and pins, spoons, boots, dolls' limbs, and chop bones. The cesspits that had once served as toilets and garbage bins yielded up the greatest wealth of artefacts, all caked in a clayey, smelly sludge. But one pit excavated towards the southern end of Leichardt Street in 1988 contained not the usual haphazard miscellany; it was neatly stacked from brim to bottom with intact champagne bottles. Nothing else – except for one strange item. On the clay floor of the pit, when the last of the hundreds of bottles had been removed, lay a crumpled wad of cloth. It was a shirt – largely decayed, but its sleeve cuffs and buttons could be made out – and it appeared to be wrapped around something. Gently the muddy cloth was peeled back to reveal a tight clump of bones and animal hair. A cat, said the bone expert. A tabby.

❧

This autumn of 1843 you've had reason to give thanks, at last, for the years you carted Phillip around on your back.

He was born with streaming dark hair like yours and a twisted foot all his own. The name that you and Jem had settled on for him was lost when old Johnny bought himself a namesake, promising a town allotment that never materialised and plenty of brandy that did. To you, though, your boy will always be plain Phillip. You carried him slung in a shawl on your back until he was nearly four, when (as a favour to Fawkner) a bootmaker fitted him with a brace and he found his feet at last.

Jem took off four years ago. Last you heard, he was in Yass – working, but drinking the lot, if you know anything. None of his wages have come your way, anyhow. After he left, you kept taking in washing and weaving rag mats, but, for a year or so now, there hasn't been much call for either. People have been managing their own washing and keeping their rags for wearing. Then two months ago your neighbour, Christo, won a contract from the council to clear the broken bottles off the streets. Everywhere, they were. Phillip cut his good foot real bad once, on a bottle neck sticking out of the Collins Street roadway. Anyhow, you convinced Christo to use you as labour: you and Phillip both, for two-thirds of a man's wage. Christo hummed and hawed, but he knew he was getting a good deal. Phillip's seven now and no burden anymore. And Christo knows you're well up to the work: many's the time he's seen you carry four copper-loads of wet washing across the street with Phillip wriggling on your back.

Now, struggling over the Eastern Hill, you curse Christo's stinginess. He got these thin sacks cheap, and all it takes is one jagged bottle neck to start a tear that cuts clean across the sack in no time. Phillip follows in your tracks with a small barrow, retrieving any bottles that escape. He lags well behind, but it's not his limp that's the problem; pushing a wooden-wheeled barrow uphill through thick scrubby bush would be bloody hard work even if he had two good feet. But he keeps his eye on your tracks and knows that he'll make up distance when you stop to rest or to add another marine to the load.

You're heading downhill now, down towards where the gaol's being built at the north end of town. But you stop a good way short of the building works. You swing your two sacks down at the foot of a massive white gum, these two making it nine for the day. The other seven sackloads are already leaning or fallen there. That'll do for today; it must be near five o'clock. Shaking the cramp from your wrists and forearms, you look down across the town, through smoke haze already thickening over the township, muffling it against the crisp, white-blue sky. Phillip and his barrow squeak gratefully downhill

towards you and empty their load with a noisy flourish against the
bottle tree. Your boy trudges wearily, stiff-armed, over to you and
leans his head into your armpit. You knead the back of his head with
your dirt-crusted fingers. 'Come on,' you say, and the pair of you start
downhill towards home. You're only too glad to keep pace with him
for a change.

Your cat Bottle (Johnny Fawkner named her, too) is getting old,
but she still engages in almost nightly battle with the possums down
near the river. Three nights ago she came home with her belly torn
open and a nasty bite under one ear. You tried to keep her inside
the hut, but she *would* drag herself around the yard, growling at the
hens. Now you find her dead beside Jem's old forge. You get Phillip
(nearly dead on his feet, poor love) to fetch an old frock of his
father's, then he leaves you crouching there under the skillion, strok-
ing Bottle's motley old coat and thinking on how the two of you came
to be here.

At six next morning, you hump the nine sacks from the big gum
downhill a little way to the pit Christo had dug the day before. It's
above six foot deep and four wide by six long (Christo used to be
a grave-digger). Usually you just up-end each sack and shake their
contents into the pit – you like the noise of breaking glass. But today
you lower yourself into the pit and have Phillip pass Bottle down
to you. You place the duck-cotton parcel on the floor of the pit and
call up to Phillip to start handing down the bottles, unbroken ones
first. Reaching and bending, you surround Bottle with bottles, laying
them neatly side by side and end to end. When the floor of the hole
is covered, except for the space at one side where you're standing,
you begin the next layer, this time placing bottles gently over Bottle
as well. This goes on, layer upon layer, until the pit is nearly full.
Then you haul yourself out and drop broken bottles into the space
where you've been standing. When you finish, it must be close to
seven o'clock and the top layer of bottles shimmers like tar where the
rising sun catches its surface.

'Fetch the shovel, love, and we'll cover her in before Christo arrives.'

I lent the Captn 4 Bottles of Gin

'Mr Escourt very typsy, Captn Coltish a little, Dr Cottar, the 2 Fergusons, Mr B and C all Elevated. This setting an example where no spirits are allowed.' When Johnny Fawkner made this entry in his journal in November 1835, he referred to an undertaking by members of the Port Phillip Association that during the first year 'no liquour [sic] of any description shall be landed on the Settlement for sale or distribution among the servants, excepting only wine for family use or medicinal purposes'. Fawkner himself was a teetotaller of a rabid stamp (although as a concession to courtesy he would sometimes allow himself a glass of 'small' or 'sifting' beer) and in a document grandly entitled 'Constitution & Form of Government' he set out hypothetical laws for the outlawing of drunkenness at Port Phillip:

> ... if any man or woman persist in this vice they shall, after properly warned, be expelled to one of the drunken towns of Sydney, Hobart or Launceston ... at their own expense.

Fawkner, you may recall, had formerly been a publican – and still owned a hotel – in the 'drunken town' of Launceston. Prominent among the stores he brought with him to Bearbrass were supplies of beer, wine, and spirits, and no sooner was his raggedy house erected than he styled it 'Fawkner's Hotel' and commenced trading. Flouting the Port Phillip Association's supposed ban on distribution of liquor to servants, Fawkner 'Gave Chas and Scott Bottle of Wine, Jas, Glass Gin' after a hard day's furrowing for potatoes in mid-November 1835. Three days later, he gave Michael Carr (himself soon to be a publican) a bottle of wine as payment for mending a cart. But it wasn't until Christmas-time that Fawkner's hypocrisy fully revealed itself.

On Christmas Day, Fawkner sold to his still-amiable neighbour,

Henry Batman, '2 Bottles Gin for Self – and 4 for Men', as well as a dozen bottles of porter and six bottles of wine – on top of which, he *gave* Batman's servants another two quarts of gin. The next day, Batman was back for two more bottles of gin and another six of porter, and in preparation for New Year's festivities he bought three gallons of brandy from Fawkner's stores. The consumption of these quantities of liquor by his neighbour was viewed with tolerance by Fawkner, provoking only a couple of mild, indulgent rebukes in his journal. Presumably for the sake of discretion, he rendered these remarks in his imperfect French: 'Mr B. & Dr Cottar buv'y une Demi bouteille de G. Chez moi, et apres la, il a quarrellee' (which I take to mean that Henry Batman and Barry Cotter bought a half-bottle of gin from him, after drinking which they fought) or 'Mr Hy B. Ivrie' (that is, drunk). It transpired though that Fawkner's tolerance was directly indexed to his cash box: he lost the custom of Henry Batman and his cohort after regular supply vessels began to provide an alternative source of liquor early in the New Year of 1836 and the deterioration of the neighbours' relationship was immediate. Batman openly scorned his former supplier and Fawkner condemned Batman's drunkenness, now that he no longer had a financial stake in it. Fawkner, through his journal, kept up a running commentary of Batman's sprees and misdemeanours:

Sunday the 21 of Febry *I think Batman was drunk ... he appeared half mad, I think with Rum. After this although on Sunday he gave a Bucket of Beer to the men and set them singing songs.*
Wednesday March 2nd 1836 *Batman & wife both drunk this Day.*
Thursday the 3rd of March 1836 *Batman & Wife not quite so drunk today. I think their grog was short.*
Friday the 4 of March *Found that Batmans grog is done although on this day fortnight he had 10 or 12 Galls.*
Saturday the 12 of March *Batman very quiet for want of grog,*

looking out for Caledonia [a supply vessel]
Saturday the 19th March 1836 Batman is utterly unfit to hold
office here, for he is devoid of Intelligence a mere bore who goes
about with a short pipe in his mouth and always drunk when
he can get the liquor and is very brutish in his address at those
times – when sober he is a Specious Hypocrite.

That last comment is rich, coming from Fawkner.

The extent to which Fawkner's temperance principles were ruled by his purse can be seen in a journal entry relating the arrival of the vessel *Adelaide* (or 'Aid Delayed', as Fawkner sometimes wrote it) in March 1836. Usually the arrival of supply ships was accompanied by riotous drinking, with Batman and others rowing out to greet the source of their next tipple and toasting the voyage, the King, and the cargo with captain and crew. On this occasion, Fawkner remarked on Batman's unusually sedate return from the *Adelaide*:

Capt. McClelland came up when Batman came – no riot no
noise all sober. Why, do you ask Why! the reason is plain there is
not any spirits on board the Adelaide.

Was Fawkner pleased? He was indeed: he knew a commercial opportunity when he saw one. 'I lent the Captn 4 Bottles of Gin,' he wrote – and, in Fawkner's language, 'lent' invariably meant 'sold'.

With his own servants also, Fawkner refused to see the connection between the liquor he issued them (as an advance against wages) and their resultant drunkenness and disinclination to work:

Friday the 1st Day of January 1836 Scott 2 Bottles Wine 1
Brandy, Charles 1 B Wine, James Gilbert 2 Bottles Wine.
Saturday the 2nd of Jany 1836 Scott neglected his work all day,
half drunk, forfeits 5/ Jem very lazy to day.

So John Scott's New Year's Day spree would have cost him eleven shillings – six for the wine and five for the next day's lost wages. During the last two weeks of January, Fawkner advanced to his blacksmith, Jem Gilbert, four bottles of brandy, one of gin, three of porter, and four of ale. Soon after, Fawkner ceased to record the issuing of liquor and rations in his journal, but by May he was noting that 'Jem did very little work yesterday but got drunk & less today', 'Jem the Blacksmith gets very lazy', and 'Jem Idling the time away'. Two years later, Jem was fined for public drunkenness.

Interestingly, the trigger to Jem Gilbert's drinking – or to Fawkner's supplying him – seems to have been the birth of his and Mary's son, four days after Christmas 1835. Fawkner – himself childless – apparently considered liquor a necessary solace to first-time fathers.* Shortly before Mary Gilbert's confinement, Fawkner recorded a more melancholy delivery: 'Mrs Ferguson miscarried, lent Ferguson 2 B of Port'. It is to be hoped that a glass or two of that reached the lips of Ferguson's poor bereaved wife.

Worshipping the false God Bacchus

SOMETHING REMARKABLE – *There was not a single charge of drunkenness at the police office yesterday. Such a fact is worthy of record for its singularity.*

~ PORT PHILLIP PATRIOT, 30 DECEMBER 1841

Once Police Magistrate Lonsdale arrived with a handful of constables in September 1836, the New South Wales Police Act was actively enforced. Section 6 of the Act read:

---

* It would probably be a mistake to imagine that Jem guzzled all that brandy himself. His wife, Mary – aged eighteen, a long way from home, and coping with a new baby in a flimsy bark hut in mid-summer – probably swallowed her fair share. Police charges brought against her in 1838 would reveal her to be fond of a tipple at any time of the day.

> *Constables to apprehend all persons found drunk in the*
> *streets, at any hour of the day, and all drunken, loose, idle*
> *and disorderly persons who cannot give a satisfactory account*
> *of themselves, between sun-set and the hour of eight in the*
> *morning.*

Such 'drunken, loose, idle and disorderly persons' were, if found guilty, fined five shillings for their first offence, ten shillings for their second, fifteen for their third, and so on. Alternatively, an impoverished drunkard could opt for a period of confinement on bread and water, on the treadmill, or in the stocks. As with fines, the length of incarceration was multiplied for repeat offences. Richard Edwards (also known as 'Clubby Dick') was fined £1 upon his fourth drunk-and-disorderly conviction in June 1839, but having liquidised his wages the night before, Dick was skint. In default of the fine, he was sentenced to six hours in the stocks.

Fifty per cent of a drunkard's fine was paid to the arresting constable, and in the absence of breathalysers and – usually – of reputable witnesses for the defence, the constable's word was all that was needed to exact a conviction and a fine. Here was a system crying out to be abused – and the poorly paid constables obliged. In 1840 Johnny Fawkner, that arch-abstainer, voiced the concerns of sober men:

> *The Police are bound to be vigilant ... but this vigilance may be*
> *overstretched; and there is one great evil arising from half the*
> *fine for intoxication, &c., being paid to the constables, namely,*
> *that it is an inducement to them to take sober men into custody*
> *and prefer charges against them ...*

This was the justice-loving Fawkner. But the smirkingly self-righteous Fawkner delighted in caterwauling the names and deeds of convicted drunkards from the pages of his *Patriot*. He played his 'Police Reports' for laughs; they were the printed equivalent of a Punch and Judy show or the throwing of rotten fruit at miscreants in the stocks. Here he is, in full throttle, in February 1839:

> [Several men], all Disciples of the jovial horn, were found guilty of the degrading worship of one Sir John Barleycorn, and in their orgies, beating each other and disturbing the peace in the suburbs of the peace loving town of Melbourne ... ordered to pay 20s each and costs ... Oh! how they will hate beer from this day out. Aye, and how rich our young Queen will soon get at this rate. Thomas Herings, assigned to Mr Brown, for his love of drink 72 hours of solitary meditation on, oh, the joys of wine, mighty wine. J. Connor, fined 5s for his bibulous folly overnight. W. Winbury sacrificed to the Queen a couple of handsome half crowns in acknowledgement of his having worshipped last evening the false God Bacchus.*

Women he flailed a little more gently:

> ... an interesting looking damsel, who stated herself to have been three sheets in the wind – added 10s to the funds. Mrs Carey, a respectable-looking woman, for having indulged a little overnight, fined 5s.
> Mary Doyle, 'whose failings never leaned to virtue's side' had just arrived from the bush and was 'tossicated'.

Take a look at the Herald or Gazette though, and it becomes clear that the previous day's drunkards list was universally regarded as fair game. Here are two examples from the Herald in mid-1841 which show how much comic mileage could be wrung from reports of five-shilling fines in the police court:

---

* Fawkner neglected to name the suppliers of the convicted men's liquor. At this time, he still owned a hotel where, for a price, all comers could join in that worship which Fawkner the newspaper proprietor condemned as 'degrading'.

Barney Carroll, a 'meet me by moonlight' kind of gentleman,
was charged with having been found fuddled in Collins-street,
leaning against a post and vigorously smoking a small lime kiln,
which ever and anon he gave his lips, and took't away again.

James Toomey, a wild Irishman, fresh caught from the bogs of Killarney, was called to account for what he appeared to consider a very innocent source of amusement, the previous night, to wit, dragging his coat by one sleeve through the centre of Collins-street and shouting, 'ullabaloo, who dares put the tip of his toe upon that, who,' upon which he was taken into custody.

One man appearing on a drunkenness charge in 1849 did not wait for the next day's papers to raise laughs at his expense:

An aborigine known as McNall* was charged with drunkenness
– spoke exceedingly good English and seemed to consider the
affair a good joke. Two hours in stocks.

James Burns, charged with drunkenness in August 1841, blamed the publicans. 'They didn't put enough of the Yarra Yarra in the rum,' he told the magistrate, 'and a small quantity set my brain reeling.' A woman named Duffy claimed just the opposite when she appeared in court later that year, charged with having concealed a roll of jaconet (a light cotton fabric) about her person in the shop of A.H. Hart of Collins Street. As the *Patriot* related the story next day:

The prisoner admitted her guilt and said, that had it not been
for 'a crop o' drink' she took on the persuasion of some men
who told her the water of this country was not good for her, she
would have been sorry to have troubled any thing belonging to
'the dacent man'.

---

*   This man would have derived his name from the butcher, John McNall.

Not too many 'Misters' and 'Esquires' made appearances in the 'Police Reports' as drunkards. Which is not to say there weren't drunkards amongst the gentry. The euphemism for the condition was 'the colonial vice' – as in, 'I'm afraid Sir John is unavailable. He has succumbed to the colonial vice.' One young squatter, John Slade Headlam, would drink twenty glasses of brandy at a sitting, poking his fingers down his throat after every fourth glass to make room for more.

Section 69 of the Police Act deemed that should any man, 'by excessive drinking, so waste his estate, as thereby to expose himself, or his family to want, or greatly to injure his health', an order could be issued that he should not be sold or served liquor for a year. No such ruling intervened to save Henry Batman and his family from ruin. His death in October 1839 made for what was arguably Johnny Fawkner's finest moment in print:

> *Died on Friday last, Henry Batman, formerly Chief Constable of Melbourne – another victim to idleness and the dose. For months past, this man devoted his whole time to gambling and drinking; and has at last fallen as sacrifice to this shrine of Moloch.**

Name your poison

As a rule, the Bearbrass gentry favoured brandy, while rank-and-file drinkers preferred (or could only afford) rum. But the choices didn't end there.

Good local beer could be had from 1837, when John Mills built a brewery in Flinders Lane, east of Queen Street, on a block sloping down to the river. He used Yarra water, of course, and his proximity to the river saved the cost of cartage. Thomas Capel and John Moss started brewing in 1838, when all three breweries were turning out 'a very palatable ale' at two shillings a gallon. Henry Condell went on to

---

*   Moloch was a Semitic deity, mentioned in the Old Testament, to whom parents sacrificed their children.

become the most successful of the Bearbrass brewers and was elected as the town's first Mayor – thanks largely, it was said, to the availability of his popular beverage at hustings and polling places.

Imported ales could be had by the bottle, barrel or hogshead – Dunbar and Sons, Ashby's strong, Burton, and Pimlico. There was Taylor's brown stout, Marsella wine, Cape wine, cherry brandy, and strange concoctions like Rum Shrub and Old Tom. The advertisements of wine and spirit merchants and publicans jostled one another on the front pages of the broadsheets. But Henry Baker* of the Imperial Inn in Collins Street was unquestionably the Big Kev of the Bearbrass liquor trade, coming up with advertisements that caught the eye of common folk. 'FOR THE BENEFIT OF THE WORKING CLASSES, SINGULAR, UNPARALLELED …' began an 1841 advert for a new local brew. For a mere fourpence, customers could have their quart jugs filled with a 'wholesome Table Ale' which, they were assured, was a far cry from the 'Tobacco water and liquor derived from stewed sugar bags' that other publicans passed off as beer. Baker was still going strong in 1847 when he urged his 'very superior wines and pure spirits' on the reading public as just the thing to mark 'a Birth, a Marriage, Death, or any other EVENTFUL OCCURRENCE'. His advertised stock included:

> *London Bitters (Fine Stomachic), Good Brandy, Better Brandy, and Best Brandy (ditto Rum & Whiskey), London Cordial Gin, Colonial Ales, Excellent Sherry Wine, Hunt's or Page's Choice Oporto Wines, Draught Red Wine, Choice Old Brandy, Pale or Brown, Holland's Gin in case bottles, Byas' or Dunbar's Bottled Ale and Porter.*

Those in the know could bowl up to a bar or race meeting booth and order a throat-scraper, an eye-opener (an efficacious hair-of-the-dog),

---

* This is the same man who applied a 50 per cent surcharge to teetotal diners for their shilling meals.

a spider (lemonade and brandy), or a stone-fence (ginger beer and brandy). With the asking price for a mixed drink in 1838 at one shilling and threepence, most drinkers took their spirits straight or with a splash of Yarra water. The shandygass, a weak blend of ginger beer and beer, was a favourite among the womenfolk.

Sucking the monkey

Had only they realised it, the 'contraband women' who stowed away inside beer casks on Bearbrass-bound ships risked an indignity greater than detection by the authorities. When a ship's cargo included liquor, there was always a chance that members of the crew would be tempted to 'suck the monkey' – that is, drill a tiny gimlet hole in the cask and suck liquor from it through a straw. In an 1844 letter to a customer, the merchant James Graham advised that he had taken precautions against just such an occurrence:

> *I have shipped this morning in the* Sally Ann *five gallons of brandy which is contained in a five-gallon keg which I have had packed in a case to prevent the sailors 'sucking the monkey' which you were afraid of.*

In 1837, a half-hogshead cask of smuggled rum was found in Michael Carr's hotel in Flinders Lane. The cask was confiscated by a customs officer and sold at auction. The person who bought it later complained that the rum in the cask had been topped up with salt water – apparently in an effort to disguise the fact that the monkey had been sucked.

Bullock drivers were known to perform a less subtle variation of sucking the monkey. But, once again, James Graham was onto them. He warned a customer in 1846, 'It is an old Colonial trick to break the bottles in a case and hold it over a panniken or quart pot to catch what leaks out.'

Champagne notoriety

The years 1839–40 in Bearbrass were later called 'the days of champagne notoriety'. The district's fledgling economy was booming. Land
in the town was at a premium, with shrinking allotments returning
burgeoning profits. The subdivided blocks were auctioned at 'champagne sales', so named because prospective buyers were invited to
drink themselves into improvidence with free beer, brandy and champagne.* The sales were often referred to as 'champagne lunches', as
sumptuous cold collations were also spread out for intending bidders.
In fact, anyone who fancied a free feed and a bellyful of grog could
sidle into the auction room or marquee and partake. Champagne
lunches became a byword for wanton extravagance. The accepted
form was for 'anyone who was disengaged' to saunter in, take a bottle
of his preferred drop (regardless of how many stood open already),
knock off its top with a knife, and chug-a-lug the contents.†

Champagne characterised the era – maybe even shaped it. When
squatter Niel Black arrived at Bearbrass in 1839, he was greeted by the
sight of young men sipping 'thin champagne'. Even bullock drivers
got in on the act, as Thomas Strode, in his lavish style, relates:

> It was no uncommon occurrence for a bullock driver to pull up
> his team opposite a public house, call for a case of Champagne,
> which he would have opened in the street, and filling his
> pannikin with the coveted aristocratic liquor, assist any passers-
> by who were inclined to join him in his dissipation, with a
> profuse liberality pay the landlord the paltry £9 for the dozen
> bottles supplied, disposing of with the greatest sang froid,
> flourish his whip with an extra crack, and then move with his

---

*   Garryowen called it 'sham-pagne', claiming it was really gooseberry wine.
†   Drinking from the broken neck of a bottle was less dicey than it sounds. In those
    days, the glass ring that formed the lip of a bottle was applied separately after the
    body had been moulded in a piece. The lip could therefore have sheared off fairly
    cleanly when struck. But even so …

team in a most exhilarated state, having found an easy way of
getting rid of his money in a gentlemanly manner.

This story appears to marry up with an item from the *Patriot* of March 1839, in which a likewise exhilarated bullocky, in showing off his dexterity with a cattle whip, 'nearly severed (from his head) the EAR of a gent who was passing by'.

Bearbrass's brief flare of opulence left behind debris that would taunt the townsfolk when the local economy plummeted into depression in 1841. As early as 1840, Fawkner's *Patriot* complained of champagne bottles littering the streets:

Turn where you will in your perambulations through the town,
it requires your constant attention that you do not bring your
ancle [sic] in contact with one of these dangerous obstacles. Nor
is the grievance confined to Melbourne alone, for we constantly
observe in the country roads the fragments of bottles stewed
about in abundance.

The greenish-black bottle glass of the period was sometimes as much as a centimetre in thickness and, when fractured, formed shards like deadly obsidian blades. Encountered underfoot, it could have penetrated even the 'lasting' footwear of those times.

Governor Gipps, visiting the stricken district from Sydney in 1842, bore out the *Patriot's* complaint, noting that 'The whole country for miles, almost for hundreds of miles, round Melbourne is strewed to this day with champagne bottles'. Legend has it that cairns of them marked the boundaries of the town, and the roadsides along (present-day) Wellington Parade and over the Eastern Hill to Fitzroy bristled with dead marines.

By the mid-'40s, the economy had recovered; but champagne never regained its favoured status – at least, not until the gold rushes once again made an art form of extravagance. In 1844, James Graham wrote to a supplier in England that 'Champagne nowadays is rarely to be met with at any table here'; this in spite of its availability 'at ridiculously low prices … even so low as 7s 6d per dozen and very good champagne indeed too.' Seven shillings and sixpence a dozen! What a come down from the 'paltry £9' paid by Strode's *bon vivant* bullock driver.

Sly grog shops

Sly-grogging was the selling of liquor without a licence. Eating houses were often outlets for sly grog, but more commonly the stuff could be bought from the householders of any number of shabby huts in the town. Every serious drinker knew someone who dealt in sly grog. A knock at the right door, a rattle of coins, and the tablecloth would be flung back to reveal a cask. The main attraction of sly grog shops was that they served patrons at all hours, including those who had been refused service by reputable liquor vendors. Sly grog shops catered to the all-night drinker, to the hopeless drunk and, often, to the customer who had more than drinking on his mind. The term 'disorderly house' was commonly used to describe an enterprise which combined sly-grogging with brothel-keeping.

One of Bearbrass's earliest sly grog dealers was Lizzie Nash. The wife of a private in the 80th Regiment, posted at Bearbrass from March 1837, Nash was certainly in the sly grog trade by October 1838 when she was 'shoved in the neck' and knocked down by a customer, Tom Lowry, as they wrangled over outstanding payment in the side parlour of Carr's public house. Nash was five months pregnant at the time. She dealt sly grog from a hut on the government block, at the south-west corner of King and Collins streets, which she shared with her husband Tom and two (soon to be three) small children. (In mid-1839, the whole town knew of the 'notorious sly grog shop kept by Mrs Nash', but the police were out to catch her in the act. A constable on surveillance duty late one night was knocked unconscious by someone displeased by the inhibiting effect of his presence.

The 80th Regiment was relieved by another early in 1840 and Lizzie Nash's husband was posted to Windsor, near Sydney. Lizzie and her children stayed behind as she was heavily pregnant. After the birth of her fourth child, she asked for a free passage so that she and the children could join Private Nash at Windsor. When her request reached Superintendent La Trobe, he canvassed Police Magistrate Lonsdale's opinion:

> *Mrs Nash having been brought up and punished since her*
> *confinement for sly grog selling, the Supt. begs the Police*
> *Magistrate to state whether the circumstances under which the*
> *offence was committed are of a nature to admit of this indulgence*
> *being extended to her at this time.*

Lonsdale replied – 'Decidedly not.'

A Mrs Roberts appeared in the police court one Saturday in November 1840, 'charged with keeping one of those detestable holes, a sly grog shop'. The *Patriot's* man on the spot reported that Mrs Roberts was 'blooming like bricks' (that is, smiling energetically) throughout the proceedings, but 'upon hearing the sentence (£50), relaxed into a scowl, which penetrated through the very desk of the police clerk'. Who could blame her? Fifty pounds was an enormous amount of money. This must have been Mrs Roberts' second offence, the fine for a first offence being only £30. That was the fine exacted in 1841 from John Mitchell, 'the keeper of a notorious sly-grog shop and brothel, in Elizabeth-street, under the semblance of an eating house'. And in a cheeky piece on the Melbourne Club in the *Patriot* that same year, Johnny Fawkner asked, 'Ah! ah!! Where's the £30 fine?' He reckoned gin was being served at the unlicensed club house in Collins Street. And he was in a good position to know: the clubhouse was next door to the *Patriot* office.

Lambing down

Workers from the bush – shepherds, shearers, bullock drivers and stockmen – might come down to town on a spree only once or twice a year, with the express purpose of blowing their wages. To that end, most headed straight for their favourite public house, where they knew they would receive every assistance toward attaining their goal. The men's wages usually took the form of a cheque or order drawn against their employer's bank. These were called 'sticking plasters' and those who bore them into town were 'plaster-men'. The bushman handed over his 'plaster' to the publican upon arrival, and the 'lambing down' or 'fleecing' would commence. Everyone entering the bar was invited to take advantage of the plaster-man's 'shouts'. Then, when his wages were almost gone, the bushman would be handed the tiny balance as spending money for the remainder of his stay in town, and would be treated to a free breakfast.

Lambing down was big business for publicans, so it was in their interest to curry favour with bush-workers. In the late '30s, Robert Fleming's Edinburgh Castle Hotel in Collins Street would fleece so many shearers at the end of a season that their 'free' breakfasts called for more than a hundredweight (50 kg) of chops and steaks.

William Bull was a farm servant and on his rare visits to town was 'a right thirsty soul'. In January 1840, he was fined fifty shillings for being drunk and disorderly. Having followed his nine prior convictions, the *Patriot* knew Bull like a friend:

> *This hero of the pint pot, during his brief sojourn amongst us, invariably pays his respects once or twice to the lock-up previous to his departure.*

At the end of a spree, the bush-worker knew that if he lounged long enough in the front bar of the public house, a prospective employer would approach him with an offer of work. Many hotels acted as virtual labour exchanges, where squatters could depend on finding bush-workers who had drunk their wages and were looking for the means to fund their next trip to town.

Public houses

William Lonsdale found, when he arrived in September 1836, that a number of unlicensed public houses were already in operation. Immediately he issued interim licences (proper ones had to be approved by the Sydney authorities) at £25 each, and the free-born Bearbrass hostelries were brought to heel by the Licensing Act.

Six days a week, public houses could trade from four a.m. until nine p.m.; during summer months, they were allowed to open two hours earlier in the morning. Publicans who held a night licence – for which they paid an additional fee – could trade until midnight. Sunday trading was strictly limited: public houses could open from one to three p.m., but no liquor could be consumed on the premises. Beer only was to be sold on Sundays, and customers brought their own jugs and pots to be filled at the bar, then drank them in the streets outside – or carried them home inside their coats if the weather was inclement.

Publicans were fined £5 if they sold liquor to a 'married person whose intemperance was known to be of injury to his family', allowed wages to be paid inside their hotel (luckily for them, no law forbade the *spending* of wages therein), or served liquor to convict servants or Aborigines. The publican's name had to be legibly painted in a conspicuous place on the hotel's exterior, in letters at least three inches high, and a two-burner lamp kept alight over the door after nightfall.

Every public house was required to have two sitting-rooms and two sleeping rooms exclusively for the use of customers. Squatter Edward Curr described the front sitting-room, or bar, of a Bearbrass hotel in 1840:

> *A lengthy apartment, in the centre of which was a long narrow deal table on which stood, here and there, a number of bottles of*

ale, brandy, champagne, &c., together with tumbler, glasses and pewter pots. On each side of the tables, against the walls, were benches running the length of the room, on which were seated some thirty men in every stage of intoxication, from maudlin imbecility to that of the maddened bacchanal, vigorous and rampant, in the first stage of his debauch.

The Licensing Act also required that there be 'a place of accommodation, on or near the premises, for the use of the customers, in order to prevent offences against decency'. This was the 'dead house', where those who were dead drunk were left to recover themselves and so avoid drunk-and-disorderly charges. According to Garryowen, the dead house was generally a 'secure, unwindowed, comfortably-strawed exterior apartment … kept tidy and comfortable, and freshly strawed each morning'. But dead houses were far from being as benign and cosy as they sounded. Their insensible occupants were easy prey for robbers and, on more than one occasion, thugs beat a drunkard to death when he revived to find his pockets being plundered. The term 'dead house' began to wear a more literal meaning.

Fawkner's hotels

Johnny Fawkner's hotel was the first at Bearbrass. From the time his house was erected in November 1835, he called it 'Fawkner's Hotel' and offered accommodation and meals to visitors and new arrivals. Liquor was served to guests and, as we have seen, was sold to other settlers, but, to begin with, there was no bar, and certainly no dead house or beer garden. Fawkner's Hotel was just a little weatherboard house halfway up a grassy slope beside the Yarra.

It was built of Tasmanian timber – broad paling walls, with a roof of palings and shingles, and hardwood floors – and set back from what would become the south-east corner of William Street and Flinders Lane. Fawkner took pride in the glazed windows, panel doors and 'good brick chimney' built by himself and Jem Gilbert. On the ground floor were six rooms, with those overlooking the river reserved for guests of rank. As the population and the hotel's patronage grew, the kitchen was cut in two and a dingy little bar opened at the back of the house. The upper storey was a stoop-worthy attic divided into claustrophobic sleeping chambers. All in all, said Garryowen (who never saw it), Fawkner's Hotel was 'little more than a clumsy and comfortless booth'. A visitor in January 1836 recalled it years later as a structure 'of a very primitive order', where cheap rum laced with river water could be had at Mayfair prices.

In August 1836, Johnny and Eliza Fawkner returned to Launceston for a spell, leaving their property in the care of two servants, William Diprose and Charles Wise. In the Fawkners' absence, Diprose and Wise handed over the house-cum-hotel to George Smith and Dr Barry Cotter, who renamed it the Port Phillip Hotel and carried on the business. Johnny was understandably enraged when he arrived back at Bearbrass in 1837, and he commenced a campaign of harassment against Smith and Cotter in an effort to regain his property. He finally drove out the interlopers by taking the front parlour by force and threshing his entire wheat crop therein, keeping the racket up day and night.

The town survey was now completed and the land on which Fawkner had built his hotel was earmarked as part of the customs house reserve. For £100, he was willing to give it up without a fight. (The front sitting-room would never be the same, anyway; wheat husks kept drifting down from the ceiling boards into his breakfast.) The government subsequently sold Fawkner's old hotel and fragments of it were soon distributed throughout the town.

Among Fawkner's purchases at the first land sale, in 1837, was an allotment on the south-east corner of Collins and Market streets. Here he built his second hotel, which Garryowen called a 'vast improvement' on the first. Built of timber and brick, it offered all manner of 'superior advantages', including splendid views from a balcony facing the river and an observatory on the roof ('... to the westward you look over the extensive plains leading to Geelong, with a background enriched by the peaks of the Villaminarta range of hills*...). The 'quaint, pyramidal' roof was itself worth seeing; according to Garryowen, it bore a resemblance to 'a half-open umbrella with the whalebone slightly out of order'.

Fawkner's second hotel was licensed in July 1838. To mark its opening, he staged a fireworks display from the observatory and excitable patrons joined in, showering the large crowd with buckshot. On the outskirts of the crowd, a group of Aborigines looked on enthralled, and Reverend William Waterfield saw an opportunity to lecture them on 'where the good and bad go when they die'.

In a side parlour off the downstairs hallway in his new hotel, Johnny Fawkner established the town's first library. The exorbitant one shilling paid for a rum-and-aqua also bought admittance to the reading room – 'Mental and Bodily refreshment unrivalled in this quarter of the globe' was how Fawkner billed it. The library's contents included 'A very choise Siliction of Books' as well as English and colonial newspapers. Garryowen told a story of an Italian count with the improbable name of Mynheer-von-Bebra, whom Fawkner appointed librarian. When he accused the Count of stealing coins from a cash drawer, Fawkner was dealt aristocratic upper-cuts that blackened both his eyes. The mysterious von-Bebra may actually have been Christian Ludolph Johannes De Villiers, a former South African bushman and founding Superintendent of Native Police at Port Phillip. De Villiers drank too much and one day in February 1838 confronted Fawkner in his library. The two exchanged blows and De Villiers came off second-best – flung out in the street on his backside.†

---

* You Yangs
† Fawkner was slightly built, but evidently he knew some canny wrestling throws. On another occasion, he threw John Batman's servant (and Eliza Batman's future husband) William Willoughby, who was a biggish man. Willoughby described how his wiry attacker 'seized me by the arm and in some manner got himself under one of my legs and forcing it up caused me to fall back on a chair'.

Fawkner, of course, was a teetotaller, but when pressed by a genial patron to 'have one on me', he would accept with good grace and pour himself a tot from a bottle above the bar. 'Your health,' he would propose with glass raised, then would toss back the contents in a swallow. 'Fine fellow, old Johnny,' the generous customer would muse as he paid for the round, never thinking that he'd just been toasted in cold tea and charged for best brandy.

But Thomas Strode, original printer of the *Gazette*, reckoned that *he* had Fawkner's number. In his unpublished memoirs of Bearbrass, written shortly before Fawkner's death, Strode vented his spleen with a tasty piece of scandal that credits Johnny Fawkner with pioneering lap-dancing and casts doubt on his reputation as a puritanical git:

> ... *a certain boniface in bygone years who now assumes the garb of sanctity, supplied his questionable customers who visited the dancing shed attached to his hotel with pots of porter, whilst a portion of the frail sex present were to be seen in the costume adopted by Eve on her entry into Paradise, and who would often become transfixed to the spot with a fit of grovelling sensuality until aroused from his phantasmagorical reverie by the voice of his helpmeet calling on him to attend the less exciting duties of serving male customers at the bar with gills of rum and pints of 'arf and 'arf.* *

Entertaining though it may be to picture the old 'doubly convicted scoundrel' creaming his corduroys at the Pink Pussycat Dancing Shed (incorporating Fawkner's Hotel), I just can't see it. I mean, *what* dancing shed? But then, Fawkner's capacity for hypocrisy *was* legendary – so make what you will of Thomas Strode's story.

---

* 'Half and half' was a blend of half bitter and half malty ale; the term was also sometimes used to describe a drunkard – presumably a reference to blood-alcohol content.

Fawkner gave up hotel-keeping in April 1839. Who knows – perhaps the hypocrisy of the situation got too much even for *him* to live with.

Carr's Governor Bourke Hotel

While Fawkner's Hotel was the first on the ground at Bearbrass, Michael Carr's Governor Bourke Hotel was the first to be granted a licence by Lonsdale in October 1836. Michael Carr was a sawyer by trade, originally from Dublin and, although the licence was in his name, his wife Kitty was very much an equal partner in the business. Built of sods and timber, the Governor Bourke was dank and dark, with not even the appointments of Fawkner's first hotel – but Carr's hotel was popular. Mind you, it was the sort of popularity that showed up mainly in police reports. It was evidently a 'round up the usual suspects' kind of a place: absconding servants often turned up there, fights broke out, police were assaulted, and thefts occurred regularly. As Chief Constable, Henry Batman might have asked questions as to why this was so, had he not himself been one of the Carrs' best customers.

Michael Carr himself was implicated in the smuggling of a cask of rum from a ship anchored in the Yarra early in 1837. The contraband was found in Carr's public house, concealed under two mattresses in a room adjoining the tap room. Carr insisted that the rum had merely been left with him for safekeeping when two former lodgers, William Jemott and Robert Wilson, headed up-country to work. Jemott and Wilson were sent to prison for six months while Carr was fined £30 as an accessory.

In mid-1838, Michael Carr had cause to go to Sydney for a few months, leaving Kitty in charge of the Governor Bourke. While he was gone, she found herself in strife. In July, Tim Hall, a bush-worker lodging at Carr's, claimed that she had stolen a possumskin pocket book containing £22 9s (his year's wages) and his Certificate of Freedom.* Hall appears to have been a moderate drinker and had not

---

* Granted to convicts who had completed their term of sentence.

come into town looking to be fleeced. He arrived at Carr's early one morning, left his belongings, and went off to catch up with friends at the Mounted Police Barracks. Late in the afternoon, he returned to Carr's and ordered a pot of ale. He presented his order for £22 9s, but Mrs Carr said she couldn't cash such a large amount; so he returned the order to his pocket book, inside his jacket, and paid instead with some small change. Assisting Kitty Carr behind the bar was a man named Hugh Lowry (likely a brother of, or perhaps the very same, Thomas Lowry who flattened Lizzie Nash at Carr's). Hall told the magistrate:

> I was sitting on a form during the whole transaction with Mrs Carr on one side and Lowry on the other ... We three were talking and Lowry and Carr were skylarking and joking with each other, shoving and taking hold of each other across me and rubbing their sides alongside me.

When Hall reached into his jacket to fetch out his pipe, he found his pocket book missing. Immediately he turned to Mrs Carr and demanded, 'Kitty, have you got my money?' at which she laughed and replied, 'It's safer with me than with you, luvvy.' It would be returned to him in the morning, she said, and, reassured, Hall drank on until bedtime. Next morning however, Kitty Carr denied having his pocket book; she had been joking, she said. When he persisted, Hall told the court, she told him that 'if I did not go out of town immediately I should get murdered', and Lowry echoed the threat. Hall's friend, Corporal Owen Nowlan of the Mounted Police, was with him before the pocket book was found to be missing, and Nowlan's evidence suggested that Kitty Carr and Lowry were not the only ones who'd had the opportunity to lift it. Hall and Nowlan had taken a drink at the nearby Ship Inn (a sinkhole of even lower repute) after the pocket book was last seen, and there'd been a number of other drinkers in the tap room at Carr's when Hall's property was missed. In the end, the case was dismissed, leaving Tim Hall to get used to the fact that he'd worked a whole year for nothing.

Three months later, with her husband still in Sydney, Kitty Carr was accused of stealing clothes worth £8 from a box belonging to a lodger named William Nicholson. The box was in the right-hand parlour, which was used as a sitting-room by day and a bedroom at night, and at eight-o'clock one morning, after he'd been lodging there several weeks, Nicholson found that the staple securing the lid of the box had been drawn and the clothing was gone. Missing were a blue body coat, four waistcoats, three white shirts and one red-striped one, two pairs of trousers (one of blue cloth, the other of corduroy), and six pairs of socks. Some days later, the hotel's cook, John Yates, told Nicholson that, when 'passing through Mrs Carr's sleeping room', he had seen the lodger's clothes spread out on her bed. Nicholson confronted Kitty and she admitted having removed the clothes from his box, but, as she suspected that he had not 'come by them honestly', she would keep them until her husband returned from Sydney. Now here's a funny thing: Nicholson agreed to let the matter rest. Kitty Carr must have been *some* coquette. But when Michael returned, the game was up. Clothes? What clothes? Nicholson went to the police. But, although his evidence in court was corroborated by two other witnesses, the case was dismissed and Kitty Carr's unblemished record remained.

And a good thing for her that it did. Had a charge of theft been proved against her, Kitty Carr would have been in no position to become Bearbrass's first female hotel licensee, following her husband's death in October 1839. Michael Carr was just thirty-six when he died, and Fawkner farewelled him with a tribute headed ANOTHER VICTIM OF INTEMPERANCE:

> *This man … has been some three years destroying a strong constitution by continual indulgence in the murderous vice that is ruining many, viz. – Constant Habitual Drunkenness.*

The Highlandman and Royal Highlander hotels

Another of the early Bearbrass licensees was Jemmy Connell. Like
the Carrs and Johnny Fawkner, he had been trading in liquor before
Lonsdale arrived. His hotel was the Highlandman (sometimes called
the Highlander), near the south-west corner of Queen and Little
Collins streets. Connell had a servant named James Gill who, in
July 1837, was supposed to be fencing his master's allotment when
he was seen 'having carnal knowledge of' a four-month-old calf. Gill
was charged with bestiality and sent to Sydney for trial, and Jemmy
Connell hired a married man to finish the fence.

The Highlandman's licence was transferred in 1845 to a new
public house, owned by John Shanks, on the site of an earlier one (the
Melbourne Hotel) in Flinders Street, just east of King. The new hotel
was named the Royal Highlander and gave its name to the adjacent
Highlander Lane. The hotel was demolished in 1912, but Highlander
Lane remains.

The Lamb Inn

George Smith, formerly a farmer, was issued one of Lonsdale's temporary licences in October 1836 for his Port Phillip Hotel. This was the
former Fawkner's Hotel, which Smith and his partner Barry Cotter had
acquired from the men to whom the absent Fawkner had entrusted
it. After being driven out by Fawkner's agricultural revenge, Smith
bought land on the north side of Collins Street and built a new hotel
which he called the Lamb Inn. The main portion of the hotel was
constructed of materials from Henry Batman's former house which
had obstructed the course of the newly defined William Street. The
Lamb Inn was licensed late in 1837 and Thomas Strode, arriving the
following year, described it as:

> *a very humble affair, being formed of lath and plaster, with the*
> *rough coat of mould marked in sundry ingenious and fanciful*
> *stripes ... its rooms were few and narrow, and its sleeping*

accommodation scanty and confined; its little parlour serving for
every meal, was usually crammed with settlers from the bush ...

In fact, the Lamb Inn became renowned as 'a roystering place for
shepherds with cheques' and its name may or may not have been a
play on – or even the origin of – the term 'lambing down'. George
Lloyd, a visitor from Van Diemen's Land who made the mistake of
lodging at the Lamb Inn in 1839, saw an apposite significance in the
name:

Never was a sign more inappropriate.* Instead of affording rest
and shelter to the weary traveller, the orgies that were kept up
day after day and night after night within its walls, converted it
into a perfect den of drunkenness and vice.

For the Lamb Inn was not just the fleecing depot for thirsty bushmen;
it was the headquarters – The Den, in fact – of the band of gentlemen
rowdies who called themselves the Waterford School.† Out of the
Waterford School emerged the Melbourne Club, which was founded
at the Lamb Inn on New Year's Day, 1839.

By 1840, the Lamb Inn had been extended, the rooms which
Strode had counted as 'few' now numbering thirty-one. Advertising
his hotel for sale in January that year, Smith described a spacious
dining room, coffee room, cellars, coach-house, groom's room, hen-
house, and extensive stabling. It fetched a price of £7,000.

The new landlord of the Lamb Inn added a billiard-room which,
in the early '40s, served in lieu of a public hall. It acted as a polling
place, court sessions were heard there, and it hosted the town's first
coroner's inquest, in 1841. Georgiana McCrae's son, then a young boy,
many years later remembered the Lamb Inn as the place 'where I saw

---

*   Evidently, Lloyd had construed the inn's name as a reference to the lamb of God,
     'which taketh away the sin of the world' (John 1:29).

†   See Chapter 4.

my first dead man: a bushranger, stretched out on the billiard-table, with a bullet through his head'.*

From spiritual to spirituous

Two public houses with religious origins were the Queen's Arms and the Caledonian. An early Bearbrass builder of Wesleyan Methodist faith built a tiny brick chapel at the north-west corner of Swanston Street and Flinders Lane. The chapel had supposedly been built to hold a congregation of one hundred and fifty, but it could accommodate less than half that number in comfort. A visiting preacher wrote that, 'were I going to remain here I think that instead of suffocating myself and congregation in so small a place I should turn out of doors', while Garryowen would liken the assembled Wesleyans to 'herrings in a cask'. After two years, they moved to a more commodious chapel in Queen Street and the original one was bought by Thomas Monahan and converted into a pair of 'cottage residences'. These went on to form the rear portion of Monahan's Queen's Arms Hotel in 1847, the kitchen taking up a good part of the former chapel.

The Caledonian Hotel, on the south-west corner of Swanston and Lonsdale streets, began its life as the home of the Reverend James Clow, first Presbyterian minister at Bearbrass, in 1838. There was nothing modest about this churchman's house. It had thirteen capacious rooms (plus servants' quarters and outbuildings), with dormer windows set in a steep, shingled roof, french windows, and a wide verandah along the front. After not much more than a year, Reverend Clow and his family moved on, hoping to lease their home as a lodging house or seminary. Instead it became the Caledonian Hotel. In 1845, the Caledonian began a new life as a temperance hotel, under the stewardship of a Mr Tankard.

---

*   *Georgiana's Journal*, p. 27.

Four hotels to an intersection

Everyone had heard the claim that, during the gold rushes of the 1850s, Melbourne had 'a pub on every corner'. But in the late '40s, Bearbrass was already on its way to achieving that impressive Monopoly score. In April 1847, the town had a hundred public houses – one to each corner at some intersections. John Bourke (a former overland postman) applied for a licence that year for a newly erected hotel on the corner of Queen Street and Flinders Lane. Chief Constable Sugden, in opposing the application, stated that there were already eight public houses within a hundred yards of that corner. But the Licensing Board apparently figured, 'Well – what harm can another one do?', and granted Bourke his licence.

CHAPTER 8

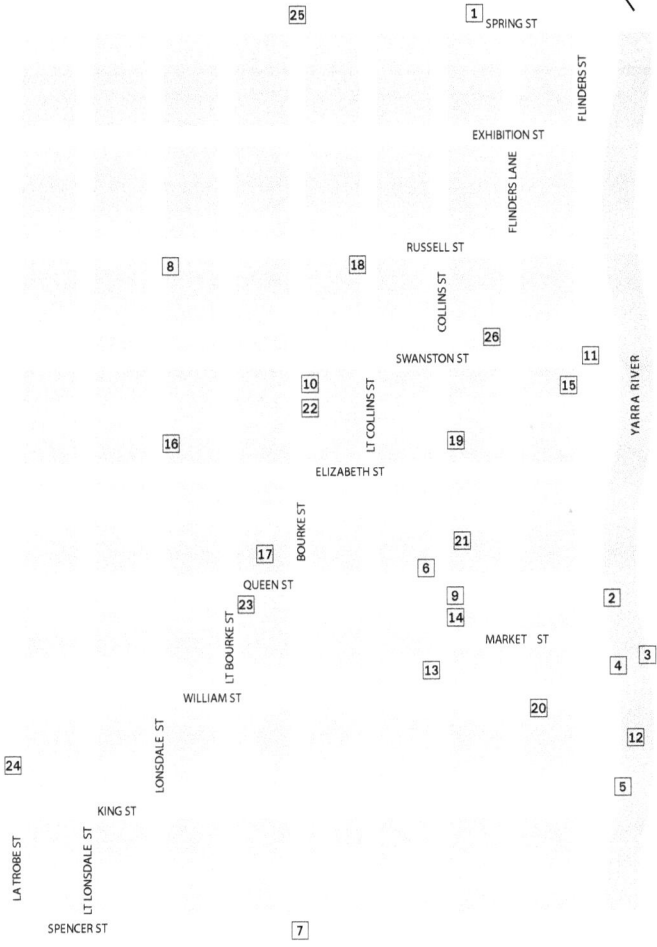

25

1 SPRING ST

FLINDERS ST

EXHIBITION ST

FLINDERS LANE

RUSSELL ST

8   18

COLLINS ST

26

SWANSTON ST   11

YARRA RIVER

10   LT COLLINS ST   15

22

16   19

ELIZABETH ST

BOURKE ST

17   21

QUEEN ST   6

23   9   2

LT BOURKE ST   14

MARKET   ST

13   3

WILLIAM ST   4

20

LONSDALE ST   12

24   5

KING ST

LA TROBE ST

LT LONSDALE ST

SPENCER ST   7

1. Treasury Gardens, or the Manna Forest

2. Proposed site of Palmer's 'floating baths', 1843

3. Riddle's bath house and lounging shed, 1844

4. Kentish's baths, 1848, and Victoria baths, 1850

5. The Yarra Yabbies swimming club met at Cole's Wharf

6. Umphelby's Angel Inn had the town's first billiard table

7. The winning post of the original racecourse

8. St George and the Dragon Hotel, landlorded by the gallant George Say

9. Site of a staged dog-fight, 1840

10. The Eagle Tavern, its clientele the nemesis of barrel-rollers, 1847

11. The Princes Bridge scaffolding was popular with amateur gymnasts, 1849

12. A Mr Quinn crossed the river on a tightrope in 1849

13. Lamb Inn, original meeting place of the Melbourne Club

14. The Melbourne Clubhouse, scene of 'incessant depravities'

15. The Port Phillip Clubhouse, formerly 'Hodgson's Folly'

16. Prostitutes strutted opposite St Francis' Church in 1849

17. A brothel in 'the notorious Vinge's Lane', kept first by the Willises, then by the Tootes

18. The 'den of infamy' that spawned the 'Brass Gong Affair' of 1847

19. The Australian Hotel, into whose bar Janey Moor staggered after a laudanum overdose

20. William Harper's British Hotel, venue of the town's first musical recital, 1839

21. The Royal Hotel, in whose ballroom the town's first polka was danced

22. The Pavilion, later renamed the Theatre Royal and Royal Victoria Theatre

23. The Queen's Theatre, birthplace of the Twist

24. The Flagstaff Hill dunny was ignited as part of the revelries that greeted news of Separation

25. Eastern Hill, venue of the Separation Celebration Sports

26. Bearbrass VIPs watched the Separation procession from this point

CHAPTER 8

Bearbrass at Play

The Manna Forest

Leave the city and take a walk or a tram to the Treasury Gardens. You might expect that their proximity to the State Government offices would make these gardens a wretched place, their tree roots unsettled by the proximate agitation of adding machines down the generations and their ambience irradiated by a bad bureaucratic vibe. But on the contrary, there's something beatific about the Treasury Gardens. I've seen men in suits stroll hand-in-hand there, and Laurie Levy in saintly contemplation of the duck pond. I've never seen power-walkers in the Treasury Gardens. No sooner, I suppose, do they launch their first thrusting stride than the serene spirit of the place overtakes them, plucking at the velcro fastenings of their wrist weights and lulling the walker to a dreaming gait. Mighty Moreton Bay fig trees line the pathways and pelt down their hard little fruit as a further deterrent to hasty footwork. If you don't mind being donged by an occasional fig, take a seat beside a path; otherwise, the lawns invite sprawling in dry weather. The constant play of a fountain in the duck pond adds to the great *feng shui* of the place (and makes you wonder where the nearest toilets are – they're at the far end of the gardens, in Lansdowne Street). The sparrows are friendly, the possums active – even the John F. Kennedy memorial, down by the pond, seems benign. (The narcotic quality of the gardens frees you momentarily from that most haunting of questions: 'Did Oswald act alone?') The site of these gardens was once known by townsfolk as the Manna Forest, because of the honey-like sap of the ghost gums that grew there. But 'manna' can also mean spiritual nourishment. So let us think of this place as the Manna Forest still – a name not only more mellifluous than its present moniker, but also more apt.

∽

Mama said you could go with Billings to the Manna Forest, just so long as you all understood that you'd have to *walk* all the way back. If Henry couldn't manage, you'd have to carry him. 'Yes, yes, of course. We don't mind,' you told her. Billings didn't look too happy about having you lot along. Tom sat up front and tried to impress him with his shanghai while the rest of you joggled around in the back, but clearly Billings couldn't have cared less. (This was work to him: he didn't want a crowd of half-boots getting under his feet while he was getting firewood. What was he, a nurse-maid now?) Mama had wrapped the band saw in an old pillow slip and told Nennie (that is, Agnes) to tuck it under her legs in the dray, so that the littlies wouldn't be wanting to play with it.

It wasn't long before you left Flinders Street behind and headed away from the river into the thickening bush, along a rutted track. 'Look at the manna on that one!' shouted Tom, pointing to a dripping mass high up on the trunk of a white gum.

'And this one,' said Josie, pointing to another. 'We could just about reach it, I think.'

'Let us off here, Billings!' ordered Tom, in imperious imitation of your father, and Billings jerked the reins so sharply that you all flew forwards and Mary bit her tongue. You clambered out, Nennie comforting Mary, and Billings trundled off without so much as a nod.

Nennie reckons she can make a treacle cake using manna instead of treacle. She says it'll take about half a pint of the stuff. 'First,' says Tom, 'we need a good sharp stick.'

'How's this?' you ask, holding up one about a foot long and the thickness of a broomstick.

'Right. Give it here.' Tom sharpens it to a stumpy point with his pocket-knife. 'Now, which one first?'

Josie's over at the tree she spotted from the dray. 'I can nearly reach,' she says, spidering her fingers as far up the trunk as she can.

'Here, let me.' Tom pushes her aside and easily prises off the sticky gob of sap himself. 'Where's that jar, Nennie?'

'Oh no,' wails Nennie, 'I left it behind!'

Tom throws stick and manna to the ground and grinds his boot into it. 'Bloody stupid girl!'

'Tom!'

Mary, who's still whimpering over her bitten tongue, gives a renewed yell.

'Here, Tom,' you say, scrabbling in your trouser pocket, 'we could use my hankie.'

'What, and have a snot cake instead?'

'It's clean!' you protest, but Tom takes no notice. He's busy trying to get the manna off the sole of his boot. He scrapes his foot back and forth angrily in the dirt. Then, 'GRORRG!' he explodes and stamps off, picking up leaves and twigs with his right boot as he goes.

The rest of you are relieved. It's almost as bad as having Father along, going anywhere with Tom these days. He manages to spoil everything. You all decide that the manna cake can wait until another day. With the help of Nennie and Tom's sharpened stick, you each get a good-sized lump of sap to suck on (Mary gets the first one, to sooth her sore tongue), then Josie pipes up, 'What about a game of Parrots up a Gum Tree?'

'Yay! Can we, Nennie?'

'Well, we'll have to find a tree with low enough branches – but strong ones,' says your big sister.

Between the five of you, you find a good sturdy gum with a branch low enough to swing yourselves up on and others within easy reach. You climb up four branches and perch there, about twenty feet up. On the branch below you is Josie, her skirt tied in a chunky knot at her waist, and below her is Mary, with Nennie and Henry on the branch nearest the ground. On the count of three, you launch into a raucous chorus of chirruping and squawking while Nennie sings 'Five Parrots Sitting up a Gum Tree'.

From a distance comes a shout from Tom: 'Pipe down, you lot! You're frightening all the birds away!' Good job, you think – better than letting him bung them with his shanghai – and you pitch your squawks a bit louder.

An hour or so later you're still up there, trying to make a gum-leaf whistle and keeping a watch out for Billings. Nennie has helped the others down and they're playing hopscotch. Then, 'Here he comes!' you shout and scramble down, missing the last branch altogether and landing on your backside. You can hear the clip-clop and uneven rumble of the dray approaching and the five of you hide in the scrub by the side of the track. When the dray comes in sight, out you all jump, shouting, 'BOO!' Mister, the dray horse, doesn't so much as twitch a nostril.

Billings says crossly, 'You still here, are you? Well, like your ma told you, there's no room for you in back.' It was true: the dray was full – overfull, even – of firewood, all odd lengths.

'Never mind,' Nennie tells him, 'we'll walk back with you.'

'Just to keep you company,' you say, with a laugh.

'Don't you go scaring th'old horse,' grumbles Billings.

'Not to worry,' says Nennie, feeding the dray horse a morsel of manna she'd been saving. 'Mister's used to us, aren't you, Mister?' And the five of you – Nennie carrying Henry, and Josie pulling Mary by the hand – run ahead of the dray all the way home.*

Yarra yabbies

*Persons bathing within view of any public wharf, quarry,
bridge, street, road, or other place of public resort, within the
limits of the town, between the hours of 6 in the morning and 8
in the evening, shall, on conviction, forfeit and pay a sum not
exceeding £1 …*

So ran Section 21 of the Police Act. This was pre-Speedos, remember,
so 'bathing' generally meant taking to the water naked.† There were
those at Bearbrass who enjoyed a swim, or who couldn't be bothered
heating water for a hip-bath, or who (like the televisual Mr Darcy)
got a bit steamy after a long stretch in the saddle – and mostly they
observed the law and took their dip early in the day, before anybody
else was about. Or they'd find a spot up-river, out of sight of townsfolk going about their business. But when it came to summertime
and dust flew in the hot glare of the afternoon, there were those who
couldn't resist the wide, wet, cool expanse of the Yarra. 'Section 21 be
buggered,' was their attitude.

The summer of 1841 was a scorcher, hot for unremitting weeks on
end. Nevertheless the *Herald* felt duty-bound to blow the whistle on
the skinny-dippers at the Falls:

*We beg to call the attention of the authorities to the indecent
practice of allowing persons to bathe in the river, immediately
above and below the custom house falls at all hours of the*

---

*   The Welsh family lived in Yarro Cottage – 'a cottage of some pretensions' – in
Flinders Street East, around about where the Phoenix Hotel stands today. The
children's father, Paddy, after whom Tom styled himself, was the principal
director of the Port Phillip Bank and was described by a contemporary as 'a
grasping selfish creature'.

†   The thoroughly draped and swaddled Particular Baptists were an exception, of
course.

> *day. Ladies in consequence are deterred from walking on the*
> *banks of the river which would otherwise become a fashionable*
> *promenade.*

A fashionable promenade on the banks of the Yarra? Sounds familiar. At any rate, a few pairs of bobbing buttocks were the least of the indelicacies in store for ladies and others who thought to take their leisure on the Yarra banks in 1842:

> *Occasionally the toil-worn denizen of this crowded town, in*
> *his endeavours to recruit and restore his exhausted energies, by*
> *breathing an untainted atmosphere, is perchance, induced to*
> *follow the windings of the Yarra Yarra. Here it often happens*
> *that his walk is spoiled by the sight of two or three bloated and*
> *putrid carcasses of dogs, pigs, or other animals, floating down*
> *the stream with the tide ...*

A correspondent to the *Patriot* calling himself 'Natator' went bathing with some friends (and the odd putrid carcass) one afternoon, 'about a stone's throw above the slaughter houses'. He was breaststroking contentedly when he 'was threatened by a *soi disant* constable with being taken to the watchhouse, from thence before the "Beak" and peradventure a seat in the *stocks*'! 'Natator' went on:

> *In a climate like this it strikes me that every facility should be*
> *given to parties desirous of enjoying so healthy an exercise ...*

Now John Palmer had the same idea and proposed to erect 'floating baths' above the Falls. The town council objected strongly, arguing that Palmer's patrons would be bathing in the town's drinking water, but he pushed on with his plans anyway. The *Patriot* in November 1843 described the floating baths as a wooden structure supported by two pontoons:

... and though rather lop-sided in appearance at present, we
doubt not when properly ballasted and brought to a level they
will be found to answer the purpose and prove a great source of
comfort and luxury to the inhabitants.

Palmer never did get the ballasting sorted out. Two weeks before
Christmas, the floating baths listed sharply, tearing the whole structure almost in two.

While the floating baths were foundering, John Riddle sought
permission to build a bathing enclosure, seventy feet long, on the
opposite bank of the Yarra. The site Riddle proposed was *below* the
Falls, and this made all the difference in the eyes of the town council.
If people wanted to bath in mutton leavings, good luck to them.
Approval being forthcoming, Riddle's baths opened in January 1840.
'Respectable' patrons could bath in the large enclosure, forty feet in
length, for sixpence a day or could subscribe for three months for £1.
Those deemed less respectable paid threepence, or twelve shillings a
quarter, for a dip in a smaller pool. The baths were constructed so
that a constant flow of water passed through them, keeping impurities
on the move. A boat ferried patrons from the north side of the Yarra,
and for those arriving from the southern suburbs on horseback, stabling and fodder were provided. Tickets to the big pool also admitted
their patrons to a 'lounging shed' where, after a few bracing laps, they
could enjoy 'a cup of Mocha and a mild havana' before returning to
the rigours of commerce and domestic life.

But the average Bearbrass oick preferred to keep his threepence
and take his chances with Section 21. After two seasons (they were
open only during the warmer months) Riddle's baths closed down,
having failed to turn a profit. A wool-washing works took over the
site, pumping out greasy sludge to defy swimmers.

Nathaniel Kentish built new baths in 1848, on the town side of the
river, opposite the wool-washing works. But even before they opened
for business, Kentish's baths burned down, it was supposed in retali-

ation for his failure to pay the builders. The Victoria Public Baths, on the same site, opened for business in the middle of winter 1850, on the strength of a claim that 'cold water bathing every morning is the finest fortifier against all the ills and diseases that either body or mind are liable to'. The new baths featured showers and *douche* baths as well as a large central swimming pool. In a bold step forward, the Victoria Baths were open to the women of Bearbrass, being reserved for their exclusive use between ten a.m. and noon each day. The baths were open from six a.m. to eight p.m. daily, except during divine service on Sundays.

The price of a swim at the Victoria Baths was sixpence for all comers, putting it beyond the pockets of most working men and women. But those who bathed in the Yarra proper now risked big fines, not just the few shillings of old. Patrick Annand, a tinsmith, was a member of a swimming club – an informal group of, mainly, tradesmen – who called themselves the Yarra Yabbies. They would meet after work at Cole's Wharf, strip off on the steps, and swim laps under cover of the wharves – not wanting to offend the tender sensibilities of wharfies, bullockies and seamen who frequented that part of town. A priggish young constable arrested Annand as he emerged from under the wharves one afternoon in February 1850. Unable to pay the £5 fine, the tinsmith was confined for the rest of the summer in the hot gaol on the hill, where the most water he would see was two inches, once a week, in the communal bathing trough.

Gambling & public house games

By law, public houses could not contain a skittle-ground* or ball-court, any dice, cards, bowls, quoits, or other objects that could be used in gaming. But in the '30s and early '40s, there was a tendency on the part of licensing magistrates to overlook the addition of skittle-grounds and ball-courts to public houses. These entertainments seem to have been

---

* Similar to a bowling alley, but on a smaller scale.

viewed more as sport than a form of gambling. In the licence renewal hearings of May 1844, however, the magistrate acknowledged that 'skittle playing was a healthy exercise', but felt obliged to enforce the law and insisted that the William Tell, Australian, and Farmer's hotels would be relicensed only if their skittle-grounds were removed.

Constable James Dwyer caught two men playing cards at the Governor Bourke Hotel after closing time one night in December 1836. Kitty Carr was in the room, and there was a glass of grog on the table. Michael Carr, as licensee, was fined £2 for allowing gambling on his premises, but the charge of selling liquor out of hours was not upheld: Kitty said the drink was hers. Ed Steel, the convict scourger, was caught taking bets on the toss of a half-crown at Moss's public house the next year. He forfeited a month's pay – plus the half-crown, which one of the arresting constables pocketed, 'as evidence'.

In July 1839, Johnny Fawkner was all a-froth over Jack Armstrong's recently opened ginger beer saloon and billiard room in Queen Street. It was 'a Hell – a petite Crockford's',* and he urged the constabulary to 'keep themselves on the alert respecting this low sink of iniquity … opened solely for the simple, but speedily ruinous purpose of play'. Regardless of what else may have been going on there, Armstrong's billiard table was quite legal, billiards being the exception to the anti-gaming laws. For £10, and with the say-so of the police magistrate, a publican could buy a permit allowing billiards to be played on his premises. Edward Umphelby (often called Humphilby) brought the first billiard table to Bearbrass, installing it in a large parlour at his Angel Inn, on the north-east corner of Collins and Queen streets, in 1838.

'The best billiard table ever imported to this Colony' was auctioned by the creditors of Stanway's Hotel in Flinders Street in 1846. This is how their advertisement described it:

---

* Crockford's was an exclusive gambling club in Regency London.

An Imperial Petrosian twelve foot BILLIARD TABLE, by Thurston,
with eight massive turned legs made solid, and French polished,
Indian rubber cushions, and best superfine cloth; together with
balls, cues, marking board, circular cue stand, rests, and spirit-
level, seats covered with hair seating, patent revolving six burner
solar lamp, with shades and glasses complete.

This magnificent object was bought by John Brago, also known as 'Jack the Nipper', who established a billiard saloon at his Horse and Carriage Repository* in Lonsdale Street. Brago was a masterly player. Between ten a.m. and two p.m. each day, when the repository was at its quietest, he taught billiards 'scientifically', and he must have been good for he charged pupils eight shillings an hour. In November 1849, he offered prize money of £20 to any man who could beat him at his table, with a return bout to be played at the table of his opponent's choice. Two weeks later Jack sailed for California – 'in the hopes,' said the *Patriot*, 'of being able to pocket something better than balls.'

The hoots and the huzzas of the mob

Horse-racing, as 'the sport of kings', was well regarded by the authorities and had its place at Bearbrass almost from the first. Its place, to begin with, was the grassy flat to the north and west of Batman's Hill, now occupied mainly by railyards. There the town's first race meeting was held, over three days in March 1838. The course was marked out with stakes and saplings, commencing up the line near the present-day North Melbourne station and sweeping round through West Melbourne to the finish line, under the swooping roof of Spencer Street station. Two bullock drays lashed together made a grandstand, and a select few publicans had booths cobbled together from tea-tree and canvas. Punters who were in the funds bought smokes from the

---

* That is, a nineteenth-century carpark.

'cigar and light' boy for sixpence and drank 'spiders' at one-and-three-pence a shot.

The horses themselves were mostly wiry working animals from the bush. Mrs Datagalla, belonging to John Batman, won the Town Plate on the first day of the meeting. On the second day, Fawkner suffered ignominy when his mare, Yarra Lass, was trounced in the Beaten Horses' stake. Edward Umphelby's Miss Fidgett broke her neck at the final jump in the steeplechase and Umphelby's wife, Mary Ann, sobbed over the dead mare after Barry Cotter applied a fatal shot. The jump where Miss Fidget came to grief was for the rest of the season dubbed 'the Weeping Mary Hurdle'.*

The town's first cricket club was formed in November 1838, with the first official fixture played on the 17th of that month, not far from where the old Royal Mint building now stands in William Street. An informal match was staged in March 1840 between the married men of the town and 'their more unfortunate brethren, the Bachelors of Melbourne'. Unfortunate or not, the bachelors displayed the greater stamina and skill, soundly thrashing their opponents.

In 1843, the Scotsmen of the town formed the 'Caledonian Shinty Club of Australia Felix' – shinty being a game similar to hockey, so named because of the cry of *shin ye!* when a score is made. Matches were played on St Andrew's Day and at regular Caledonian gatherings for some years to come.

The working classes marked holidays and celebration days with rollicking sports meetings, featuring events such as catching the greasy pig, greasy pole-climbing, sack races, and wheelbarrow races. In 1838, Johnny Fawkner wondered whether regular sports days might act as a cure for habitual drunkenness among 'the labouring population'. This proved not to be the case, but sports days were nonetheless, in the

---

*   Uncannily, the position of the Weeping Mary Hurdle bore some relation to that of the Spencer Street station luggage locker in which Picasso's *Weeping Woman* was stashed in 1987.

parlance of the times, 'good clean fun', as well as a boon to publicans.

On Boxing Day 1846, George Say staged a sports gathering in the roadway outside his St George and the Dragon Hotel in Lonsdale Street. Attractions included 'that truly English amusement, Grinning through a Collar', goat-racing, and a great novelty – a wheelbarrow race for boys in blindfolds. The advertised program of events concluded with the promise that:

> G.S., in order to convince the public that he is by no means deficient in GALLANTRY, will produce some articles of feminine adornment, the right to which will be contested by a race between Elderly Ladies.

By 'elderly ladies', he meant those over forty.

A greasy pole was a spar, about twenty-five feet (8 m) in length, well coated with lard and stood on its end. At the top was fixed a hat containing a £1 note, which served both as target and prize. Sometimes two poles were erected side by side and the contest was between two men – who would reach his target first? All kinds of aids were resorted to: handkerchiefs tied around the hands, dirt or sawdust sprinkled on the pole, a good gob of spit in each palm. Few ploys succeeded. Some sports days passed off without the £1 being claimed. At the New Year's Day sports at Emerald Hill in 1850, a magpie flew off with the money just as a red-faced Ned Crumball had shinnied within reach of the hat. Needless to say, the greasy pole was a real crowd-pleaser.* One newspaper told of 'The cries, the laughter, and the "up again, boy" ... the hoots and the huzzas of the mob'. And that was *before* the refreshment tent commenced business for the day.

---

* And why not revive it as a Moomba event? Or as a permanent fixture in Federation Square? Surely a margarine manufacturer would leap at the chance to sponsor the world's first monounsaturated greasy pole.

Street games

Between sports days, those who were not of the cricket-club set made their own amusements. The newspapers brimmed with complaints at the shenanigans of the 'street arabs', 'half-boots', 'urchins' and 'idle vagabonds' – children and youths whose playing pitches were the streets. A neverending cause of ire was that, to the street urchin, Sunday was as good a day as any for kicking a ball or tossing coins on the front step. And that was Sabbath-breaking, or 'profaning the Lord's Day'.

To be fair to the papers, though, there *was* more to the street antics than ball-games and coin-calling. For a start, there was dog-fighting – a 'disgusting exhibition' of which was staged at the corner of Queen and Collins streets on a Tuesday evening in April 1840. 'As usual,' said the *Patriot*, the bloody spectacle attracted 'a large concourse of idle vagabonds', laying bets and urging the animals on. Then there was the random firing of pistols and fowling-pieces. Not ride-by shootings – nothing like that; just firing into the air as an expression of elation, of celebration, of boredom. Every New Year's Eve, lead shot would rain down on the streets of Bearbrass.

Gum-branch shanghais and yonnies (smooth pebbles) were prized by 'half-boots' who would make a sport of window-breaking. In 1845, the *Patriot* made light of the craze for shattering windows.

> EXTRAORDINARY – *The Glass in the windows of uninhabited houses in Melbourne appears to be of a more brittle texture than in any other portion of the Globe. Only leave a house untenanted for a fortnight and upon visiting it again not a whole square of glass will be found. Whether this can be accounted for on the principle of atmospheric pressure, or the playfulness of the juveniles of the Town, or whether it arises from a wish to increase business among the glaziers is doubtful.*

Firecrackers were the must-have toy of 1847. Ha'penny bungers, they were in those days – two-a-penny at the big merchants' stores. 'A favourite practice,' lamented the *Herald*, 'is to set squibs in the key-holes of several doors at night, and to cause a simultaneous explosion.' And barrel-rolling was popular that same winter. Half a dozen or so 'idle scamps' broke into the shop of a cooper in Bourke Street one night and rolled his barrels and casks about the streets. One of them dragged a barrel up the hill to Queen Street, where he found a ginger cat lounging in the gutter. He popped her inside and gave the barrel a mighty shove. The stunned cat flew out halfway down the hill, but the barrel careered on until it reached the Eagle Tavern, near the top of the block that is now the Bourke Street Mall. Its thunderous approach brought drinkers scrambling from the bar and, apprehending the cause of the ruckus, they seized three of the boys (the rest had scarpered) and dealt them a sound thrashing on the spot.

For those who were really game, there was the extreme sport of *flaming* barrel-rolling. It required a tar-barrel, a match, a pair of sturdy boots, and a foolhardy disposition. Once the barrel was alight, its 'rider' propelled it along the roadway with kicks, oblivious to the sparks and spits of flaming tar that must have showered back on him. The police and press were rightly outraged, fearing that a burning barrel could ignite a wooden building and stonker half the town.

Even kite-flying – a harmless enough sport, you'd have thought – was prohibited within the town. A flapping kite could cause horses to bolt, as in this incident in November 1847:

> *On Saturday last, we perceived a horse and dray going at*
> *railroad pace down Lonsdale-street and on enquiry, ascertained*
> *that some urchin had frightened the animal with a kite.*

As the Princes Bridge neared completion in 1849, young galoots would perform daredevil gymnastics and balancing feats on the slender wooden scaffolding that supported the arch. Fifteen-year-old

Izaac Walton slipped and escaped injury only by catching hold of a piece of rotten rope. Doubtless Izaac and his mates were among the crowd of five thousand that gathered a couple of months later to watch 'a singular feat of rope-walking' by Mr Quinn, a celebrated rope dancer from Radford's circus in Van Diemen's Land. A tightrope was stretched across the Yarra from Queen's Wharf to the south bank. 'What are the odds,' taunted the *Patriot*, 'that he does not get a cold bath?' But the performance went without a hitch, Quinn taking less than two minutes to make the crossing with an open umbrella in one hand and a wriggling Chihuahua in the other.

Clubs

Almost indistinguishable by their antics from the low-born vagabonds were the high-living gentlemen rowdies. These were primarily young squatters, whom inherited wealth, the certainties of class, and a preference for brandy over rum, set apart from the common run of larrikins.

Originally, the Lamb Inn was their headquarters and the Waterford School their *alma mater*, but with the formation of the Melbourne Club in 1839 the focus shifted to the Club House, formerly Fawkner's Hotel. Garryowen recalled that in the early '40s, the Melbourne Club was 'the focus of every nocturnal kill-time' – that is, practical joke – 'that could be conceived'. Its members sawed through verandah posts, broke windows, pulled down shop signs, removed door knockers, staged drag-races on horseback, and, when things got really dull, they fought duels. Nor were they above poking firecrackers through keyholes or rolling barrels down Collins Street, just like their working-class counterparts.

The office of the *Patriot* was right next door to the Melbourne Club House, so that Johnny Fawkner could not but be aware of the 'incessant depravities' committed by the so-called gentlemen members. The Club House had no licence to serve liquor but, with members and friends in high places, they hardly needed one. Fawkner fumed and occasionally burst into print – under the whistle-blowing *nom de plume*, 'Bob Short' – with sarcastic exposés of the goings-on next door.

The same Melbourne Club today presents as the epitome of refinement and exclusivity, a far cry from its origins in brandy-fuelled tomfoolery.

Bearbrass gentlemen who owed their wealth to commerce rather than inheritance founded their own club in 1839. A guest of the Port Phillip Club in the early '40s described its members as:

Impersonators of the tradition of fine old English gentlemen, buttoned up in black, and blue, and drab; drinking their decanter of port on the hottest days with abnormal dignity.

The Port Phillip Club House was in Flinders Street, between Swanston and Elizabeth. Originally a mansion named Yarra House, it had been built in 1839 for John Hodgson, but at such enormous expense that the building's completion left him bankrupt. Yarra House became 'Hodgson's Folly'. When the Port Phillip Club folded in 1843, the building became a boarding house, then the Port Phillip Club Hotel. The rambling old hotel survived until 1960, when it was demolished and replaced by the tacky Port Phillip Arcade.

The celestial nymphs of Flinders-lane

A newly arrived immigrant calling himself 'A Friend of Chastity' wrote to Superintendent La Trobe in 1849. He described himself as a person of considerable experience in the world, who had travelled widely and 'witnessed much infamy' in foreign parts. But the 'dens' of Bearbrass, he declared, far eclipsed any that he had hitherto encountered. Prostitutes strutted in Lonsdale Street, opposite St Francis' Church, shouting obscene invitations to passers-by (much in the manner of Melbourne Club members ten years earlier). And the newspapers so relished their duty of exposing the trade of 'brothelizing' that their type compositors could set the word *notorious* in a single flourish with their eyes shut.

Bearbrass had a surplus of single men, making prostitution as inevitable (though not as readily sanctioned) as the sale of liquor. In 1838, Fawkner's servant Mary Gilbert accepted payment from a sailor for allowing him to 'take liberties' with her. Catherine Reardon was repeatedly before the courts in 1839 on charges of keeping a brothel. And in the early '40s, Margaret Donovan (alias Farrington, alias Casey) kept 'a notorious house of ill-fame'. As well as charging lodgers by the half-hour, she dealt in sly grog, and harboured runaways like Dickie Higgins, whose capture on her premises cost her a £20 fine.

The *Gazette* in 1840 drew police attention to:

> ... *a house tenanted by little Waggoner, the constable, and a woman with whom he is at present* par amours, *[where] the most riotous and disorderly scenes occur almost nightly. The precise nature of these unseemly disturbances is, of course, unknown to our informant, who can judge them only by the noise with which they are accompanied* ...

When Samuel Willis and his wife appeared in court charged with keeping a disorderly house in a lane between Bourke and Little Bourke streets:

> *One witness, a near neighbour, swore to having been frequently annoyed by persons frequenting the house in the night, but whether these disturbances consisted of men or women, or a mixture of both sexes, he could not positively swear, being rather aged and unable to see well in the dark.*

The old fellow was unlucky enough to live in Vinge's Lane, the Soho of 1840s Bearbrass. The Willises were committed for trial in Sydney, but their place was filled by Elizabeth and Peter Toote (or Tuite). Within a year, the Tootes' 'nest of infamy' had been raided and they too were sent to trial on charges of keeping a common brothel. Needless to say, the *Patriot* entered into the spirit of things:

> *The facts of this case are of too gross a nature for publication*
> *... it appears that scenes of the most revolting nature were there*
> *nightly carried on, and that it was also a receptacle for the most*
> *notorious thieves in Melbourne.*

The *Patriot* went on to condemn the Tootes for allowing drinking and 'fiddling' to take place on their premises. Both husband and wife were sentenced to two years' gaol with hard labour. Peter received, in addition, a £50 fine for sly grog dealing and suffering gypsy music to be performed.

In 1847, merchant James Graham complained that the allotment behind his store, on the north-west corner of Little Bourke and Russell streets, had been minutely subdivided and was occupied by a 'perfect nest of wretched hovels and a complete den of infamy'. Soon after, an anonymous correspondent wrote to the *Patriot* on the subject of the same 'den of licentiousness'. Its occupants he referred to as 'some half-a-dozen abandoned characters' engaged in 'nocturnal debauchery'; but what he really objected to was the 'singing, yelling, dancing and fiddling' emanating from a public house in the quarter. The letter ended with a bombshell: 'I have been told, Sir, that the landlord of the house is the Chief Constable for the District'.

Chief Constable William Sugden was described by Garryowen as 'a tall, straight, good-looking man, who strutted like a retired dragoon through the streets'. His reputation was as a fair and effective law-keeper, so here was a revelation indeed. The *Patriot* correspondent who side-swiped him was possibly Peter Davis, an auctioneer residing in Bourke Street East. Soon after the letter was published, Sugden charged Davis with public disturbance for using a gong at his auction rooms. In reporting the charge, the *Herald* remarked that it was strange that Davis should be singled out, as gongs were employed by every auctioneer in the town.

Occasionally the men of the press found it in their hearts and loins to spurn the word 'notorious' and treat prostitution with just a lick of light-hearted indulgence. The *Herald*, in one instance, sighed over a constable caught '"romancing" with some of the celestial nymphs of Flinders-lane'. The misfortune of a country lad obviously caught a reporter's imagination and the tale, as he spun it, is worth relating in full:

> *Friday morning, John Murray, a slashing chap fresh from the*
> *bush, was confronted at the Mayor's court with a Cyprian**
> *well known to Constable Swindell as Grace Fadden. Johnny,*
> *it appears, having spent the last half year in ruminating upon*
> *'Love's young dream,' upon his arrival in town managed to*
> *get himself introduced to the fair Grace. On Thursday night,*
> *believing 'nothing half so sweet in life' as a star-lit walk, he*
> *strolled with his lady-love along the banks of the winding*
> *Yarra; but the ill-starred lovers were not destined to any lengthy*
> *enjoyment of their contemplated ramble, two constables having*
> *intruded upon their retirement. The delinquent not having the*
> *indulgence of a 'night licence' to perambulate at such an hour,*
> *John was ordered to hand out £5.*

Grace, in other words, was a convict servant out after nightfall. As an 'old offender', she was sentenced to gaol for three months.

In the early 1840s, just as the economic depression began to be felt in Bearbrass, shipload after shipload of immigrants arrived to find themselves without work or wages. After a time, the government found employment for many of the men on public works, but unmarried women had to fend for themselves. The large store-house in which the female immigrants were housed was declared by the

---

*   Meaning, of course, a prostitute – 'Cyprian' being a reference to Venus, goddess
      of love.

government surgeon to be 'a Brothel on a large scale'. John Dickson, a doctor of more benevolent disposition, sympathised with women who were driven to prostitution. In a report to the government, he wrote that, 'having lost cast at home, from the circumstances of one or two bastardies, [they] seek asylum in the Colonies'. This, believed Dickson, was the background of seventy per cent of the unmarried women immigrants, and most found no asylum at Bearbrass, just more ignominy. In the words of one magistrate, the town was 'crowded with single women – their career one of crime and misery'.

Take Meg Helton, for example: 'a young woman of emaciated body and contused countenance'. Seven times in two years she appeared in court under various charges of misconduct, and in March 1843 was before the magistrate again. The charges this time were drunkenness, living by prostitution, frequenting and dancing at taps and public houses, and 'being the most dissolute character in the metropolis' (that last added by the *Herald* for good measure). She was sentenced to a week in prison – then home again to the streets.

Then there was the story of Janey Moor – called by the *Herald* 'one of those misguided females ... who endeavour to eke out the slender thread of their miserable existence by inveterately following up those abandoned courses into which they have unhappily lapsed'. Janey attempted suicide by taking a large dose of laudanum (a tranquilliser combining opium with alcohol). After swallowing the stuff in Little Collins Street, Janey dragged herself into the Australian Hotel near by, and dropped insensible at the bar (no novelty to the publican, that). But she survived, and was gaoled for her attempt. Probably, she went to the river next time, stuffing the bodice of her already-heavy frock full of stones, then wading in. A good few of the women who sought asylum at Bearbrass would find it at last in the Yarra.

Does your mother know you're out?

As we have seen, fiddling and dancing as enjoyed by the rougher classes were dismissed by the Bearbrass press as mere evidence of dissipation and vulgarity. But the more refined styles of music seem to have given little more satisfaction.

The town's first formal music recital – or soirée – took place at William Harper's British Hotel in William Street in December 1839, with tickets priced at half-a-guinea each, to keep out the riff-raff. Thomas Strode criticised the venue: 'The room itself was well adapted to the purpose, being low and badly lighted …' And Johnny Fawkner's *Patriot* next day gave greater coverage to 'the noisy, drunken, blackguard language and outrageous conduct of a fellow professing to be a gentleman' – a reference to Strode – than to the performance of the players.

Glee singing was popular during the early '40s, perhaps as a panacea to insolvency. In August 1841, Mr Clarke invited 'gentlemen amateurs' to join his glee class on Tuesdays at seven p.m. Five months later, the group gave its first professional performance, at a concert farewelling Monsieur and Madame Gautrot (visiting recitalists) at the Royal Exchange Hotel. Next day, the *Patriot's* critic remarked that 'the voices of the singers obviously came from throats more accustomed to swallow beer and brick-dust, than eggs and butter', suggesting that Mr Clarke's drive to attract *gentlemen* pupils to his glee squad had failed. They did however, said the *Patriot*, give an admirable performance of a glee entitled 'Life's a bumper' – a bumper being a full glass of ale.

In a concert at the Victoria Saloon, Little Bourke Street, in January 1842, a gentleman pianist 'obliged the refractory audience with "Peace in the Valley", but alas!' reported the *Patriot*, 'there was no *peace* for him'. The rowdy drinkers 'advised him to "try a beef-stake" – to "lay down"' – and even went so far as to ask 'if his mother knew he was out'.

Balls were the one form of dance entertainment that the press saw fit to comment upon. The grand ballroom at the Caledonian Hotel in Lonsdale Street was the toast of the ball-going crowd in the early '40s, but when it fell into the hands of tea-drinkers, John Cowell's stump-marred Royal Hotel in Collins Street won favour. Its ballroom was christened with the Squatters' Ball in January 1845, and the following year the town's first polka was danced there. There was no grand civic hall in Bearbrass, but the halls attached to the various churches regularly played host to balls. Naturally, no liquor was served on these occasions. In May 1848, a fancy dress ball was staged at the Protestant Hall – 'At the Request of Many Highly Respectable Families', according to the publicity pitch.

> *The Ladies' Private Room will be under the charge of*
> *a respectable female. Observe!!! Should any person of*
> *objectionable character be introduced the Stewards will exercise*
> *a right to remove them from the premises.* NO MASKS ALLOWED.

The queerest place imaginable

In 1839, Thomas Hodge was a barman at the Eagle Tavern in Bourke Street. He was keen on amateur theatricals and persuaded his boss, James Jamieson, to build a wooden theatre on the adjoining allotment. Hodge was given the management of the theatre, which he named the Pavilion, and in 1840 he applied to the government for a licence. His application was refused as Superintendent La Trobe, the town's magistrates, and church authorities believed that, based on the examples of Sydney and London, the staging of popular entertainments would harm community morals. Thomas Hodge argued that his theatre's performances would, rather, improve the state of morals in the town, but the opposition remained. He managed eventually to win a temporary permit, late in 1841, allowing the staging of charity performances only, but these soon came to a halt when police raided an exhibition of 'ballet dancing' and closed the theatre down. Hodge took up hotel-keeping at the Victoria Saloon, but a few months later was again in strife for staging 'indecent dancing' performances.

Perhaps Hodge himself had been the impediment to the granting of a theatre licence. The new management secured a licence early in 1842 and changed the Pavilion's name to the Theatre Royal. Sydney

actor George Buckingham was appointed stage manager and he produced and performed in variety shows that combined singing, dancing,
comic recital, tragedy, and farce. Buckingham, his wife, daughter, and
son (who presented 'a comic medley' at the age of three) were the
principal troupers, along with local amateurs and visiting professional
performers. Regrettably, the wholesomeness of the performances did
not rub off on the audience. The magistrates and Superintendent La
Trobe had their worst fears swiftly realised. Coarse, drunken behaviour and fist fights – even riots – attended every performance.

The theatre was a tall wooden shed – 'the queerest place imag-
inable', according to Garryowen. The whole structure swayed like a
coal-freighter on windy nights, and patrons in the gallery complained
of sea-sickness. Heaven help anyone seated below. Even on windless
nights, it was best to keep one's hat on in the theatre. Those in the
pit who were well-mannered or foolish enough to remove their hats
during a performance would have them used as spittoons by hoo-
ligans in the dress circle above. Bald spots likewise made excellent
targets. The carrying of umbrellas – by playgoers and performers alike
– was advisable on rainy nights, as the roof leaked prodigiously.

According to the Port Melbourne pioneer, W.F.E. Liardet, 'smoking
used to be carried to such a pitch in the pit that it bore the appearance
of the crater of a volcano in roaring action'. The smokescreen not only
made it difficult to see the stage, but caused performers to be gripped
by fits of coughing. Peter Snodgrass, a Melbourne Club dandy, took
the atmosphere a step closer to inflammability in May 1842 by throwing fireworks into the boxes and seriously alarming the ladies therein,
'one of whom was considerably injured by the bursting of one of the
squibs'. The renowned gourmandising magistrate, Major St John, was
on the bench when Snodgrass fronted up on a charge of disturbing
the peace. St John excused Snodgrass's behaviour, declaring himself
'not surprised that young men should misconduct themselves in such
a manner when … the boxes which should have been reserved for
families were filled with women of improper character'. We can be

certain that Snodgrass's acquittal was toasted in gin at the Melbourne Club, and that a fat lamb or two, killed and dressed were delivered to Major St John's residence before the week was out. (Snodgrass was a grazier and able to accommodate such bribes with ease.)

In an attempt to cast off the theatre's association with past vulgarities, its name was changed again in early 1843, to the Royal Victoria Theatre. The intended change of image, in line with Major St John's remarks, is apparent from advertisements:

> *Amateur Theatricals – to be held at the Victoria Theatre. 'The Rich Man of Frankfurt' and 'Why don't you Marry'. The greatest care will be taken to preserve the strictest decorum and order, a number of gentlemen have proffered their services to attend the doors and arrange everything for the accommodation of ladies.*

But to no avail. The following month, May 1843, La Trobe and the full bench of town magistrates refused to renew the theatre's licence.

Just three months later, a visiting Sydney actor and theatre manager named Conrad Knowles talked the authorities into granting him a limited licence, on the condition that he hire several 'special constables' (that is, bouncers) to ensure that order was maintained. Knowles brought legitimate theatre to Victoria, including the town's first professionally staged Shakespeare production. The occasional variety show would draw rowdies back to the theatre, but, on the whole, Knowles managed to keep the theatre 'fit for the reception of respectable families'. He died suddenly in June 1844 and the theatre lapsed into its former disrepute, 'through mismanagement, and the bad conduct of one of the actresses, who frequently appears upon the stage in a state of intoxication'.* In August 1845, renewal of the

---

* A Mrs Cameron sounds a likely candidate. On Boxing Night, 1844, she featured on stage in two minor roles: as Elizabeth Stanton, a young orphan betrothed to the son of a magistrate in 'Tom Cringle; or the Wrecker's Lair', and as the devilishly named Miss Long Clacket in a 'laughable farce' entitled 'The Ringdoves'.

Victoria Theatre's licence was refused for the last time. The *Patriot* was jubilant:

> ... *respectability triumphed over blackguardism in the attempt to revive from its ashes the old brothel known as the Victoria Theatre ... Although there were one or two loose fish upon the bench, the upright, honorable and moral portion of the Town Magistracy scouted the idea of pandering to the depraved appetites of 'Family Men' and degraded females.*

The management gave up the struggle and the shonky old barn was thereafter used as a stable.

A more solid theatre – solid both in terms of masonry and respectability – was built between 1843–5 by missionary-turned-publican, J.T. Smith, at the north-east corner of Queen and Little Bourke streets. Smith was granted a licence for his Queen's Theatre, on the understanding that he would stage entertainments of a strictly 'chaste and moral' nature and that guards would keep the low-life muzzled. The success of the Queen's Theatre was assured when George Coppin and his company arrived in mid-1845. Coppin leased the theatre from Smith and performed to packed houses for a year. Coppin was an accomplished classical actor, but he owed his Bearbrass popularity to his talents as a comedian. The handbill for a play called *Old Kentucky Nigger* gives an insight into what made a Bearbrass audience laugh:

> MR COPPIN *will appear as the* OLD KENTUCKY NIGGER *and screech the celebrated nigger melody* JIM BROWN, *with his unequalled* CYMBAL POT-LID ACCOMPANIMENT *and extraordinary* LOUISIANA JUMP *and* OLD KENTUCK GRAPE VINE TWIST, *making a display of toe and heel genius 'surprising to de white folk and sartin death to all Long Island niggers.'*

(And you thought Chubby Checker invented the Twist.) By 1850, George Coppin had moved on, but the Queen's Theatre continued to pull crowds with the kind of acts that wouldn't look out of place in a Melbourne International Festival program:

> *Grotesque Chichachachechochuchawkracer; or Ethiopian Comic Dance, by Mr Young; Treasons of the Sultana; Fireworks; Mr J. Purdon performing his wonderful feats on the SLACKROPE; and the Farce of Sylvester Daggerwood, or the Mad Actor.*

Can't you just see Chunky Move performing the Grotesque Chichach achechochuchawkracer and Glenn Robbins in the Farce of Sylvester Daggerwood?

In the Bearbrass years, the Queen's Theatre was never the scene of the kind of riot and roistering that were its predecessor's downfall. But, come the gold rushes, all that would change.

Separation at last!

The first public meeting in the long campaign for the separation of the Port Phillip District from the colony of New South Wales took place in June 1840. Of course, Johnny Fawkner had never seen Bearbrass as an outpost of the cursèd Sydney; for him, the campaign for separation began the moment he visualised a settlement at Port Phillip with him in it. Likewise John Batman. The distance separating Bearbrass from Sydney made it apparent from the first that if the southern settlement flourished it would one day demand a colony of its own. And that day soon came. From 1846, the push for independence gained strength until, on Monday, 11 November 1850, separation was finally announced.

The Separation Bill had actually been passed by British Parliament in London on 1 August, but the news took fourteen weeks to reach Bearbrass. It arrived unobtrusively. English newspapers dated 4 August were brought up from a ship that had just come into port, to the desk of Edmund Finn (alias 'Garryowen'), a reporter for the *Herald*. Late in the afternoon he began leafing through them, looking for items to include in the 'English News' columns of the next day's edition. Then, on page five of *The Times* (sandwiched between an amendment to the Dog Act and an advert for a virility cure), his eye lit on a short paragraph stating that the Separation Act had been passed. Finn hauled the *Herald*'s compositor out of the pub and had him set an Extraordinary edition of the paper, using the biggest type he could find. By nightfall, most of Bearbrass had heard the news.

Next day, every building in the metropolis was decked out with bunting. Hot-air balloons, ten feet in diameter and emblazoned with the word SEPARATION in letters two feet high, were released from Flagstaff Hill, to the applause of five thousand rejoicers. All over the town, public houses had been open all night, fuelling revellers with 'Separation Salutes', a cocktail of gin and ginger beer, drunk to the toast – 'VICTORIA!' One enterprising brewer had bottled (or, at any rate, labelled) a special Separation Ale in anticipation of the news, and empty bottles littered the roadways as they had in the days of champagne notoriety.

In the evening, beacon fires, prepared weeks before, were set alight at Flagstaff Hill* and on hilltops all around the town, at Geelong, and throughout the interior. This was the signal to all citizens of the new colony of Victoria that independence had been achieved and the celebrations begun.

On Wednesday, Separation Celebration Sports were mounted at Eastern Hill, where Parliament House now stands. As well as the usual greasy poles and sack races, there was a cocker spaniel stakes, won by Superintendent La Trobe's Byron, and a bunion competition in which Flinders Lane neighbours, Maria Spiggot and Fanny Anstey, drew for first prize. An elderly gent was disqualified from the latter

---

*   The dunny at the Flagstaff Hill signal station had been accidentally incinerated during a trial run a few days earlier.

contest when he tried to pass off his gouty swelling as an enormous bunion. The sports concluded with a greasy pig chase, which caused by far the greatest diversion of the day. Not only was the poor animal coated with lard, it was painted red as well.

> *Some of the first who seized it and fell on it were covered with red paint from top to toe; frequently five or six fell over each other, and after capsizing several women who crowded rather too closely to witness the fun, and several children who were sprawling in the dust, and shouting at the top of their voices, the grunter escaped from his pursuers, who were completely knocked up.*

The exhausted animal was finally captured next day by two constables in Brunswick Street, Fitzroy.

Thursday, most townsfolk spent recovering from their exertions, attending thanksgiving church services, and preparing for the grandest day of celebration yet. Friday the 15th had been proclaimed a general holiday, and there was to be a procession through the town, followed by the official opening of the Princes Bridge, a public feast, more games, and a fireworks display in the evening. Superintendent La Trobe's wife had 'one of her neuralgic headaches' on Friday morning and, 'upset by the saxhorn band' – which had awoken the La Trobes at six a.m. – 'and fearing any cannonading', she asked her friend Georgiana McCrae to act as the Superintendent's consort for the day. So Georgiana, resplendent in Madame La Trobe's swansdown-trimmed black satin polonaise jacket, took her place beside La Trobe (who had swapped his flowered dressing-gown for something with epaulettes) in the open carriage. The official party watched the entire procession – estimated to have stretched for three miles – from a stand at the north-east corner of Flinders Lane and Swanston Street. Of the musical contributions, Georgiana wrote, '… no doubt, if the two lots of instrumentalists that followed the saxhorn band had been more *d'accord* the music would have been better'.

Mayor August Greeves' contribution to the Separation celebrations was to have been an enormous oxen pie, six feet in diameter, borne on a dray pulled by ten of the pie-filling's brethren. But that morning's *Herald* broke the news that:

> *Bullock Pie has vanished from the list of our Separation*
> *Rejoicings, there being no time to make the dish to contain the*
> *ox, or to build the oven to bake the pie, that the Mayor was to*
> *have given; but his Worship has kindly promised to hand over*
> *the extreme value of a 'fat ox' to the General Rejoicing Fund.*

After the procession had crossed the Princes Bridge, La Trobe declared the bridge officially open, and the crowds began to move off. Some of them headed for the sports at the cricket ground on the South Melbourne side of the river, while others made for the refreshment tents in the Botanic Gardens, where two thousand sticky buns were distributed to 'children of all denominations'. One of those buns, 'saved up' by young Nellie La Trobe who rode in the carriage with her father and Georgiana McCrae, was later found to have attached itself to the swansdown on the sleeve of her mother's best polonaise.

Months earlier, Mayor Greeves had appointed an 'Illumination Committee' to oversee street decorations and fireworks for the Separation celebrations, and their labours culminated in a monster fireworks display on Friday evening.

Dancers at the exclusive Separation Ball, two weeks later, were treated to the inaugural performance of John Wilkie's 'Separation Polka', a piece of music described as 'very tastefully got up' and 'proof that the arts are not neglected in Victoria'.

Official notification of Separation did not reach Sydney until January the following year, and it took a further six months for a Victoria Electoral Districts Act to be put in place. But finally, on 1 July 1851, Victoria was officially declared a separate colony. Another holiday was declared (one which would be observed for almost fifty years to come), after which the people and government of Victoria settled down to enjoy the fruits of their maturity.

The End of Bearbrass

Just four days after Victoria's separation became official, the
authorities announced that gold in payable quantities had been
found in the new colony. Bearbrass was forgotten in the magnificent
chaos that followed. The period prior to the gold rushes has been
likened to pre-history, and this book has given that era's lost civilisation
the name of Bearbrass. From its chrysalid state as Bearbrass – a modest
provincial city in a colony just finding its feet – Melbourne emerged
into the glare of international acclaim, as the capital and port of the
world's richest goldfields.

Soothsayers and optimists had been predicting a splendid future
for the city since the earliest days of Bearbrass. Thomas Strode, when
contemplating the move from Sydney in 1838, was advised that,
'before many years elapse Melbourne will become the Metropolis of
the Southern Hemisphere'. The *Cornwall Chronicle*, out of Launceston,
ventured the opinion in 1839 that, 'It is by no means improbable that
Port Phillip, at some future day, will raise to be the Queen of the
Australian Colonies … the Garden of New Holland.' In 1850, on the
brink of Separation, the city was 'destined to become the New York

of the future United States of the South'. Boldest of all was Charles Williams, who declared in 1840, 'there is no doubt Melbourne will yet surpass London'. What prompted such a prophesy? Williams was a real estate man trying to flog land in Bourke Street.

In 1848, a tract titled *The Emigrant's Friend* was issued in London, offering advice to those considering a life in the Antipodes. The Port Phillip District, readers were told, was 'a land of plenty, but a land of industry', with an economy soundly based on agriculture, rather than on mines and speculation. The District's colonists were applauded for 'carrying out well-matured plans of ultimate prosperity':

> *not led away by golden dreams of mineral wealth, they look to a rich and well-watered soil for that gold, which industry procures from the cultivation of it ...*

Early Bearbrass landowner Sylvester Browne had come close to divining the city's future when he likened the city in 1840 to 'a goldfield rush without the gold'.

The search for gold at Port Phillip was underway as early as 1842. Jem Gumm, a one-time servant of both John Batman and Johnny Fawkner, lived the life of a hermit in the Plenty Ranges (the Eltham and Warrandyte of today) and was known as 'Gum the Gold-hunter'. Mining was illegal, all mineral wealth being the property of the Crown, but when police searched Gumm's hut they found no gold, only a crucible.

Since the mid-1840s, Charles Brentani, the watchmaker and jeweller of Collins Street, had been paid discreet visits by shepherds and fencers who worked in the Pyrenees region, between present-day Maryborough and Ararat. A shepherd down from Daisy Hill (Talbot) – flushed, but not with drink – would be led to Brentani's back room where he would place on a table a grimy screw of cloth. With eager but efficient fingers, Brentani would untie the unprepossessing package and spread out its edges to reveal a tiny huddle of gold nuggets.

During 1848–50, Brentani and others mounted expeditions to the Pyrenees in search of gold, but without payable results. In February 1849, a publican named Roach told the *Herald* of a nugget – 'larger than any yet exhibited in Port Phillip' – shown him by a gold-seeker recently returned from the Pyrenees. William Clarke, landlord of the Waterman's Arms in Little Collins Street, was shown 'some splinters of quartz with a metallic substance attached' in June 1850, by a man who claimed to have found them within four miles of the town.

Since 1849 the Californian gold rushes had been big news, and shipping notices in the Bearbrass press huzzahed, 'CALIFORNIA! CALIFORNIA!' in boldest print. At the outbreak of gold rushes in New South Wales early in 1851, it looked as if the Port Phillip District would be drained of its labouring population. The local authorities had no choice but to promote gold discovery in their own district. In no time, the Gold Field Committee had firm evidence of payable gold at Anderson's Creek (Warrandyte) and in the Pyrenees, but announcement of the local finds was held back until Separation became official. Then, on 5 July 1851, the tumult was unleashed.

The vision of orderly progress for the new colony, together with certainties of social position and status, were exploded as surely as kegs of gunpowder in the loft of the Sporting Emporium. 'The present is a period pregnant with good or evil,' was the gloomy greeting given to gold by the editor of the Melbourne-based *Illustrated Australian Magazine*. As the town began to empty, he warned of gold's 'baneful and pernicious effect' on human morals, but comforted himself and his readers with the prediction that 'the novelty will soon pass away [and] the majority will return to settle in their peaceful homes'. Contributing to the same journal, 'Timon' concluded his poetic regret of the gold discoveries with the line: 'I – to all who heed my verse, Stamp thee as VICTORIA'S CURSE!'

Gold changed everything.

❦

Just like the novice diggers of 1851, I have forsaken Melbourne in favour of the goldfields. And like the lucky ones, when there's money in my kick I still head into town to blow it on a spree: a show, fancy food, fizzy drinks, and the dictates of fashion. When I'm there, in Melbourne, I can't help noticing – again, as the gold-gripped diggers must have done, through their patina of booze – how the shape of the place is shifting. In the fifteen years since I moved away, Southbank and the casino have stretched the town across the Yarra, while Swanston Walk has cut a new kind of desolate divide through the centre. Docklands and a surgically enhanced Collins Street have drawn the metropolis further westwards than ever before, and drawn the eye too – Telstra Dome and the new Southern Cross station swooping and blinking like Luna Park rides. Perhaps it's because the heart of my life is elsewhere nowadays that it seems to me as if Melbourne is losing *its* heart.

But while the physical landmarks change, the Bearbrass touchstones are still there for me. I chart a meandering course from the railway station in Spencer Street to the present centre of the city: along the lower end of Flinders Street, and through Market Street, Bank Place, Chancery Lane, and Equitable Place. On the way, veils of more recent rememberings drift across my mind-map of Bearbrass, so that Mary Gilbert and that cranky git Hooson inhabit the same streets as the ghost of myself-when-young, lounging with a boy poet on the ledge of his third-floor garret window, sharing the dregs from a wine cask bladder.

Strange that my train ticket gives my destination as Melbourne when really it's Bearbrass I'm visiting.

FURTHER READING

To readers who wish to know more about Bearbrass, I recommend the following books:

Aboriginal Melbourne: Discovering the lost land of the Kulin people by Gary Presland (McPhee Gribble, 1994; originally published as *The Land of the Kulin*, 1985) – dealing with pre-Bearbrass Melbourne, this book takes the reader yet another layer beneath the surface of the modern city.

Michael Cannon's *Old Melbourne town before the gold rush* (Loch Haven Books, 1991) – the comprehensive Bearbrass handbook, profusely illustrated.

The Chronicles of Early Melbourne, 1835 to 1852 – Historical, Anecdotal & Personal by 'Garryowen', alias Edmund Finn (published in two volumes by Fergusson and Mitchell, Melbourne, 1888; reissued, with an index, by Heritage Publications, Melbourne, 1976) – the definitive early Melbourne reference book, crammed with good yarns.

More readily available and less intimidating in size is *Garryowen's Melbourne*, edited by Margaret Weidenhofer (Nelson, Melbourne, 1967), containing selected excerpts from Garryowen's *Chronicles*.

The Melbourne Scene, 1803–1956, edited by J. Grant and G. Serle (Melbourne University Press, 1957) – a collection of documents and extracts, including many items from the Bearbrass era.

Historical Records of Victoria, volumes 1–6 (Victorian Government Printer and Melbourne University Press, 1981–91) – six bulky volumes of material gleaned from early government records held in the Public Records Office of Victoria (and not nearly as boring as they sound).

Paul de Serville's *Port Phillip Gentlemen* (Oxford University Press, Melbourne, 1980) – a look at the Bearbrass gentry and their up-country brethren.

Martin Sullivan's *Men & Women of Port Phillip* (Hale & Iremonger, Sydney, 1985) – a harsher view of the Port Phillip gentry and their relations with the labouring classes.

Melbourne's Missing Chronicle, being the Journal of Preparations for Departure to and Proceedings at Port Phillip by John Pascoe Fawkner, edited by C.P. Billot (Quartet Books, Melbourne, 1982) – Fawkner's first year at Bearbrass, in his own inimitable words.

Liardet's water-colours of early Melbourne by Susan Adams and Weston Bate (Melbourne University Press, 1972) – detailed, characterful depictions of Bearbrass by pioneer Frank Liardet.

Pioneer Merchant: The letters of James Graham, 1839–54, by Sally Graham (Hyland House, Melbourne, 1985) – lots of business talk, but peppered with insights into town and family life in Bearbrass.

William Westgarth's *Personal Recollections of Early Melbourne and Victoria* (originally published by George Robertson, Melbourne, 1888; reissued by Rippleside Press, Newtown, n.d.) – memoirs of another pioneering merchant who went on to become one of the colony's most illustrious citizens.

Old Melbourne Memories by 'Rolf Boldrewood' (George Robertson, Melbourne, 1884; Heinemann, Melbourne, 1969) – as plain Thomas Browne, the author arrived at Bearbrass in 1840, aged fourteen.

Georgiana's Journal. Melbourne 1841–1865 – the journal of early settler Georgiana McCrae, edited by her grandson, Hugh McCrae (ETT Imprint, 1992) see also Brenda Niall's biography, *Georgiana* (Miegunyah/ Melbourne University Press, 1994)

Peter Mews' *Bright Planet* (Picador, 2004) takes Bearbrass into what-if? territory. Read this novel for a closer-imagined acquaintance with Kitty Carr, Johnny Fawkner (and his raunchy daughter-who-never-was), William Nicholson and his barista-boy, and Edwin Robins of the blue-speckled trousers.

In 1868, Thomas Strode, like Garryowen a Bearbrass newspaperman, wrote his own account of the town's early days. He named it 'Victoria: Annals and reminiscences of bygone days, historical statistical and social ... by a Melbournite of '38'. It was never published, but the hand-written manuscript is now in the National Library of Australia. The La Trobe Library at the State Library of Victoria has a copy on microfilm, and it bears reading not only for the old man's memories, but for his unblunted enmities and enthusiasms.

Also available on microfilm at the State Library of Victoria are complete copies of the Bearbrass newspapers: the *Melbourne Advertiser*, *Port Phillip Gazette*, *Port Phillip Herald*, and *Port Phillip Patriot*, as well as the *Argus*, which commenced publication in the late 1840s. With a rainy hour to spare, you can get inside Bearbrass through the hand-cranked pages of its broadsheets.

ACKNOWLEDGEMENTS

The author acknowledges the following sources:

Excerpts from the letters of James Graham are reprinted from *Pioneer Merchant: The Letters of James Graham, 1839–45* by Sally Graham, Hyland House Publishing, South Yarra, 1985. The originals of the letters are held by the University of Melbourne Archives.

Excerpts from government records of the Bearbrass era are reproduced from *Historical Records of Victoria, vol. 1: Beginnings of Permanent Government* (ed. Pauline Jones), and *vol. 3: The Early Development of Melbourne, 1836–1839* (ed. Michael Cannon), Victorian Government Printer, 1981 and 1984.

Excerpts from John Pascoe Fawkner's journal originally appeared in *Melbourne's Missing Chronicle*, edited and with an introduction by C.P. Billot, Quartet Books Australia, Melbourne, 1982. The original manuscript of Fawkner's journal (MS 3224) is in the collection of the National Library of Australia.

Excerpts from the journal of Georgiana McCrae come from *Georgiana's Journal, Melbourne 1841–1865*, edited by Hugh McCrae (Imprint Classics edition 1992), and are reproduced with the permission of ETT Imprint.

Excerpts from the reminiscences of Georgiana's son, George Gordon McCrae, first published as 'Recollections of Melbourne and Port Phillip in the early '40s' in the *Victorian Historical Magazine*, 1911 and 1912, are reproduced courtesy of the Royal Historical Society of Victoria.

Excerpts from Thomas Strode's memoirs are taken from his unpublished manuscript, 'Victoria: Annals and reminiscences of bygone days, historical statistical and social … by a Melbournite of '38', in the collection of the National Library of Australia (MS 19).

INDEX